THE
TEMPLE
DOWN THE
ROAD

Other books by Brian Matthews

Non-fiction

A FINE AND PRIVATE PLACE: A MEMOIR

AS THE STORY GOES

LOUISA

FEDERATION

OVAL DREAMS: LARRIKIN ESSAYS ON SPORT
AND LOW CULTURE

THE RECEDING WAVE: HENRY LAWSON'S PROSE

Fiction

QUICKENING AND OTHER STORIES

MAGPIE (with Peter Goldsworthy)

THE TEMPLE DOWN THE ROAD

Brian Matthews

VIKING

an imprint of

PENGUIN BOOKS

Viking

Published by the Penguin Group (Australia)
250 Camberwell Road, Camberwell, Victoria 3124, Australia
Penguin Books Ltd
80 Strand, London WC2R 0RL, England
Penguin Group (USA) Inc.
375 Hudson Street, New York, New York 10014, USA
Penguin Books, a division of Pearson Canada
10 Alcorn Avenue, Toronto, Ontario, Canada M4V 3B2
Penguin Books (NZ) Ltd
Cnr Rosedale and Airborne Roads, Albany, Auckland, New Zealand
Penguin Books (South Africa) (Pty) Ltd
24 Sturdee Avenue, Rosebank, Johannesburg 2196, South Africa
Penguin Books India (P) Ltd
11, Community Centre, Panchsheel Park, New Delhi 110 017, India

First published by Penguin Books Australia,
a division of Pearson Australia Group, 2003

1 3 5 7 9 10 8 6 4 2

Text copyright © Brian Matthews 2003

Text and cover design by Brad Maxwell © Penguin Group (Australia)
Cover photograph by Megan Ponsford
Typeset in 11.5/18 pt Fairfield LH Light by Post Pre-press Group, Brisbane, Queensland
Printed and bound in Australia by McPherson's Printing Group, Maryborough, Victoria

National Library of Australia
Cataloguing-in-Publication data:

Matthews, Brian (Brian Ernest).
The temple down the road.

Bibliography.
Includes index.
ISBN 0 670 91178 X.

1. Melbourne Cricket Ground (Vic.). 2. Melbourne Cricket Ground (Vic.) – History.
3. Cricket grounds – Victoria – Melbourne. I. Title.

796.0689451

www.penguin.com.au

For Ted Fitzgerald and Ray Tynan
and in memory of Dick Owen

CONTENTS

PROLOGUE   I

PART ONE   17

PART TWO   127

PART THREE   203

EPILOGUE   297

AUTHOR'S NOTE   302

SELECT BIBLIOGRAPHY   303

PHOTOGRAPHIC CREDITS   307

INDEX   308

I'D BE DELIGHTED TO HAVE A CHAT WITH YOU
ABOUT THE TEMPLE DOWN THE ROAD . . .

Tim Lane, sports broadcaster,
in an email to the author

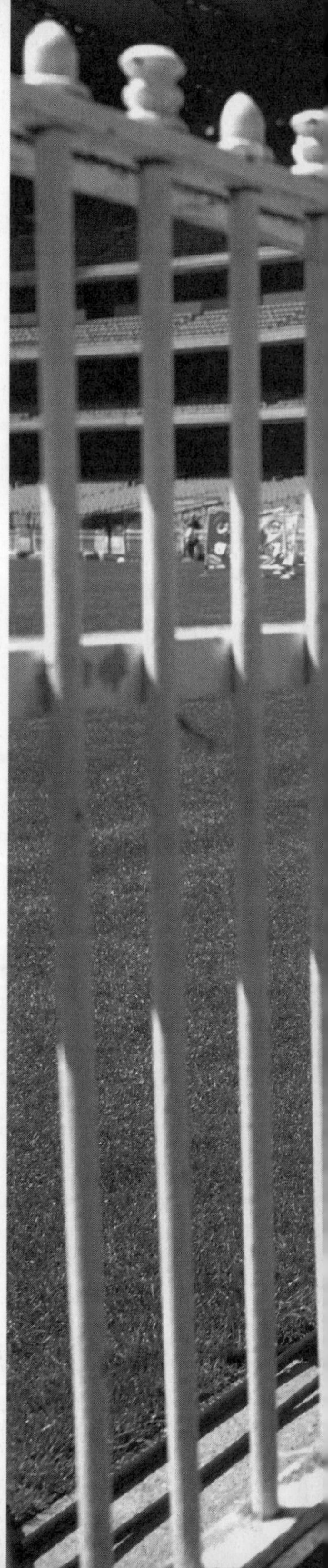

PROLOGUE

What can be said with complete confidence
is that the MCG is no meretricious show-off.
It has always had a grand allure – a distinct
sense of being a place where great events
uncover greater deeds.

Steve Waldon, 'The Last Word',
The Age, 16 July 2003

At exactly the halfway mark of the 1966 Victorian Football League season, I went to the MCG to watch Richmond play St Kilda. It was one of those stirring MCG days – a cold but flawlessly blue June sky arching over the lofty, flag-fluttering grandstands of the stadium towards which, from all directions in long sunlit lines, a huge crowd was advancing. Squatting magisterially in its manicured paddock of plane trees and grassy slopes, the 'G' looked ready for anything, inured as it was to practically every great sporting moment and contest in the history of the city of Melbourne. In the glittering pantheon of those diverse sporting encounters, this meeting – between the Tigers and the Saints – would rate only modestly. But 'on the day', as the coaches say, it loomed very large indeed.

Beaten Grand Finalists in the previous year, St Kilda were undefeated after eight rounds and had a massive percentage. Only slightly off that pace, Richmond had six wins, one loss and a draw behind them as they burst on to the famous ground to take on the League leaders. Notorious for anticlimactic performances when heroics were required, the Saints wilted under Richmond's seven-goal burst in the second quarter and spent the rest of the afternoon vainly trying to catch up.

As I battled my gloomy way into the Cricketers Arms after the game with what appeared to be about eleven thousand others, I overheard a bloke say, 'That's the end of St Kilda, mate. They're buggered for this year. You watch 'em go down.'

About three months later, as 101 655 people poured from the MCG after the 1966 Grand Final, I made a quick detour back to the Cricketers (along with, it seemed, about half the crowd from the game) in the mad hope that fate would bump me into that bloke again. St Kilda had just won their first (and still only) Premiership by one point. They hadn't 'gone down' after all. I knew if I came face to face with that false prophet I would be able to say something satisfactorily memorable while avoiding the crudely triumphalist or simply obscene, attractive options though those were.

Strangely enough, I didn't spot him, and soon, having given up on my attempt to tryst with fate and coincidence, I was inching my way across the footbridge with the other half of the crowd. At the highest point of the bridge, I paused to look back. Stopping on the footbridge after a Grand Final, when it is carrying its load of departing spectators, some of whom are, in the nature of things, in a state of despair or advancing depression and others either euphoric or suffering medium to advanced alcoholic befuddlement, or both, is neither smart nor socially aware. When, consumed with elation and vague idealisms, I paused on the footbridge on that Grand Final day in 1966, disgruntled Collingwood supporters immediately complained, some abused me and swore, and others told me in a variety of different yet unmistakable ways to get moving. St Kilda supporters conversely, buoyed by victory, booze and endorphins, would have evinced no surprise at all if I had announced that I was about to flap my arms and fly off the bridge into town.

Pressed against the solid wall of the bridge and with the crowd flowing past me like the tides around a rock, I looked back. Imperturbable as ever, the MCG was settling down into the luminous evening, its tall and curving lines blurring while the light drained from the sky and the cold air flooded invisibly through the trees. As I gazed, the flagpoles and lofty stands were transmuted to cathedral spires in the dusty, gothic and transforming light. Transfixed, I saw the soul of the place, not as just the site of this or that famous victory or defeat, but as Melbourne's imaginative home, its dream, its . . .

'Can you move on a bit, sport,' came an amiably frustrated voice. 'Everyone's bloody trippin' over you.'

I moved on. Behind me, the MCG melted into the mystery of another dusk and its ghosts from the Wurundjeri tribe and the Police Paddock and other distant days began to populate the darkening air.

Most of Melbourne's four million people are aware of the Melbourne Cricket Ground – the MCG as it is commonly known, or, with affection, simply the 'G'. It would be difficult for even the most disengaged to claim complete ignorance of it, because its towers and flagpoles and jutting girders and steep curve of walls are all visible from the city and, on certain days and nights, its noise and clamour are clearly audible too. Not to mention on summer evenings, when a one-day international cricket match moves into its second half and the 'G' flowers with light under an enormous moon and a purple sky drained at last of heat. Or in winter, on a Friday night, when the light towers blaze in the cold air and shouting fans are scarfed in their own frosty breath, or rain slivers down through the light in silver lines.

The MCG from its early days was one of those places that increasingly became, in the minds of Melburnians, part of the city's essential identity, its personality, in much the same way that Notre Dame is indistinguishable from ideas of Paris and Parisians; or San Marco and Santa Maria della Salute are laid claim to by even the most irreverent of Venetians; the way St Paul's transcends class and denomination to be all things to all Londoners; or, in more recent times, the winged silhouette of the Opera House has replaced the Harbour Bridge as shorthand for Sydney. In this same way the MCG is quintessentially Melbourne. The sense of ownership everyone feels about it has made it 'the people's ground'; not that it is ideologically egalitarian – on the contrary, membership of the Melbourne Cricket Club is achieved only after doing time in a very long queue, and there are now many privileged echelons at the 'G' above the base status of General Admission. Nevertheless, it is in everyone's imagination; it is part of the people's dream of Melbourne.

You can be dismissive of the 'G', but it's very difficult to ignore it or cut it completely from your mind. The MCG, like all big stadiums, is a dramatic physical presence. But it has also entered our language and our lore. Modern dictionaries recognise the process whereby language reflects changes in society's perspectives and levels of tolerance. What was once regarded as taboo or unacceptable or subliterary gains acceptance because it has become part of the collective consciousness, and to ignore it would be to ignore changes in the nature of that consciousness and ignoring those changes, in turn, would be to overlook significant shifts in the mores and behaviour of the community.

So, in 'Australia's national dictionary', *The Macquarie Dictionary*, third edition, we find words like 'fair dinkum' (adj., colloquial: *true, genuine*), 'fuckwitted' (adj., colloquial: *foolish, stupid*), 'pussy' (noun, colloquial: *the vulva*), 'ratshit' (adj., colloquial: *useless, broken . . .*) and much more.

In the same way, the MCG (which, incidentally, appears in *The Macquarie Dictionary* in that form) has long since gone beyond its status as a site, or architectural entity, or even major sporting stadium.

It is now part of the Melburnian (and Victorian and Australian) mental and imaginative world. It has entered what the Aboriginal people would call our 'Dreaming'. It is not just the place where we saw Australia beat the Poms or Fitzroy beat Melbourne; or where we attended a papal mass or Billy Graham's massive revivalist show; or where we heard the three tenors warbling effortlessly around the Members' wing. It is not only the sum of its history since Governor La Trobe granted the Melbourne Cricket Club permission to remove trees in order to establish a cricket ground. Or even since the tribes of the Kulin nation gathered in what the white man when he arrived would call the 'Richmond Paddock' and, later, 'Yarra Park' for dance, ceremonial, grievance airing and consultation: '. . . long ere the settlement was formed,' wrote a settler, William Thomas, in 1840, 'the spot where Melbourne now stands and the [river Yarra] flat on which we are now camped was the regular rendezvous for the tribes . . . twice a year or as often as circumstances and emergencies required . . .'

In those days, at about the time that John Batman came ashore on the Yarra bank, the 'Port Phillip District' – as the Europeans would call it – was wholly owned and controlled by the Kulin nation. Five related Aboriginal language groups made up this entity, and their sway extended around the bays and north to Euroa. The coastal tribes were the Wathaurong, inhabiting the Bellarine Peninsula and the Otways; the Woiworung, who lived on the flats of the Yarra and its tributaries; and the Boonwurrung, who spread along the Mornington Peninsula, around Westernport Bay, east to Wilsons Promontory and north to the foothills of the Dandenongs. The inland tribes of the Kulin nation were the Taungurong of the Goulburn River valley and environs and the Ngurraiillam from the Campaspe River to east of the Goulburn River.

The Woiworung consisted of five clans and each clan was closely connected with a section of the terrain. Two of these clans, the

Wurundjeri-willam and the Wurundjeri-baluk, inhabited the river flats and the country towards Westernport respectively: they were often seen around the edges of early Melbourne, and so the settlers came to refer to the local inhabitants, wrongly, as Wurundjeri and not the Woiworung.

Although he did not suspect it, Batman's place for a 'village' was exactly the area where the tribes of the Kulin nation had been regularly gathering for many years before the arrival of the white man. After the invasion, they continued for a time to use their favourite and familiar grounds on both sides of the river, which the first Europeans called the Freshwater but which the people knew as Bay-ray-rung or Birrarung – the River of Mists. Batman's surveyor, John Wedge, renamed it the Yarra Yarra in 1835 because he was convinced that was the Aboriginal name for it. And so, as they had done for generations, the Koories continued to congregate on either side of the Freshwater/Bay-ray-rung/Yarra Yarra and in 1844, for example, a great throng of Woiworung was camped on the site of what became the MCG and the Richmond Cricket Ground. It was their accustomed and familiar place.

A hundred and fifty years later, Aboriginal footballers, running down the race to tread for the first time on the MCG turf and steeling themselves for the noise, the space and the tension, found instead a great sense of intimacy as their feet hit the grass of the oval, as if it were, instead of the most famous stadium in the land and an arena of fearful exposure and nerves and achievement or failure, their accustomed and familiar place.

For myself, I think my very first visit to the 'G' was on 2 January 1948, the second day of what was then the New Year's Day Test Match. India was the opponent, making their first-ever Test tour to Australia. In the Second Test in Sydney, Indian bowler Vinoo Mankad entered cricket folklore when, after having repeatedly warned Bill Brown for backing up too far at the bowler's end in a previous India v. an Australian XI match and then again in the opening overs of Australia's first (and only) innings of the Second Test, he ran Brown out by suddenly aborting his bowling run-up and breaking the stumps with Brown backing up yards down the wicket. The phrase 'doing a Mankad' passed into cricket language, always uttered with a certain amount of disdain, since it was a manoeuvre, even after warnings, that seemed to be on the very edges of sportsmanship and the spirit of the game.

This famous incident gave a little controversy to a tour in which India was outclassed by more or less the team that Bradman would take to England and which would become known as 'The Invincibles'.

My only memories of my first sight at the 'G' are of the size of the stands, of the hugeness of the place, as I saw it then, and of Keith Miller, who came in at number five (Bradman had made 132 the previous day) and made 29 – a sensational cameo innings that included three sixes, two of which I recall flying into the first deck of some grandstand – the Grey Smith, I suppose. I seem to remember the ball rebounding hugely off the high grey concrete wall of the grandstand balcony. But who knows. It's a funny thing, memory.

Those summers of 1947 and 1948 seemed to be longer and hotter than they are now, and they came flooding back to me when I began to recall Miller's big hits and that day at the 'G'. Going to the MCG was a very unusual treat for me at that time. I was much more likely to be found mucking round at St Kilda beach or on the jetty, or, though my mother disapproved, sneaking into the St Kilda Baths, then as now the cynosure of controversy and notoriety, although for different reasons. I remember the sight of all the blokes lounging and swimming stark naked (we're talking men's baths, needless to say), and I recall the paunchy chap who told me and the kid with me that when the man-o'-war jellyfish stung you, whatever part they stung went stiff. He then gave us an inventory of all the bodily bits that went stiff in response to the ministrations of a man-o'-war. I reported this to my mother, leaving out the embarrassing bit, but she extrapolated easily from the general drift, and that finished for good my visits to the Baths.

In those days, there seemed to be hundreds of man-o'-war jellyfish treading water around the pylons of the pier. In idle summer moments I had often tried to spike them with my homemade flounder spear, hanging upside down from the pier's edge with my legs pinioned by a trusty mate.

This eye-popping scrutiny had rendered them very familiar to me. They had a sort of bluish ruff instead of a neck, which constantly rippled and undulated. Out behind them streamed long, wispy, translucent tentacles. Everything about them looked flaccid and resistless.

Despite the lesson in what might be called 'traumatised erectile function' delivered to me in the Baths by the naked expert on jellyfish stings, I remember deciding it was a great mystery how so flabby a creature would manage to make *anything* stiff.

But what was even more dramatic was the stingray scare. It all came back to me while I struggled to refocus on Keith Miller, his wild black hair tossing as he pulled the ball over square leg. I remembered the man who was killed by a big ray when he stepped on it in the shallows at St Kilda beach. The numerous sightings and a couple of wounds and near misses. Those hot dusks when I would splash around in the shallows while my father swam. The lap of the benign bay waters, the crowds, the women with dresses tucked up into their bloomers, babies wallowing, dogs zipping and bounding, laughter and chat as the sun sank on a scorcher at the end of a Melbourne working day. And me, dashing into the dip beyond a sandbar and seeing it – a stingray, dead set, going hell for leather out to sea through water up to my knees. And those knees turning as boneless as a man-o'-war.

Then I was running, sprinting through the splash and drag of water to tell my father.

'Stingray!' I gasped. 'Stingray, Dad.'

He was talking to a mate and having a smoke at the water's edge, standing there, both in their damp togs. And he didn't believe me. Nothing I could say then, nothing I said later, would convince him that one of the terrors of the deep had winged its way past my ankles, the long deadly tail flicking like a rudder, leaving eddies of sand on the bottom.

Ambushed though I have been over the past few years by memories of those days, this one had lain as deep as a ray itself, perhaps because at the heart of my stingray memories lurked an experience of the direst terror.

Such shadows from the depths have to creep up on you, like the floppy, ribbony man-o'-war. You can't let them burst out of the darkness fully formed, or . . . or what?

But back to the MCG from which, after all, we have strayed only a few miles around the bay.

The next time I went to the 'G' was in December 1948, and this time I didn't miss the Don. My father took me to Bradman's testimonial game. It was a rollicking, almost carnival event – social cricket, but played by the best in the land. Sid Barnes bowled a tennis ball at one stage and Don Tallon made 128 of his total of 146 runs *after the tea interval*, chasing 101 in an hour. They failed by one run and, in a game in which the two sides made 836 all up, the improbable result was a tie.

The sensation that I vividly remember, however, was Bradman's mishit when he was on 97. The ball skied to Colin McCool, who not only expertly dropped it but managed to kick it, as if clumsily stumbling, further towards the boundary. The batsmen ran three, and I saw the Don make 100. I nearly lost my father, though. Chain-smoking through the latter part of Bradman's innings, constantly assuring me that even if he made 50 or so we'd been privileged to be there, insisting that we couldn't expect a century every time he went to the wicket, then grabbing me so hard by the arm that it hurt when the miscue floated towards McCool. 'If he catches it, they'll lynch him,' my father said hoarsely, as the ball hung forever in the high blue air of the 'G'.

I returned to the MCG on 3 January 1952 to see the last day of the Fourth Test against John Goddard's West Indian team, which included Worrell and Weekes and the rampaging spin pair, Ramadhin and Valentine. Australia had won the first two Tests and West Indies the third. Australia, needing 260 to win, were looking down the barrel by tea on what was to be the last day, having been murdered by Ramadhin and Valentine. The last two were in – Doug Ring and Bill Johnston. Ring could bat a bit, and Johnston was a famous 'bunny'. Edging, snicking, lofting the ball over the increasingly agitated fieldsmen, running three where there should have been only two and one where there was scarcely a run at all, the partnership, masterminded by Ring, who did most of the hitting, realised 38 – enough for Australia to win by one wicket.

Thirty thousand people watched this remarkable rearguard action, many of them rushing across from offices in the city as news of the afternoon's play and Australia's desperate plight spread. I was so tense as Ring and Johnston tightroped their way through over after over that I was unknowingly kicking the seat in front of me, one of the long green jarrah seats in the old outer – a rat-a-tat, rat-a-tat of anxiety – until one of the blokes sitting on it turned around and, no doubt gratefully venting his own worry on a ready-made juvenile scapegoat, said, 'Stop kicking the seat or I'll break your bloody neck.'

But after 1952, following a short MCG-less interlude while I struggled through secondary school, my recollections of the 'G' are bound up in memories of a great friendship. In my last year at school (1953), I had shared several classes with a saturnine, brilliant bloke named Ray Tynan. We got to know each other in that final school year and became great mates when we went on to Melbourne University.

Ray was a Richmond supporter, but he was also one of those people who just liked to see some good footy. As a matter of fact, he was open to experience generally, in a way that I was too timid to contemplate, then at least. Ray was a year older than I was and when we met at school he was repeating his matriculation while I was making my debut. His results had been excellent, but he was repeating because his father thought he was still a 'bloody ignoramus' at the end of his first year. I came across him when he was lounging his way through matriculation for a second time to become better educated.

Nothing could have been further from my thoughts than an additional year, although my father, like Ray's, was all for it. I wanted to get shot of school. I hadn't liked much of it, and I couldn't wait to leave. So, I worked hard to get the scholarships that would mollify my father and launch me into the university, for which – because I was too young, stunningly unsophisticated and embarrassingly lacking in confidence – I was entirely unsuited. Second-year matric would have made all the difference.

Ray's urbanity and consequent greater willingness to give almost anything a go meant that we were not all that close during our first university year. Ray played a lot of billiards and snooker and made a wide circle of friends. I buried myself in the library, working away each day with massive ineffectiveness, and got to know a few others whose lack of self-esteem and anxiety about exams might have been something like my own, although perhaps they were simply hard workers. But Ray and I kept in touch and, by the start of the university term in 1955, we were very much in tune and already plotting the overseas trip that we would eventually make together six years later.

Ray was fascinated by the rise of Melbourne in the Victorian Football League (from eleventh in 1953 to losing Grand Finalists in 1954) and was confidently predicting they would dominate for years to come. He went to the MCG on the Queen's Birthday to see Richmond, 37 points in front at three-quarter time, succumb to a paralysing Melbourne last quarter and lose by more than two goals. (I meanwhile was at the Junction Oval watching St Kilda finish eight goals behind Footscray.)

Ray decided we should go to the Grand Final that year and, if possible, to every remaining Grand Final during the 1950s. And we did, which was how I came to see the dominant years of the Melbourne Football Club, which played in the six Grand Finals from 1955 to 1960 and won five of them. We punctuated this sequence by going to the Olympic Games in 1956, and each summer we watched Sheffield Shield and Test cricket from Bay 13.

Ray and I became, like most of our peers and so many of the population of Melbourne, MCG habitués. The MCG was one of 'our' haunts, as familiar as a favourite pub or cafe. We weren't alone in this attitude, of course. Most of Melbourne, we soon discovered, especially – but by no means only – most of *youthful* Melbourne, felt exactly the same way.

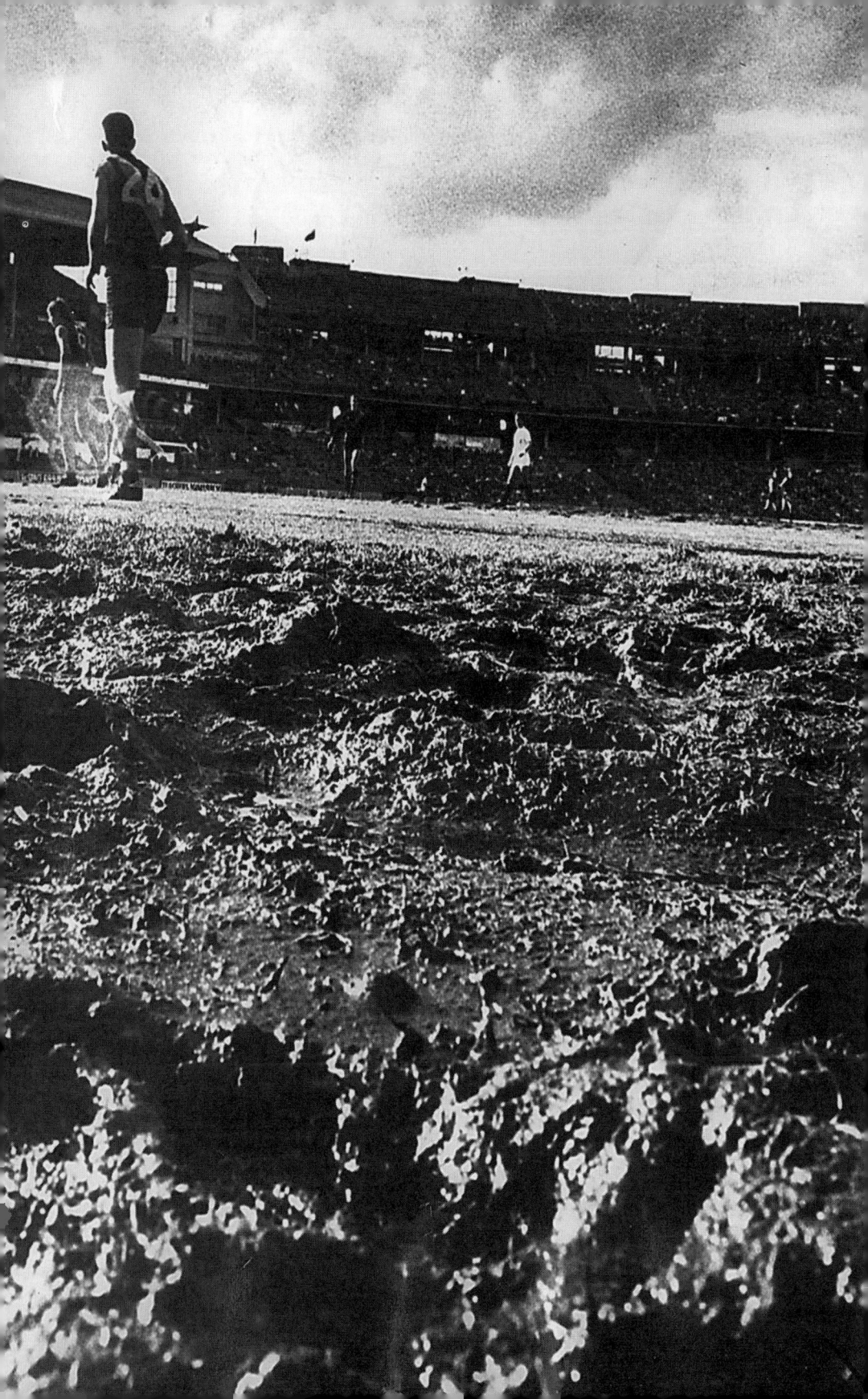

PART ONE

If the ghost of Tom Wills ever visits the
Yarra Park, he would be intrigued to see
the huge stadium enclosing the ground
on which he had often played cricket and
[would be] delighted to know that football
is now played there . . .

Geoffrey Blainey, *A Game of Our Own*

AND NOW FOR the Great Big MCG Show of Tom Wills presented by Magic – over one night only.

It is dark night and deepest winter. *Melbourne* winter – as it used to be thirty, forty years ago, a creaking, cramping cold tightening on flesh, needling at bone. Astringent, eye-smarting fog swirls up from the Yarra, the river of mists, folding Southbank and Flinders Street Station into lumpy grey parcels, squatting on Princes Bridge and swallowing headlights and the snailing, clanking trams like a black hole gulping light, clotting Swanston and Flinders streets, coiling downstream thick and damp into the parklands, entombing the motionless trees of Yarra Park. On Eastern Hill, St Patrick's Cathedral spire is a mere point of warning light. Further down the slope, the Hilton is a scarcely visible glow and, in the valley below, the darkened, silent MCG is wrapped as if by Christo, tower to tower, roof line to roof line, in an obscure, bitter and formless shroud.

There are ghosts everywhere in this murky, noiseless and muffled winter night. They are crowding around the MCG, the great stadium that all of them have known at different times down the years, for it has been many things to so many people. And from their insubstantial and milling ranks emerges that one figure who, above all, must be Phantom to the MCG's Opera. Materialising from the gloom only a stone's throw from the fog- and night-muffled heart of twenty-first-century Melbourne, he is leading the ghostly throng back into the 'G' – all those multitudes, and not just footballers and cricketers, that the ground has accommodated for their many purposes over its time in Yarra Park. He is taking them back there to relive, remember, reproduce – in the space of one haunted fog-mantled night – the great times, the culture and the metamorphoses of the MCG before the dawn chases all shades and ghosts back into their mysterious and unreachable darkness. The Phantom is Tom Wills.

THOMAS WENTWORTH WILLS's grandfather, Edward Wills, was a highway robber whose sentence of death had been commuted to transportation for life. Edward eagerly grasped his second chance and, in partnership with his wife – a free woman – he became a successful small businessman in Sydney. Tom's father, Sydney-born Horatio Spencer Wills, was a printer and publisher who hankered after land and duly acquired some on the Molonglo Plains close to Canberra, when that highly structured urban and constitutional experiment was not even a gleam in anyone's eye.

Horatio moved his family to Victoria – the Port Phillip District, as it then was – when Tom, who was born on 19 August 1835, was about four and a half. They settled in the Western District of Victoria on a property near Ararat called 'Lexington'. Here Tom Wills began to reveal his phenomenal sporting abilities, playing cricket with his cousins and other children of the district and probably a species of football using stuffed possum skins with the Aboriginal children living in the area. Tom also learnt the language of the local Aborigines and became fluent in it.

After a stint at Rugby School in England, where he distinguished himself as a cricketer, less so as a scholar, he returned to Melbourne and in early practice sessions at the MCG quickly bore out all the rumours about him as a magnificent cricketer. He played – and dominated – for the Melbourne Cricket Club and Victoria, which he captained in eight matches, and when he was free to do so played with several other clubs. For Wills, the cricket season became a rather frenetic, crowded, eventful and invariably successful interlude in the year. When cricket stopped for winter, Wills, of all people, must have felt terribly let down. Perhaps this sense of emptiness, combined with his naturally restless and questing intelligence when it came to all things sporting, moved him to wonder how cricketers might occupy the winter months. His suggestion, embodied in one of his characteristically flowery letters, would change the history of sport in the infant colony and then in the nation.

Like many a sportsman who followed him, Wills found it difficult to accept the quieter life after years of fame and crowded sporting endeavour. But he had other demons as well, which drove him to alcoholism and a horrible death.

BRANDISHING A – a wand, is it? Surely not, but a something – some-thing shiny, glinting in his upraised right hand, batonlike, Tom Wills strides at the head of the columns of the past, melting through the 'G's closed gates, and leads them – all the multitudinous makers of MCG history – on to the fog-curtained oval.

He stands in the centre of the arena, where in modern times the umpire holds the football in the air as he prepares to start a match; where batsmen gaze around the field before taking guard; where Wills himself won games off his own notoriously heavy bat, or with his own bowling. It is as if he is pausing to remember, running tracts of history – the 'big picture' – past his ghostly mind's eye in the instant between the siren's opening blare and the footy hitting the middle of the centre circle and lifting up into . . . into . . . the whole world and all its mad possibilities and connections . . .

WHACK, THE BALL thumps the earth and up it goes, right into the northern hemisphere. And here is – not Wills, for the moment, but *me*. I am in Venice for the first time in my life and I am at the airport, having just arrived on the flight from Rome. I have instructions to follow. First, I must find a phone (the mobile being still an idea on some boffin's drawing board) and ring Professor Bernard Hickey. It is Hickey who has issued the instructions and, for the next six weeks, providing I can find him, I'll be working with him at the University of Venice – at Ca' Foscari, as it is known. In those days – December 1974 – you had to buy *gettone* (small coinlike plugs that dropped into the slot where you would think coins might go) to use the phone. Forgetting this, I try several times in vain with *lira* coins before noticing the sign.

Equipped with *gettone* after a struggle with a bored person behind the sixth counter I enquire at, I return to the phone and dial the number. Engaged. I try again immediately. Engaged. I go for a nervous short stroll and return to the phone. A bloke in overalls and cement-dusted work boots is using it, waving and gesticulating and shouting. It sounds like a knock-down, drag-out terminal fight, but he is probably just ordering more cement. I wait five minutes or so, and he seems to show signs of finishing. Or, at least, he has launched into a furious crescendo of what sound like obscenities and death threats but are almost certainly only confirmation and summary of his order.

As I wait for his peroration, I realise why the Italians are and have always been so good at opera. Italian life unfolds each day, not with the rational continuity of the novel – so preferred in Anglo-Saxon society – or the Scandinavian cold spareness of the short story, but with traditional opera's volatility, its shameless addiction to the non sequitur, its grand gesturing style, its impatience with the mundane.

The cement man finishes with a last verbal flurry and leaves the booth, throwing an amiable 'Buongiorno' to me over his departing shoulder.

I dial the number. Engaged. As I slam the receiver down in desperation, I remember that the ringing sound on European phones is a series of tones similar to our engaged signal. I ring again, listen to the 'engaged signal' and a cheery voice eventually says, 'Pronto.' It is Bernard Hickey. Relief. Instructions.

'Take the airport bus to Piazzale Roma. There you will see the boat stops. The vaporetti. Take line one – linea uno – to fermata quattordici: Stop 14. It's easy. Non e difficile.'

After enquiring at, and on two occasions abortively boarding, the five or six buses on offer, I find and ensconce myself on the correct one. Piazzale Roma – a bustling, vast space of cars, buses, pedestrians, touts, layabouts and buzzing, nipping Vespas and Lambrettas, where only white lines define roadways and paths, so that everybody and everything goes everywhere – is the bus-line terminus, so no worries about when to get off. Scarcely noticing or realising that I am looking down on the waters of the Canal Grande, even if this is not its most alluring stretch, I anxiously discover *linea uno* and buy a ticket.

Off we go with that rise and fall of diesel chugging that becomes ever after one of the remembered sounds of Venice, so that you will have a moment's acute, debilitating nostalgia in Russell Street one day months later as the scream of a bus's engine momentarily duplicates the note of a labouring *vaporetto*.

The Canal Grande unfolds before me and all anxiety melts in the slow, curving revelation of wonder after wonder – Byron's house, Ca' d'Oro, Ca' Foscari, Rialto . . . And the last wonder is at Stop 14: a towering, elegant dome floating, it seems, above the water's edge where the Canal is soon to widen into the Lagoon. I will discover that this is the stunning Santa Maria della Salute. But also at Stop 14 is Hickey – who has his own elegant style and, while not describable as towering, has an impressive rotundity reminiscent at least of domes. My work and my never-ending love affair with Venice, '*La Serenissima*', have begun.

. . . There was a downside to being, as Venice was in the fourteenth century, the main European port of entry for the rich trade from the East. Arriving ships brought more than their commercial cargo and left behind them less visible yet much more potent and durable testimony to their visits – not surprisingly, since galleys would berth with crews 'horribly infected' and dying at their oars. Seventy disastrous epidemics attacked *La Serenissima* in 700 years. In 1348, the Black Death at its peak claimed 600 Venetians a day. Near the other end of that seven-century spectrum, in 1630, Venice suffered a sixteen-month encounter with the plague during which 45 000 Venetians died. Little wonder, then, that as the plague – for no reason that anyone understood – began to wane, a grateful, religious and superstitious people was moved to thank the Lord or, in this case, the Mother of God, for deliverance.

Architects were invited to submit plans for the building of a church that would stand as Venice's act of thanksgiving for salvation at last from the plague. A young Venetian architect, Baldassare Longhena, submitted the successful design and his Church of Santa Maria della Salute – Our Lady of Health – rose spectacularly on a peninsula between the Canal Grande and the Canale delle Zattere, where it stands today as one of Venice's more breathtaking and talismanic monuments.

Santa Maria della Salute was extraordinary in Longhena's time, and it remains distinguished and arresting even among the wonders of contemporary Venice. The building is octagonal, with an imposing dome that can be seen and recognised from many vantage points along the Grand Canal and beyond the Lagoon. Inside, you can walk right around it in a circle, circumnavigating the central space, which is like a small oval, and passing on your left (or your right, depending whether you go clockwise or anticlockwise) a series of specially dedicated altars and chapels. It is an immensely exciting and elegantly beautiful place, whether seen from inside or from afar. And it is there because some-one reflected upon the importance of the people's health, the gift of physical wellbeing.

Tom Wills, a couple of hundred years later and a hemisphere away in colonial Melbourne, would have recognised Baldassare Longhena's inspiration and seriousness; perhaps he even knew about the Venetian architect, because Wills was a highly intelligent and well-educated man. At any rate, it was a concern for the health and fitness of Melbourne's cricketers that prompted Wills to write a famous letter to the journal *Bell's Life* on 10 July 1858. This letter is well known to anyone with an interest in the history and origins of Australian Rules football but it nevertheless should be quoted whenever the MCG is discussed or dreamed about.

Sir: Now that cricket has been put aside for some months to come and cricketers have assumed somewhat of the chrysalis nature (for a time only 'tis true), but at length will again burst forth in all their varied hues, rather than allow this state of torpor to creep over them, and stifle their now supple limbs, why can they not, I say, form a football club, and form a committee of three or more to draw up a code of laws. If a club of this sort were got up, it would be of vast benefit to any cricket ground to be trampled upon, and would make the turf firm and durable; besides which it would keep those who are inclined to become stout from having their joints encased in useless superabundant flesh . . . Trusting that someone will take up the matter . . .

I remain yours truly, T. W. Wills

Wills's modest proposal had massive ramifications. It resulted in his having the chance to construct and shape the very game of football he was vaguely suggesting might be beneficial. (Just as, in the army, the men who eagerly admit to being able to play the piano are then asked to shift it, so Wills, having made the suggestion about off-season fitness, was then lumbered with the task of bringing it to fruition – although, while he probably avoided piano shifting as strenuously as anyone else, there is no hint that he either objected to the football assignment or found it difficult.)

The suggestion itself was interesting enough, but Wills's lateral way of going about the invention of football was extraordinary. Presented with an easy and ready-to-hand solution – rugby or some version of it – Wills deliberately steered away from this beckoning model. Rugby, he maintained, was too bruising a game for young men who had to ensure that they kept working during the week. And, in any case, the antipodean earth was too hard for a game that involved such dives and tackles as invariably brought players into thumping contact with the ground.

Wills's recognition that the players would not be privileged young men of leisure and private-school provenance, but ordinary workers who could not afford injury or prolonged absence from work, was one of the early and crucial blows struck for the Australian code's being a game of the people. *Populi ludos populo* was its early motto – the game of the people for the people. The seedbed of rugby in England was the exclusive, class-based public schools, and the same process was developing in the colony. It was remarkable of Wills not only to perceive the possibility for a departure from the rugby running and tackling offside rule model but also to have the force of personality to resist its implicit pressures of caste and tradition.

Intent on these lateral, heretical ideas, Wills set to work with three collaborators – William Hammersley and James Thompson, both formerly of Trinity College, Cambridge, and Thomas Smith, a master at Scotch College, Melbourne, and a graduate of Trinity College, Dublin. Strongly influenced by Wills's ideas and presumably suppressing and disowning their various Trinity traditions, these three worked with Wills to produce a game with no offside rule, no free running while holding the ball, and a system of 'catching' the ball, which would eventually offer wonderful opportunities for spectacle.

J. B. Ellis, a member of the Melbourne Cricket Club committee under Wills's secretaryship, commented, with a mixture of amazement, vague disapproval and ill-concealed admiration:

> Wills has no circumspection, nor is his thinking ever of one piece. He proposes a committee to establish a code of rules for football, saying the Victorian XI is lacking in the requisite hardiness for battle, then discounts the rugby game, saying it would result in too many injuries if played on hard grounds by men! He says we shall have 'a game of our own'. In a characteristic flourish which could only succeed in injuring the feelings of

several of those round the committee table, he then added that the offside rule was designed by the English for captains who cannot set a field!

Wills's refusal to inherit the offside rule meekly and without criticism – perhaps the single most stunning and revolutionary decision he took in proposing 'a game of our own' – was no mere whim or rush of iconoclasm but something he had thought about and consciously decided upon. The game he gradually fashioned was, and remains, one of only two football codes in the world without an offside rule.

When his father, Horatio, moved the family and stock to the Western District, near Ararat, the young Wills, comfortable and familiar in the company of the Aborigines, played a kind of football known to the Aborigines as *marn grook* – 'game ball'. It was played with a ball made of, or wrapped in, a possum skin. One of the features of *marn grook*, unsurprisingly, if you consider the natural athleticism of Aboriginal people, was leaping for the ball.

A Government Protector of Aboriginals witnessed and recorded a corroboree of the Djabwurung and Jardwadjali peoples of western Victoria in 1841, which seems to have featured a game of *marn grook*: 'The men and boys joyfully assemble when this game is to be played . . . Some of them will leap as high as five feet from the ground to catch the ball. The person who secures the ball kicks it.'

It was a game as much about air as about earth. Seen in the context of his boyhood experiences playing *marn grook*, Wills's determined rejection of the available structure and rules of rugby may be regarded as not mere doggedness but as the stance of a man who had another model in mind altogether.

The consequences for the MCG were huge though not immediate. Wills's confident assertion that the hallowed turf would benefit from a good trampling was a view not shared by the Melbourne Cricket

Club. For its first fifteen years, Australian football as practised by the Melbourne Football Club took place on a paddock alongside the cricket ground. In the one exception to this rule during those years, a game between the 14th Regiment and the Melbourne team, the Melbourne captain, Henry Harrison, was told, 'Harrison, you have ruined our ground.' It would not be the last time such a complaint was raised.

Australian Rules football quickly became a favourite of colonial Melbourne and, after the fifteen-year period of exile, the swiftly evolving, improving Melbourne Cricket Ground began its notorious double life – a cricket ground in name and origins in which football was rapidly becoming the most exciting attraction.

Like Baldassare Longhena, Tom Wills had submitted a successful plan. When, under his supervision, the game he proposed became a reality, it contributed mightily to the development and formation of the 'G', because it was adjacent to the MCG that the first match of what was recognisably the new code of Australian Rules football took place – on a patch of ground of prodigious length (it would be years before agreement was reached about the shape and size of grounds) and over a total period of three days between teams from Scotch College and Melbourne Grammar School. The result was a draw, one goal each, but the spectacle and the possibilities greatly excited Wills, who was Melbourne Grammar's elected umpire, and many others who saw it.

Wills would have been pleased, getting on for 150 years later, with sculptor Louis Laumen's tribute to that epochal game – a statue of two boys competing for the ball with Wills alertly watching on. Costing $160 000, the statue was underwritten and donated by the communities of the two schools, Melbourne Grammar and Scotch, as a Centenary of Federation gift to the people of Victoria through the aegis of the MCC. Placed outside the MCG's Gallery of Sport, the statue has become an apt chronological starting point for the popular

MCG tours. A beautiful leather-bound book recording the conception and development of the statue project was also presented by the schools to the MCC. In Venice, Longhena's work and vision are commemorated not only in his soaring structure but also in a plaque recording his achievement. Similarly, the muscular, dynamic statue is a reminder of Wills's initiative and foresight in proposing a game that would be integral to and a profound influence upon the development of the MCG.

Over time and nourished by cricket and, increasingly, by the new football code, the MCG rose spectacularly on the leafy expanse of the Police Paddock where it stands today as one of Melbourne's most dramatic and talismanic monuments. The MCG was already recognised as potentially extraordinary, even in Tom Wills's time, and it remains distinguished and arresting among the competing tall buildings and burgeoning architecture of contemporary Melbourne.

The building is roughly circular, with the Great Southern Stand and the six light towers visible and recognisable from the central city and from many vantage points along the river and in the surrounding suburban and inner-city precincts. Inside the cathedral-like stadium, you can theoretically walk right around it in a circle, circumnavigating the central space, the famous smooth green oval on which armies, rock bands, priests, popes, royalty, athletes, opera singers, cyclists, players of soccer, rugby and lacrosse, soldiers, sailors and airmen and, above all, heroic cricketers and footballers have strutted their hour. These days, corporate boxes, like small chapels dedicated to this or that aspect of the god Mammon, can be viewed on your left or your right as you pass (depending if you walk clockwise or anticlockwise).

But whether you use the internal causeway or try to walk around behind the seats, the circumnavigation inside the MCG is only theoretical because you can't walk into and through the Members' area and, on football match days, you can't walk though the AFL Members' area either. But you can still cover long, curving arcs within these constraints and, as you go, you will pass bars, food stalls, football and cricket souvenir merchandising shops, offices, first aid posts, toilets and numerous other enterprises and conveniences that people who run the MCG like to call 'facilities' or 'outlets' but which, together, become a sort of curving marketplace through which the crowds shuffle, laugh, dispute, quest – for beer, pies, toilets – and browse. It is an immensely exciting, and in its own massive, dwarfing way, a beautiful place, whether seen from inside or from afar. And it has taken on its identity at least partly because Tom Wills reflected one day upon the importance of sportsmen's health, the gift of physical wellbeing.

WILLS'S TRANCE HAS lasted only a split second, even if it has taken him around the world and centuries into the past. Now he gestures with his baton, and the MCG, blackened and silenced with fog outside, is called into life on its famous arena and around its historic stands and terraces. The Police Paddock appears and quickly transmutes into the first lineaments of the Melbourne Cricket Ground, with its modest pavilion and the first cricket match, in September 1854. And here are those two famous teams from Melbourne Grammar School and Scotch College who played the inaugural game of Australian football in the paddock just outside the ground in 1858 and, with them, the Melbourne and South Yarra football teams who played the first game on the actual MCG arena.

And here, being waved through by Tom Wills, is H. H. Stephenson's XI, colourfully sashed and dashing, the first English cricket team to play on Australian soil.

In Charles Dickens's famous novel *Great Expectations*, the criminal Magwitch, an escapee from the prison hulks, disappears into the Antipodes and, as things turn out, makes his fortune in Australia. He is eventually revealed as the magnanimous and above all mysterious benefactor of Philip Pirrip – known as 'Pip' – who, as a small boy, had helped Magwitch escape, mainly because he was too terrified to do otherwise. It comes as a grievous disappointment and shame to Pip, the mature, affluent young man, to discover the shady origins of his fortune, which he had wrongly assumed to be of a quite different and much more salubrious provenance.

Although the tale is endowed with Dickens's customary narrative genius and intricate plotting, the central device – an old lag disappearing into the depths of the impossibly distant Australian colonies then returning enriched if not, in this case, transformed – is a variation on a favourite theme of the time. The colonies were a great narrative gift in which to bury, discover, rediscover, kill off, redeem and generally play merry plotting hell with the lives and fortunes of fictional characters.

Dickens was hard at work writing and serially publishing *Great Expectations* in 1860–61. It appeared in his weekly periodical, *All the Year Round* (formerly, until 1859, *Household Words*), which he continued to produce until his death in 1870. In these two journals, Dickens published many of his most famous novels and stories. *Bleak House* appeared throughout 1852–53; *Hard Times* in 1854; *Little Dorrit* in 1855–57; *A Tale of Two Cities* in 1859. Because he was concentrating on *Great Expectations* during 1860 and part of 1861 – and remember, it was serialised, which meant constant, pressing and unavoidable deadlines – it is unlikely that Dickens would have tolerated any significant interruption. On the other hand, he was an enthusiastic traveller. He had been to America in 1842 and was following with interest that country's descent into the Civil War, which began in 1861. The plot of *Great Expectations* meant that he must have been devoting a certain amount of thought, however fugitively, to Australia. Like any novelist, while no slave to research or documentation, he needed to make Magwitch's career credible and would therefore have read at least cursorily about the convict 'system' and the fate and fortunes of old lags and their like in the colonies.

If, during 1861, Dickens had received a letter from Australia 'out of the blue', you might think he would say, 'Well, speak of the Devil' and, even if only because of the coincidence, he might have been expected to pay it some attention. If that letter was offering him, an intrepid traveller, a trip to Australia, it might assume even greater interest. With *Great Expectations* either completed or close to it, the prospect of a journey to Magwitch's happy hunting ground, where he would read and lecture in his already famous way, might have given Dickens at least food for thought.

Such a letter *was* written. It came from Felix Spiers and Christopher Pond, Melbourne hotel owners. Their idea was for Dickens to come to Australia for a reading and lecturing tour. Spiers and Pond offered him £10 000 and the usual hospitality – perks, as we would call them. It was a handsome offer, and they were right to think it might appear tempting to the novelist. It was odd, therefore, and disappointing, that they received no reply – ever.

Postal services between Britain and Australia were slow but reliable, and post within Britain was excellent. It seems unlikely that the letter did not arrive, but it seems equally unlikely that Dickens, as prodigious a correspondent as he was a writer of stories, would not have managed even a note of acknowledgement. Whatever the explanation, this breakdown in communications was to be of enormous importance for the Melbourne Cricket Ground.

Spiers and Pond were not easily put off. That commercial spirit and determination explained, no doubt, their success. When the Dickensian silence had reached unignorable profundity, they abandoned the idea of a lecture tour by the great man and turned to other possibilities. To widen the range of their thinking, they sought a lateral thinker and consulted the Hon. George Selth Coppin.

As well as being a member of the Victorian Parliament (1858–63) during his career of many callings, Coppin was the leading actor and entrepreneur of his day. He owned and embellished the exotic Cremorne Garden in what is now Richmond where, apart from botanical gardens, gas lighting, gondola transport to and from Princes Bridge, a bar and a theatre, there were sideshows, performing animals, a Fat Boy, a Bearded Lady and a man known as 'Juan Fernandez' who each night put his head into a lion's mouth. 'Rare and astonishing novelties' indeed, as Coppin promised.

He commissioned a balloon to be built by Coxwell's of Tottenham, England; and the *Australasian* – 60 feet high, 40 feet in diameter, when inflated with 31 000 cubic feet of gas – carried William

Dean on the first balloon ascent in Australia. He lifted off from Cremorne Garden on 1 February and came to earth in Sydney Road, Brunswick. If William Dean was in a mood to celebrate his flight, he had landed conveniently close to the Cambridge Arms Hotel, but the record is not illuminating.

Dean's intended partner, Professor C. H. Brown, couldn't take a trick. When it became clear the balloon would not lift off with both of them on board, he jumped out, allowing Dean to soar. When, on 15 February, Brown made his own ascent in the *Australasian*, he too took off from Coppin's balloon platform at Cremorne Garden but, with different wind patterns, landed on the edge of Collingwood, where he was attacked by amazed and fearful onlookers. Or perhaps they were neither amazed nor fearful but simply prototypically *Collingwood*.

Coppin, well ahead of his time in matters of flight and theme parks and also in the possibilities of what we know as tourism, saw the potential of Sorrento, on the Mornington Peninsula, and developed it as a resort within reach of Melbourne people. He even ran a tramway from the township to the surf beach.

This was the man Spiers and Pond turned to for advice on how to fill the silence left by the magisterial but non-respondent Dickens. Coppin was visible enough in Melbourne at the best of times, but it was particularly easy for Spiers and Pond to have their attention drawn to him since his Theatre Royal was adjacent to the two businessmen's Royal Hotel and their Café de Paris.

Coppin's immediate advice was to sign up a cricket tour and, with some difficulty and a false start or two, they duly did so. The MCG was not far from Cremorne Garden, and it is not hard to imagine that a fertile, performance-orientated mind like Coppin's must have been mentally pencilling in for future reference the many opportunities its broad arena and ever-improving capacity and accommodation offered.

Like a willing bride, when Spiers and Pond popped the question, he didn't have to think twice. So, once again, the MCG's familiar profile appeared at the end point and climax of much apparently unrelated manoeuvring when H. H. Stephenson's team of cricket professionals arrived in Melbourne aboard the SS *Great Britain* on Christmas Eve in 1861.

Feted, cheered, mobbed, scrutinised and subjected to various newspaper analyses, which arrived at a multiplicity of conclusions, not all of them complimentary, the English cricketers strode on to the MCG on New Year's Day 1862 to take part in the first England–Australia cricket match. Actually, not quite a *match* in one sense of the word: there were 11 Englishmen against 18 Victorians, but it could have been worse: a team of 22 was originally mooted for Victoria. Players wore coloured ribbons on their hats and coloured sashes and, on that first day, about 20 000 people (estimates varying downwards to 15 000 and up to 25–26 000) came to watch the fun, which included a flight by the *Australasian*.

Over the four days of the game, 45 000 people attended. If Melbourne people's reputation as magnificent supporters of sporting occasions at the MCG was not actually inaugurated at this game, it received one of its more resounding fillips. Certainly the response gladdened the hearts of Spiers and Pond whose investment was pretty well covered by that one game, after which the rest of the tour was, appropriately enough given the role of Coppin, all cop.

WILLS, MEANWHILE, on his arena of ghosts, is surrounded by Aboriginal cricketers – Tarpot, Bullocky, Watty, Mullagh, King Cole, Dick-a-Dick, Cuzens, Paddy, Harry Rose, Jellico, Peter and Red Cap. This was, with the odd alteration and exception, the team that played under his supervision on the MCG against an MCC team on Boxing Day in 1866. Eleven thousand spectators came to see them, a good crowd for a bunch of unknowns, but it was already clear that people would 'support' the 'G', that it had a magnetic capacity to draw in the people, to 'create' big occasions.

The Tom Wills-coached Aboriginal team would play three more times on the MCG in the next three years, would provide the nucleus of the Aboriginal team that toured England in 1868, and would produce from its ranks one of the greatest cricketers, black or white, of his time – Unaarrimin or, as he became known, Johnny Mullagh. Although characteristically dismissive of most of the team, W. G. Grace, the most famous player of the day, praised Mullagh highly.

Who can now know the full and detailed impact the extraordinary

English tour of the Aboriginal team had in England and at home, but lingering stories of their exploits may have influenced one of the stranger migrations to Australia. Rebecca Castledine, who was born in Bow, England, in 1876, travelled to Australia in the early years of the twentieth century, soon after joined the Adnyamathanha people and married Jack 'Witchetty' Forbes in 1914. Rebecca became a figure of great anthropological interest, compared by writer Ernestine Hill to Daisy Bates (who, though 'constantly among natives', could not, like Rebecca, 'exist in a blacks camp') and described by R. M. Williams in his *I Once Met a Man* as 'hammering, shaping, melting humanity into something worthy of life'. She is buried alongside her husband at Nepabunna, South Australia. There is some suggestion that this mysterious woman – described on her gravestone as 'Peacefully sleeping. A true friend and companion of the Adnyamathanha' – may have been inspired to make her ambitious journey and become, as she put it, 'the only real white Australian there is', because she heard tales of the Aboriginal cricket team and their progress through her homeland. A long bow, but one of those historical quirks that you hope is true.

It was probably Wills's destiny to be the mentor and instructor of an Aboriginal cricket team because of his early connections with the tribes and his understanding, both intellectual and intuitive, of them. Still, though he encountered the Englishmen at various times as well as through the agency of his Aboriginal players, Wills was not available to take on H. H. Stephenson and his men.

Early in 1861, that year during which Spiers and Pond were waiting in vain for a reply from Dickens, Wills 'went bush'. With his father, Horatio, he journeyed to Brisbane. Horatio had bought a vast tract of land a couple of hundred miles west of Rockhampton, and Wills had agreed to help him drove a mob of sheep to the new 'run'. The new station was called 'Cullinlaringo', and it was soon established and busy. In October 1861, Wills went back to Brisbane with two bullock teams and their drivers to buy supplies.

According to Wills's brother, Cedric, an explosive situation had been building in the district even before the arrival of the Willses' plant. The local Aboriginal people were intent on revenging the shooting of several of their number by a Mr Jesse Gregson and a group of native police. According to Cedric, whose account appeared eventually on page seven of the Rockhampton *Daily Record* for 8 November 1912:

It seems that Gregson had not counted his sheep for a week or so, and all this time the blacks had seen a small mob of lost sheep . . . (There were no shepherd's foot-tracks with the sheep) . . . After several days of seeing them wandering about, one morning the blacks made a small yard, drove the sheep up to their camp, yarded and killed some, and were cooking the meat on their fires. That same morning, Gregson counted his sheep and found he was short. He went out and found the blacks' tracks on the sheep track. Without following them up, he went straight back to camp and, as there was a detachment of native police that had come the day before, they at once saddled up and Gregson took them to where he had seen the tracks.

Within a short distance, they came to the camp where the blacks were eating the mutton. The blacks did not think they were doing anything wrong and never moved or tried to get away. They simply went on cooking the meat as Gregson, the police officer and the troopers rode close up and fired right into the camp. Several blacks were wounded, but the others, though frightened at the noise of the guns, did not run but jumped to their feet. On seeing some of their mates unable to rise and crying out in fright, they knocked Gregson, the officer, and the troopers off their horses with nulla-nullas . . .

The blacks left the party all stunned and carried off their wounded. They could have killed Gregson, the officer and the troopers but did not do so, never thinking that the wounded among their numbers would die. But after a day some did. Then the others decided to be revenged and attack Gregson and his party. They sent runners all over the country, and were collecting at the foot of Separation Creek, on the Nogoa, which spot was only about six miles from where my father [Horatio Wills] made his camp. It seems Gregson and my father met at times on the run and rode together. Being dressed something alike, and both wearing pith helmets, the blacks took them for brothers, and decided to attack our party, which was nearer to them. Some of the blacks – the younger men and boys – were against the murder, but the elder men threatened to kill them if they divulged their plans, and they were so afraid of the old men that they left the camp.

The boy that gave me this information showed my brother, Horace, and me where the young blacks had spent the night previous to the murder. I asked this boy whether, if my father and the bullock driver had got together and shot one or two blacks, the others would have bolted. He replied, 'Carra.' (No) The blacks were in their hundreds. Of course I had heard of what Gregson and the native police had done, and being told the same story by this boy convinced me of its truth. It was just as my brother Tom [Wills] had said. Such acts are mostly the cause of all these murders. It makes my blood boil when I start on this subject – that Gregson, just for the sake of a few sheep, committed the act which was the cause of the murder of my father and all his party, men, women and children.

Wills stayed on after the massacre, which took place on 17 October, and did not return to Victoria until 1863. He then resumed his sporting career and interests with great gusto. What he did about the grief, loss, shock, sense of waste, and the irrational and vengeful welling-up of rage is not clear. He was on occasions taciturn, given to introspection, so no doubt much of this tumult was internalised – especially the guilt, baseless though it was, engendered by the sheer luck that had seen him escape and survive.

The cost of this denial, if that is what it was, would emerge savagely, tragically and without mercy as he grew older and as sporting prowess and opportunities waned.

BUT HERE IS Wills, centre stage again, waving his shining baton now at a stiff, uncomfortable-looking figure: Prince Alfred, Duke of Edinburgh, who had the honour in March 1867 of being the first member of royalty to grace the MCG – or perhaps he was the first royal whom the MCG deigned to recognise.

Granting little time to royalty, in fact appearing almost impatient that his precious witching hours might be wasted on protocol, Wills now gestures into existence one of the most famous of the MCG's 'moments': the first-ever Test match at the MCG in March 1877. James Lillywhite's touring Englishmen emerge from the darkness to face big Dave Gregory's Australians. Wills brings to flickering life episode after episode from this historic and wonderful contest like a series of modern 'highlights'.

Here is Charlie Bannerman, who scores the first 'Test' century and is one of several Australian heroes in a tight, exciting and fluctuating match. As an opening batsman and taking strike, Bannerman faces the first Test-match ball ever bowled, but his distinction is immeasurably greater than that as he goes on to score a brilliant 165. No one else does much with the bat for the Australians, however, and their total of 245 does not look imposing against Lillywhite's Englishmen. Who, conjured up by Wills's commands, crumble before off-spinner Midwinter. He bowls a titanic 54 overs, of which 23 are maidens, taking 5 wickets for 78.

In a disastrous second innings, in which Horan's 20 is the top score, Australia struggle to 104, and the match seems ready for England to pounce. If this happens, first official Test match or not, it will simply continue a depressing record on the Australians' part of failing to drive home an initial advantage and falling apart under the weight of greater experience and pressure.

But needing to make a modest and eminently achievable 154, England manage to cope with first-innings destroyer Midwinter only to be taken apart by debut spinner Tom Kendall, whose 7/55 off 33 overs rolls through pockets of stern English resistance and leads on to victory by 45 runs.

A hundred years later, this famous game is commemorated in one of the MCG's epochal performances. The Centenary Test, played on the 'G' on 12, 13, 14, 16 and 17 March 1977, had everything. Among this match's extraordinary riches are Australia's first-innings collapse for 138; magnificent fast bowling by Dennis Lillee and Max Walker to engender a corresponding collapse by England – for 95; a brilliant, rollicking century by Derek Randall, which includes having his cap (and almost his head) knocked off by Lillee, after which he springs back to his feet and doffs the cap with an expansive bow to the bowler; wicket-keeper Rod Marsh's sporting recall of Randall after he's been given out to a catch Marsh realises he has not quite made; new boy David Hookes hitting Tony Greig for five successive boundaries; Rick McCosker having his jaw broken by a rising ball from Willis in the first innings and returning to bat down the order in the second, with jaw wired and so heavily bandaged he looks like the Invisible Man on a day off; Rod Marsh's splendid and team-rescuing second-innings century – and so on.

If the game had been scripted, it could not have been more riveting, more extraordinary, eclipsing itself hour after hour as, somehow, the big occasions on the MCG have a habit of doing. And no scriptwriter would have dared provide the ending – *a win for Australia by 45 runs, the same margin as in that first Test 100 years earlier* . . .

Cricketers temporarily fade from Wills's magic scene under a flick of his baton, and conductor Julius Herz appears, energetically orchestrating his own performance, one in a series of Moonlight concerts on the oval, begun in 1878 and inaugurating what would be the MCG's infinite musical variety in later years.

The last notes are drowned by a gasp among the ghostly crew as 'The Demon' Spofforth, moustachioed and fierce of brow, joins the parade. Playing for Australia against England on 4 January 1879 at the MCG, Spofforth ushered England batsmen Vernon Royle, Francis MacKinnon and Tom Emmett into the galleries of cricket history by dismissing them with successive balls – Test cricket's first hat-trick.

And in the same year – night football under electric light! Collingwood Rifles played East Melbourne Artillery on the evening of 6 August and a week later Melbourne played Carlton. All four teams pour on to the oval under Wills's direction.

For football – Australian football – has been thriving since Tom Wills made the famous move that helped set it all in motion, and the name 'Collingwood' has been, from the start, one to conjure with.

ONE HUNDRED AND twenty-three years after the Collingwood Rifles team took the field for their night game, at 2.30 on the afternoon of Saturday 21 September 2002, Nathan Buckley led the Collingwood football team on to the MCG to meet the Adelaide Crows: the winner would play in the Grand Final the following week.

For most of the Magpie players, Buckley included, the massive roar that greeted their appearance – not merely painful to the ears but an almost physical blow – was a new experience. It had been eighteen years since the club had taken part in a Preliminary Final, and no one was interested in remembering that, because Collingwood had suffered a 133-point drubbing by Essendon. In 1990, after a Qualifying Final draw with the Eagles and a big win in the replay, the Magpies won the Second Semi-Final, went straight into the Grand Final and won it convincingly against Essendon.

But even that event, glorious and, to supporters, long overdue, had been swallowed up by failures in the following year, a losing Elimination Final in 1992 and then a long drought – 'a miserable eight years', as club president Eddie McGuire put it, 'the darkest period in the club's history' – during which Collingwood had touched unaccustomed depths before the administrative revolution that had delivered McGuire as president, Mick Malthouse as coach, and a lean, youthful playing list. No one, not even the steely, uncompromising Malthouse, expected them to go quite so far in 2002, but as rank underdogs they had beaten Port Adelaide in the Qualifying Final, and now they were the last Victorian side standing, the only hope of preventing the first-ever all-interstate Grand Final.

As the players burst on to the famous arena behind their impossibly grim-looking captain on that sunny September afternoon, they are carrying a certain amount of Collingwood baggage. Nervously they form a tight group in front of their banner:

THE PEOPLE'S CLUB
THE EXPERTS DON'T RATE
BUT TODAY WE WILL END
ANOTHER CLUB'S FATE

Buckley bursts through it, a ritual that even before ordinary home-and-away games invariably fires up a crowd – any crowd with a footy imagination, anywhere.

When, for example, the Dalai Lama arrived at Melbourne's Tullamarine Airport from Adelaide in 1991 and was loaded onto a media-mobile and whisked from the plane to the arrival concourse, he was greeted by a huge crowd of supporters and activists and confronted by wall-sized, orange banners exhorting FREE TIBET, CHINA OUT OF TIBET, and other cries of anguish. His entourage stopped, which meant that a few hundred disembarking passengers heading for their baggage also stopped behind him.

When the impasse had lasted a few minutes, with the Dalai Lama gazing benignly at the banners and his acolytes, a warmly ironic voice rang out from the back of the growing queue: 'Y're supposed to run *through* the banner, mate, not just bloody stare at it!' Welcome to Melbourne.

But the Collingwood team, as they sprint down the ground shedding bits of their black-and-white banner, bear an added burden on this Preliminary Final day: Victorians, sinking age-old and traditional hatred of the Magpies, from whose arrogance, hubris and conceit most other clubs have suffered at some time, are rallying to Collingwood to stave off the dreaded Crows and perhaps, unthinkably, even to keep the Premiership trophy and flag in Melbourne.

. . . You only have to glance over a shoulder, or gaze across the river or look down Spring Street from East Melbourne and you'll see the MCG. Depending where you are, it may be only one or two of the light towers that come into view. Or it may be those formidable curved walls or the flying-buttress-like props of the Great Southern Stand.

From most reasonable vantage points you'll see something of it, in the same way that you get glimpses of St Patrick's spire up on Eastern Hill, or St Paul's down in the middle of the city. These cathedrals, because of their sage and solemn, hefty stone and slimly spired authority, draw the gaze of visitors and even of Melbourne's blasé inhabitants. The ebbing of the tide of faith, as evident in Melbourne as anywhere else in the world, has diminished the gravity and authority of these holy places, but Melbourne people, unlike their brothers and sisters in less enlightened cities of the continent, have another avenue to God – or at least to enlightenment, to transcendence, to – triumph, nostalgia, joy and bittersweetness.

IN THE BEGINNING and before the Crows, before the Power came upon the face of the mid-west, the name 'Adelaide' meant the capital of South Australia, the City of Churches, as it was known. The City of Churches was a title that accurately captured a physical and geo-graphical reality – Adelaide did have many churches – but also shaded into psychological territory, grasped somehow, a mood, an ambience. Conservative, stolid, moral and law-abiding, the good burghers of Adelaide were proud of their untainted colonial lineage; their emphatic separation from the fleshpots of the east (a demarcation marked not only by great and gradually more arid distances but also by a different time zone), their Englishness, which was perceived to outstrip the Englishness of other states, and the even, not to mention downright sombre, tenor of their ways.

In Adelaide, for the first fifty or sixty years of last century, life was relentlessly unexceptionable. Restaurants were few, uninspiring and subject to many constraints. Pubs were more numerous, often very pleasant, but early closing. (Melbourne in the same period had many more pubs but they closed just as early.) Theatres and concert venues were barely adequate although, of all the capitals, Adelaide was, and remains, a place of splendid music. At the halfway mark of the century, the City of Churches had come to signify to most Australians not merely that Adelaide was a much-steepled, Sunday-somnolent sort of place, but also that it was staid, puritanical, narrow and joyless.

There was a time when Adelaideans did not regard this profile as either insulting or burdensome; on the contrary, many of them took pride in it. As gaudiness, tall buildings and brashness began to flower in the eastern states (no one, not even Adelaideans, worried about Perth in those days, Brisbane was unimaginable, and Hobart quite possibly not there at all), the people of Adelaide and South Australia generally could not envisage change. The status quo was set in concrete with the name 'Tom Playford' carved severely into it. Everything would be the same for ever and ever.

Inexorably change did come, even, as some saw it, savagely. If the concrete block of the status quo was inscribed 'Playford', change arrived with the ornate autograph 'Don Dunstan'. By the end of what came to be known as the Dunstan era, which roughly coincided with the 1970s, Adelaide had a world-class Festival of Arts; a Festival Centre, one of the least fussy and best of all the capital-city arts centres, in which music and theatre at last found their proper place; a vibrant urban life that took maximum advantage of the city's marvellous compactness, casual beauty, and wonderful climate; and a standard of cuisine that broke the ground for the rest of the country and remains, fortunately, one of the world's best-kept secrets. In this maelstrom, however, and despite the fact that one aspect of the rush of change was the deconsecration of many churches (they became restaurants, discos, clubs or less respectable enterprises), the old name stuck: City of Churches. In 1970s Adelaide it could not have been less appropriate, although, as in the past, when it really was the truth, no one much cared.

Curiously, it would have been slightly more accurate by, say, the end of the seventies, to have transferred the title City of Churches to Melbourne. This was not so much because Melbourne had a great number of churches, although they were numerous enough, or because it was especially staid. It was more that Melbourne's churches were dominant, impossible to ignore. The most important and powerful and atmospheric of them were not churches at all: they were cathedrals – and there were three of them.

. . . It is just Christmas Day, and Midnight Mass in St Patrick's Cathedral, East Melbourne, is approaching the Consecration in front of a vast congregation. For the past two hours, people have been crowding through the Gothic archway of the main entrance, shuffling under the bronze and ageless gaze of Saints Patrick, Brigid and Columba, who, in turn, defer to the emblem of the Crossed Keys above them and the Papal Tiara, which shows that the cathedral has the status of a minor basilica.

Inside it, shoulder to shoulder, the faithful are cocooned in fanfares, trills, melodic rumbles and thunderous glissandos as the organ, with its 76 speaking stops, 5000 pipes and 24 Spanish trumpets, remembers its onlie true begetter, the irrepressible, outrageous, Machiavellian and, despite all his wiles, long-dead Archbishop Mannix, the phantom of the cathedral, the spectre at the feast, the genius of St Pat's. With his predecessors and successors, he gazes down from his commemorative plaque on the huge throng of worshippers, tourists, happy drunks and Christmas-party leftovers all getting their Advent responsibilities over and done with.

Squeezed tight the length of the nave and packed along the side aisles past chapel after chapel – Holy Souls, St Joseph, St Brigid and the Irish Saints, St Thomas Aquinas – the congregation ripples and tenses as the Consecration approaches. Incense drifts heady and seductive beneath the chandeliers, wafting slowly up to the dulled effulgence of the Great Western Window, where the Lord ascends into heaven thanks to the artistry in 1867 of stained-glass experts Hardman and Powell of Birmingham. A clarion call from the organ brings the crowd to its feet – Hosanna in the Highest – and then a succession of dying falls sees them shuffling out at last into the hot night, duty done, faces shining with exaltation, relief, grog, perspiration, inner strength, grace, expectation, stress, vacuity . . . They flood out into the silky darkness, the city of Melbourne at their feet lit up like a sprawling Christmas tree. Above them, St Patrick's soaring Gothic spires pointing with sobering insistence to heaven and eternity; and the gargoyles, having no gush of water to spout in the dry summer, leering and grimacing at evil spirits, daring them to come close.

In the centre of the city at that same moment, another congregation is flooding out into the night, Advent duties fulfilled and only celebrations remaining. Above them, the thirteen bells of St Paul's Anglican Cathedral, cast by Mears and Stainbank in 1889, ring out in the key of C sharp. Gothic transitional in style, mixing Early English with Decorated, St Paul's Cathedral, on the corner of Flinders and Swanston streets, dominates one of Melbourne's busiest intersections.

On the other three corners are the leaning and geometric angularities of Federation Square, the colonial solidity of Flinders Street Station and the newly refurbished Young & Jackson's – one of the oldest and until recently one of the most notorious pubs in the city. From the upper levels of any one of these vantage points, you can glimpse the third cathedral in the daytime and pinpoint it on certain nights when its ceremonials are in progress by the penumbra of light and sound in which it sits like a jewel.

Melburnians are not especially renowned for their religious observance, not since halfway through the twentieth century, anyway (though crowds flock to St Pat's annual Footy Mass to hear the scriptures read by Demons, Saints, Lions, Tigers and Eagles). But many of the large number of people who attended midnight or other ceremonies at St Pat's and St Paul's on Christmas Day will be up and about early on Boxing Day and will join thousands of other worshippers at that third cathedral, a brisk ten-minute walk from St Paul's, a longer but pleasant downhill haul from St Pat's. We might jokingly call this third cathedral St G's, but its adherents often refer to it simply as the 'G' and it is known to the world as the MCG. Just across the way from the central business district and visible from it, especially at night when its six light towers turn dark into day, the MCG, one of the world's great stadiums, has exerted upon its neighbouring city an influence and a spell at least as mysterious and as potent as its more established Christian rivals. The 'G' has been a presence in the city long before its growing physical size made it visibly so. Like its Christian rivals and counterparts, the MCG is a place of ritual, worship, exaltation, mystery, wonder and comfort. If, unthinkably, there had been no MCG, we would have had to invent one.

All three cathedrals had slow starts. William Wilkinson Wardell, one of the leaders of the English Gothic Revival, and William Butterfield were the architectural brains and creators behind St Pat's and St Paul's respectively. The secular cathedral, starting more slowly and haltingly, had to endure two uprootings before finally accepting one of two sites in the Police Paddock offered by Governor La Trobe. St Pat's too had a stutter: the foundation stone of the original building was laid in April 1850, but this structure was pulled down and restarted in bluestone when the gold rushes began to supply more ready cash for such enterprises. St Paul's started life as a wooden chapel in 1836;

this became the bluestone St Paul's Parish Church after 1848 until it was demolished in 1885 when prosperous times allowed the present cathedral to be built. The 'G', on its expanse of nearly four hectares, also profited from gold in the form of rising membership for the resident Melbourne Cricket Club, the increasing availability of cricketers as migration increased and, in 1854, a new building venture: a handsome, small pavilion became the first structure – the foundation chapel – of the secular cathedral. Like the original St Paul's, it was made entirely of timber but would undergo in coming years a series of massive metamorphoses.

In those early days, as if to signal the infant MCG's incipient status as one of Melbourne's cathedrals-to-be, pigeons began to arrive and to strut and waddle round the ground and the nearby parkland and to nest and breed and call the place home in the manner of all pigeons haunting cathedrals – that is, as if they owned it.

THE AMERICAN POET Gertrude Stein once wrote, 'There are pigeons on the grass, alas!' to which her countryman – essayist, short story writer and cartoonist James Thurber – memorably objected, 'Pigeons aren't alas. Pigeons are just pigeons.'

You would think pigeons would be at and around the MCG in about equal numbers to the seagulls. Pigeons after all are city dwellers and the 'G' is a mere hop, dip and glide from Federation Square or St Paul's for a fit pigeon. And pigeons haunt cathedrals; that is their particular wish and talent, and it would make no difference to them that the MCG is a secular cathedral. Knowing St Pat's and St Paul's intimately, and being shrewd observers of the comings and goings of human beings, the pigeons of Melbourne would be wholly *au fait* with the MCG and its place in the people's lives, minds and hearts.

Well, there *are* pigeons at the 'G' – pigeon fancier and commentator Bill Lawry often spots them and identifies their particular branch of the family while on TV duty – but they appear in nothing like the numbers that their northern brethren and sisterhood amass in European public and holy places. Take Italy for instance.

In Italy there are 56 million people and 126 million pigeons. The latter look anything but *alas*. They are plump and have high levels of self-esteem. They can be found sunning themselves in some mouldering medieval embrasure, or preening beneath the gaze of an immemorially ogling gargoyle, or tucking into grain thrown by tourists in the very shadow of signs saying, '*Non dare da mangiare alle piccione*' (which ought to mean 'Don't you dare mangle our pigeons' but actually says don't feed them).

Most of the rest of the time they engage in intricate courtship manoeuvres or in the actual copulation to which these preliminaries inevitably lead. So inevitably that pigeon courtship rituals should be studied for their application to the human condition, where the *absence* of such inevitability is the subject of ancient song and story and endless contemporary expressions of male regret and frustration.

The pigeons of Italy reflect in some ways aspects of the highly attractive national character. They spend a great deal of an average day in intense, prolonged negotiations about food and quite a few more of their waking hours eating and enjoying it. With the same alacrity as their Italian human counterparts, they retire for a nap when post-prandial torpor threatens, conceding to the siesta somnolence induced by digestion. They are superficially religious, preferring the shelter of transepts, ambulatories, naves and sacristies, or if forced to rough it, any of the interstices, grots, crannies, secret conduits and dark nooks created by the external requirements of thousand-year-old cathedral architecture. They can often be heard warbling subdued approval deep in their puffed-out chests during sermons and embroidering the silences and chimes of cathedral ceremonies with their random garglings.

And yet, rather like many of the Italians themselves, the pigeons of Italy are hedonists at heart, a sybaritic lot for whom religious observance is a gesture towards eternity which simply makes sense as, with the passing of pigeon time, libidos wane, feathers flag and their sheen dulls.

Antipodean pigeons, many of which can be seen at the MCG, although they are not as numerous as the seagulls, seem less reflective, more easily pleased with leavings and rubbish and the broad, spireless expanses of supermarket car parks. They rarely congregate at deep fine leg or in the forward pocket, preferring the pickings at crowd level – although a cricket match was once delayed when pigeons in large numbers flew in to eat grass seed that had been scattered in order to jive up the wicket area.

In that way pigeons have, they would respond to human interruptions, arm-waving and clapping either by taking off, completing a circuit of the ground then landing again exactly where they'd been, or by rising a few metres in the air then settling back to get on with the seeds.

MCG pigeons, like MCG crowds, are generally easygoing and amiable. Although it is in the pigeon's nature, anywhere in the world, to look either slightly complacent or pompous – both attitudes being suggested by that puffed-out curve of chest – MCG pigeons have a faintly ironic look to them. It is as if they find it difficult to believe that so many people would come to this huge, complicated building to watch other people run around on the grass at breakneck speed or, at other times, inexplicably stand more or less stationary on the oval for long periods punctuated by sudden flurries of chasing and throwing.

Gertrude Stein would probably not have burdened MCG pigeons with an 'alas'. They are far too self-possessed, *dégagé*. All cathedrals have pigeons, but the MCG's pigeons are non-believers – as secular as the 'G' itself.

ALL THINGS CONSIDERED, it was not difficult for the 'G' to be on many people's minds as the Preliminary Final between Collingwood and Adelaide approached. They were either thinking about it already or the spires and flags of the stadium rising into their city-bound view reminded them.

But the MCG on that September day was not a magnet for Victorian supporters alone. At least 20 000 Croweaters flocked into Yarra Park, heading for the famous turnstiles, bursting into the concourse and up the stairs to gaze upon the hallowed oval. They came in planes, trains and automobiles, or, starting a few days early, hitchhiked; they filled all available accommodation and camping grounds along the highway and then packed out motels, B&Bs and hotels in Melbourne. Some were without a roof, some were without a ticket, some were without both, but they all had one destination in mind: the MCG. No pilgrimage to a holy shrine was ever more popular, more determinedly and reverentially undertaken, more dependent on blind faith.

If any of these football-rabid seekers came from the Adelaide

THE TEMPLE DOWN THE ROAD

Hills township of Aldgate, they probably would have known of their local B&B and thereby hangs yet another MCG story . . .

Doug Rumble was one of those many fortunate people whose father had put his name down at birth for membership of the Melbourne Cricket Club. In due course, as he approached young manhood, Doug suddenly found himself near the head of that illustrious queue. His membership was confirmed, and from that day on he was able to watch football matches, Grand Finals, Test and interstate cricket from the comfort of the Members. No doubt his lifelong connection with the MCC was one of the influences, even if not the most important, that contributed to Doug's being a very handy cricketer. More than handy: he was a first-class wicketkeeper for Fitzroy in the district cricket competition, a useful batsman and a generally talented all-round sportsman.

When it came time for the MCG's ubiquitous green wooden seats to give way to plastic – those same long green benches with a number for each seat that I knew so well in my youth and one of which I had repeatedly kicked in my anxiety during the last day of the Fourth Test against the Windies in 1952 – Doug decided on a whim to buy a job lot of them. After all they were made of jarrah and, despite their long service through scorchers and downpours season after season, they were in fair nick. And so a load of the green-painted and numbered jarrah ended up in Doug's backyard and, in the manner of such compulsively 'magpie' acquisitions, was duly forgotten.

Some years later, Doug was tragically killed in a skiing accident and his brother-in-law, Geoff Reddall, eventually tackling the sad task of clearing up the loose ends and leftovers of a life, came across the timber from the MCG seats. It was still in reasonable shape, and so, with the same compulsive collector's spirit that had motivated Doug, he decided to take it home: you never knew when it might be useful.

In Kingsland Road, Aldgate, halfway up the steep hill and just next door to the church hall, Geoff Reddall and his wife, Hazel, run a B&B. Set back in the bush, with a rustic path and a bridge across a tiny stream leading up to the front door, Geoff and Hazel's, as it is universally known, is a quiet and beautiful little retreat only minutes from the main road and Aldgate's cluster of shops. Geoff and Hazel live at one end of the building in spacious, timbered and sunny rooms, and their private quarters are closed off from the reception area by a sturdy, stable-style door. The top half opens for Geoff or Hazel to deal with an enquiry, or the whole door swings to allow passage to and fro. It is made of green-painted jarrah, with numbers appearing here and there incongruously and at random. The paint is split or flaking in various places and the surface is weathered by years and by use, no attempt having been made to spruce up the original condition of the wood (though seen from the 'private' side, the door is beautifully planed and polished). This is Geoff and Hazel's MCG Door – not so much a mere feature as a minor sensation when it is revealed to curious questioners (and no one fails to ask) that the timber came from the old MCG seats in the outer, the long, green, pewlike seats so many of us remember before the plastic took over. It is a long way from home, but the green door stands as a double monument to the 'good old days' at the MCG and to Doug Rumble.

. . . Among many of the staff of the MCG – caterers, cleaners, ground staff – the Preliminary Final is known as 'the people's Grand Final'. This is because, especially in the past decade or so, the actual Grand Final has been very much dominated by corporate and similar interests. The grassroots supporters, it is said, don't get enough of a look-in and, in any case, it is expensive for an ordinary punter to buy Grand Final tickets for a whole family or even simply for a spouse or a couple of kids. But the Preliminary Final is more accessible, less 'corporate', as a general rule, more the preserve of real barrackers – the people who support the teams that are playing. If this was true, the presence of Collingwood in the Preliminary Final – especially its more or less *unexpected* presence – was going to guarantee a big grassroots crowd and an electric atmosphere. And so it proved.

No other stadium could have endowed this contest with such panache, drama, intensity and colour. Walking to the ground, people glimpse the tall light towers from a long way off and quicken their pace. Arriving by tram, they stream across the new footbridge, leaping the railway and Brunton Avenue; or, from Richmond Station, the scarfed and beanied cavalcade crushes, huddles and spurts its way along the avenue. Multicoloured hordes advance in waves downhill across the park from the Hilton Hotel tram stop and Jolimont Station, flitting, edging or lumbering between the lines of cars inching into the car park. Crowds mill around the food vans near the Members and pick their way impatiently round the television trucks nosing together against the Members' Reserve wall, cocooned in their cables and wires.

Thick fingers of queues jut from the ticket windows, and stampedes of people intent on more distant gates filter through their ranks and set off round the high, curving bastions of the 'G' towards the Olympic and Great Southern Stand gates where, like two tidal currents clashing, they meet in a surf of black and white and red and yellow and blue.

Footies are flying through the air between small boys and bigger boys and grown men showing how it's done. Shouts of 'Go, Pies' rise randomly from the shifting throng; occasionally 'Go, Vics' from someone taking the larger view.

But it is not an unusual line here at the 'G' this September day, because only Collingwood stands in the way of an all-interstate final. Brisbane, due to play that night, are unbackable, and Adelaide, the dreaded Crows who plucked the flag from St Kilda in 1997, then came from nowhere to do it again against North Melbourne in the following year, are the favourites on this afternoon against the Magpies. It is the sort of script that seems so often to unfold at the MCG, as if, like the great monuments and battlements of the old world, it had stories and drama oozing from its very stones.

In brilliant September sunshine, a crowd of 88 960 – in MCG terms, a mere handful short of a full house, but a handful that would prevent the game's being televised live – pours into the 'sacred citadel', as the *Herald-Sun* sports writer Derek Ballantine called it, dropping easily into the ecclesiastical imagery that the 'G' seems so naturally to elicit from its acolytes.

They see the Pies hit the ground running, only to lose their early advantage as the Crows settle down. Adelaide is 17 points in front seventeen minutes into the second quarter and looking in control, but two goals, minutes before half-time, put Collingwood back in the game.

The opening stages of the third quarter are frenetic. Scores are level three times in the first eight minutes. Bassett, a back man moved into the forward line, scores twice for the Crows, but Fraser's third goal in the quarter for Collingwood ties the scores, and the Pies then begin to look good, especially after an inspirational 65-metre goal from Anthony Rocca. Six Collingwood goals to one in the third quarter set Collingwood up for the win no one expected and, after coping with a brief, last-ditch attack from the stricken Crows, they cruise into the Grand Final by 28 points.

There were many, like the Carlton member who said he would rather 'barrack for Iraq than Collingwood' and the St Kilda supporter who said, 'I wouldn't support those arrogant bastards if they were play-ing for the free world', who could not bring themselves to applaud. But however ambivalent the feelings and attitudes of many as the last of the rollicking black-and-white crowd wandered away across Yarra Park, the truth was that Collingwood had played a starring role in yet another MCG extravaganza. And they would be back in a week!

As the final siren was drowned by the roar of most of that 88 960 crowd, there were several onlookers who, whatever might have been their allegiances or lack of them, were taking a completely different view of the day's events.

One of these is Michael Birmingham, Assistant Retail Manager for Spotless Services (Catering) at the MCG. Like all the ecstatic Collingwood army, Birmingham's mind switches instantly to the Grand Final as the siren goes, but for professional not partisan reasons. A win by an interstate club in the Preliminary Final in general means that the Grand Final attendance becomes more corporate. Such people tend to come later and eat and drink at the higher end of the 'food chain'. A win by Collingwood, as has happened on this September Saturday, means that all the basic food outlets – the pies, hot dogs, chips, and so on – inside and outside of the ground, will be 'hit hard'. This is of course generally true at a Grand Final, but the differences are significant when it comes to catering for interstate as against local contenders. And with Collingwood's thousands of formerly knee-jerk and lukewarm sup-porters emerging from the woodwork, and the many thousands more who want a Victorian win and are prepared to swallow anti-Collingwood bias to get one, this Grand Final promises to be a special challenge.

As Michael Birmingham listens to the siren and the accompany-ing deafening roar of triumph and looks out over the famous oval (not something he has done much of during the game – he's been too busy), he is already calculating the run of the coming week. Six days to Grand Final Eve, when everything to do with the catering, that is *everything*, has to be ready . . .

Someone else for whom that final siren is a clarion call is Jason Edmonds. He is in charge of cleaning the MCG – not just the arena and the stands and seats, but the park outside and the roadways surrounding the park. Not just that, but all the nearly 200 corporate boxes, the toilets, the kitchens, the snack bars, the Members' area, the carpets, all the glass, the floors, walkways, the concrete of the terraces . . .

Edmonds's job starts as soon as the ground has emptied. His team of 200 casual workers will work through Saturday night and Sunday morning to move the rubbish left behind by the people's Grand Final, tonnes and tonnes of it. 'If you walked in here on the Monday morning after the Preliminary Final,' he tells me, 'you'd regard the place as clean.' But of course, I would be wrong. They would only just have started. For Jason Edmonds too, it's going to be a crowded week . . .

Tony Ware is another who has watched this game with a perspective that goes beyond its quality as a spectacle and its ramifications as a contest. Ware is the head groundsman at the MCG. He is best known for his preparation of the wickets on which interstate, one-day international and Test cricket teams play each summer. Boxing Day is one of his most important challenges, and he starts thinking about it as early as July, because the nature of the winter will have an important influence on the work that will have to be done not only to prepare the wicket area for that famous Test match but also to ensure the quality of the outfield. Ware has to worry about weather and temperature and lines painted on grass and a whole lot of other things. Air, whether ripping through in a gale or clinging with heavy humidity, and fire, in the form of the sun's summer searing, and water, flailing in rainstorms across the roofs of the grandstands – all of these three ancient elements preoccupy and absorb Tony Ware. But the one that might be his passion is earth – how it looks and behaves, what it will and will not grow, how hard or soft it becomes in all its seasonal fluctuations. Still, the football season keeps him just as much on his toes, even if in different ways.

And now, as the siren sounds to end the Preliminary Final, he is already mentally running through the moves – the negotiations with the very earth itself – that will have to be carried out in the next six days to produce yet another manifestation of the MCG's magic, that great cathedral-like space and its broad, oval, green nave.

All three men, in their different ways, have good reason to be reflective as Nathan Buckley's team of temporary heroes leaves the ground and subsides gratefully and triumphantly in the dressing room.

Around them, the 'G' goes quiet. Shadows deepen. A few sea-gulls wheel in, and the air grows cold. As it has done so many times before, the great stadium dissolves into the sharp spring dusk and waits its hour.

ON THE FOLLOWING Monday, 23 September 2002, that 'hour' is a bit nearer and, with the pressure of work mounting, Michael Birmingham arrives at the MCG at 7 a.m. On the walls of his small office in the Catering Section near Light Tower 1 are prints of Picasso's *Cason del Buen Retiro* and Monet's *Le Jardin de l'artiste*. He inherited the Monet with the office, but the Picasso is his and is a favourite. A place of quiet relaxation (*buen retiro*) and a peaceful garden setting are scenes worth contemplating, even if only for a stolen few minutes during what is annually one of the 'G's biggest weeks.

Equipped with the first of the day's coffees, he organises his files and papers and contemplates the order of things. After the nearly 90 000-strong Preliminary Final, he will have to check stock levels and work out what to order for the even bigger challenge of the Grand Final.

Experience and historical evidence are important guides governing the process of making estimates, but they are nevertheless estimates, and there is room for error. As Birmingham finishes his coffee and gets down to work, the MCG is waking up around him . . .

Jason Edmonds's team have worked all night Saturday and well into Sunday morning and, as Edmonds walks around the ground on Monday, he can feel satisfied that the first part of the job has been, as usual, well done. Now they turn their attention to the 'pre-event clean', they are concentrating as much on having the 'G' shining and pristine for the Grand Final as on mopping up after the Preliminary Final. Imagine the spillages after a game like the Collingwood–Crows encounter, he says: stains from Coke, beer, coffee, ice-cream, sauce and who knows what else have to be scrubbed from every concrete surface. The toilets, every last one of them, have to be cleaned, soap containers replenished, toilet paper replaced, mirrors polished. And much, much more. And there are six days to go . . .

Tony Ware blesses the weather. The ground has suffered the usual divots and wearing patches from Saturday's game, but the warm sunshine and crisp spring nights and the absence of significant rain have all helped preserve the hallowed turf in good order. Still, there is much to be done. Mowing, rejuvenation of sections of grass, line marking.

And for Tony Ware there is a bigger picture. Outside the ground, in a special enclosure near the Gallery of Sport, are the 'drop-in' pitches being nurtured for their transfer to the oval in summer. This system – removing the wicket area at the end of summer and dropping new pitches in for the cricket season – allows the centre square to be well grassed and firm even during a wet winter. In the old days, which in this respect, at least, were certainly not 'good', the turf wickets, softened by rain and churned up by boot stops in at least two games, but sometimes more each weekend, became a gluepot covering the entire middle of the oval.

Unlike his two colleagues in catering and cleaning, Ware must have a place in his thinking not just for the coming week and its culminating Grand Final, but also for the months ahead, the coming of summer, the unmistakable *craaack* of the ball on the middle of the bat, the huge curve of the crowd around terraces and stands, like a pointillist painting full of sunlight, and, above all, the smooth, fast-running grass, the green tops and the dry yellow pitches, the moisture and the rollers – all the mystery and mystique of earth, air, fire and water that blend to make cricket the fascinating game it is. Terrestrial chess.

Wind is the movement of air. Air moves because the sun heats the
Earth's surface more at the equator than at the Poles; it is also
influenced by the Earth's rotation. The result is a pattern of rotating,
continent-sized masses of air called the 'general circulation'.
Greg Laughlin, *The User's Guide to the Australian Coast*

MELBOURNE IS A windy city. In any of the four seasons strong winds
can set the tone, but August and September are often the windiest
months. In summer, the prevailing wind is a southerly and in winter,
it is mainly from the north. In the southern spring, which begins in
September, the MCG hosts one of its greatest festivals – the Grand
Final of the Australian Football League – and from late spring in
November right through the summer months and into Melbourne's
luminous autumn, interstate and international cricket matches attract
large and small crowds during long days under a burning sun or rowdy
nights under lights.

. . . When England began their first innings during the afternoon of the second day of the Second Test at the MCG in January 1963, the air was thick and clammy, heavy with humidity. Storms flickered round the horizon and the indistinct grumbling of thunder, softened by distance, was like a far-off war rolling closer. On his way to taking 6 wickets for 75, Australia's great all-rounder Alan Davidson immediately cut into the Pommy opening batsmen, dismissing Sheppard lbw for a duck and clean-bowling Pullar for 11.

This brought the English captain, Ted Dexter, to the crease. Known as 'Lord Ted', partly because of an apparently haughty and disdainful mien and partly because of the aristocratic mastery and elegance of his batting, Dexter took guard and prepared to face the remaining six balls of Davidson's over. The first swung late, fizzed past the tentative edge of the bat and thumped into wicket-keeper Barry Jarman's gloves. The next ball, dipping into the damp clinging air, pitched just short of a length and shaved the off stump as Dexter began to play at it and then in the last split second convulsively got his bat back out of the line. Four to go. The first of these reared awkwardly from a good length and flew over Dexter's gloves. At the next two Dexter played and missed by unbelievable fractions – all at sea.

Visibly frustrated, Davidson walked back to his bowling mark as a growing crescendo of buzzing, barracking and sheer excitement welled up around the stands and terraces. Thunder edged closer, lightning seemed to crackle. In a sort of blue light – half sun, half reflection from the approaching anvils of cloud – Davidson turned briskly at the top of his run and without a pause moved smoothly in for the last ball of the over. It was faster than any of the others, well up, again swinging late: Dexter's groping blade fanned so close that the slips fieldsmen gasped and grimaced, but by some aberration of physics the ball missed the off stump. Amid a huge, gusting sigh from the crowd that gradually turned into prolonged, standing applause, Dexter took three or four steps up the pitch towards Davidson, stood up very straight, and raised his bat to the bowler like a gladiator saluting the emperor.

FOR ALL HIS obvious aplomb and command, Wills seems to be taken by surprise. What can surprise a ghost? Nothing, you would think. But circus-master Wills seems to falter as a strange collection of characters begins to materialise at the cricketers' gate ready to walk on to the oval. They are wearing what look like kilts! and in some cases odd headgear and bizarrely coiffed hair. It is as if Wills resents an intrusion that looks like it might be even more exotic than his own beloved team of Aborigines. And, by and large, this group, now winding towards the centre of the ground, is considerably more exotic than anything seen before on the MCG. They are cricketers. And they are Fijian. And some are even royalty.

IN 1904, EDWARD J. MARSDEN, an Australian on business in Suva, was asked to stand in as an umpire in a match between a Fijian XI, from Bau, and the Suva Cricket Club's European team. Although the Fijians were beaten, Marsden was 'so impressed by the magnificent promise shown by the team, looking very smart in their short white *sulus* (like a Highland kilt) and cricket shirts', and by meeting the team's captain, Ratu Kadavulevu, that he 'proposed the idea of collecting a purely native Fijian cricket team, spending some time in coaching them, and making a cricket tour through the chief cricket centres of Australia with them'.

The idea caught on, fired by Marsden's enthusiasm and skill as a coach – he was himself a splendid cricketer whose illustrious career for South Melbourne was, in the opinion of all the pundits, leading to state and national selection had he not been so much absent from Australia.

And so, on 27 November 1907, Ratu Kadavulevu's Bau team, as it was known, accompanied by Edward Marsden, left Suva amid great ceremony and 'tearful farewells'.

The *Sydney Morning Herald* reported on 28 November, under the heading THE MIGHTY CAUCASIAN PLAYED OUT, that the Bau team had played the Suva Cricket Club, 'which consists of white Government officials', and had beaten them by 14 runs (thus avenging that earlier loss when Marsden had umpired and been impressed) and, after experiencing 'strong headwinds, high seas and heavy rainfalls through the Friendly Islands', the team duly arrived to a warm welcome.

So began the tour of the Bau team. They were a sensation in Sydney, as a *Sydney Mail* report noted: '. . . everyone says, "Have you seen their hair and their calves?" Both are enormous and uncommon to a degree. They approach the field of play as if it were the field of battle, with a wild war cry, and clad in garments chiefly of grass, which appear inadequate but interesting and are in reality quite sufficient.'

Ninety years before Tony Lockett's thighs and groin were preoccupying Sydneysiders, Fijian calves were all the rage.

The Bau cricketers, whose genuine ability was often overlooked in favour of their extraordinary appearance, custom and lineage, played through country New South Wales and after many adventures, including a trip to Brisbane, stepped down from the Sydney Express at Spencer Street Station in Melbourne on 16 January 1908. 'The Fijians all possess prominent and picturesque hair', noted the *Age*, while the *Argus* greeted 'Prince Kadavu's dusky cricketers from the Pacific'.

On the night of their arrival the team attended Hegarty's Baths – probably with some alacrity as several of them had complained of Melbourne's heat which, they said, lacked the light breezes that made Fiji's heat tolerable – where they played water polo against members of the Melbourne Swimming Club.

Next day they began a country tour, which was a sort of circuitous creeping-up on the cynosure of all cricketing tourists, the MCG, as if in unknowing imitation of that mythical progress from the bush to the

'G' so beloved of Australian sporting lore. Their first stop was Maryborough, where the *Maryborough Standard*'s lack of interest in the team's form with bat and ball – it noted instead with scarcely concealed relief that 'Every member of the team has been converted to Christianity, and one of their players is a native clergyman' – might have been prescient, as the Fijians beat Maryborough by 44 runs. Then on to Castlemaine, where the *Castlemaine Leader* adjusted the balance by pointing out that 'In all matches played up to the present the visiting cricketers have proved themselves adept in every branch of the game, and those who attend the match tomorrow may rely upon witnessing a first-class game. The Fijians will be attired in their native costume and will wear neither hats nor boots.' The match was drawn.

And so at last they came to the MCG to play a Victorian XI selected from the Melbourne, Prahran and North Melbourne district teams.

Rarely had the MCG seen such sights. The *Herald*, while giving overall a full, interesting and fair report of the event, could not contain itself at times. Reporting that Edward Marsden would be wicketkeeper for the Fijians, the *Herald* writer explained that 'Meleti, the native 'keeper, finds it hard to reconcile the fast bowling of Prince Pope and Joni Siqila with his bare legs, guiltless of pads, and in important matches it was found advisable to borrow a substitute, as Meleti cannot break himself of the bad habit of backing mechanically towards longstop'.

It was not, however, unusual for Marsden to take the field, under Prince Kadavu's captaincy, as wicket-keeper. Marsden, as the one true begetter of the team and the tour, had played in their first game, as the *Sydney Morning Herald* explained on 7 December 1907, 'to give the men confidence in their first encounter', and he played on many occasions thereafter, including in the important fixture at the

MCG. Marsden, the *Sydney Morning Herald* went on, was 'honoured as a chief among the natives, who call him Matakibau, i.e. the distinguished visitor, who is permitted to consult with the highest chief'.

Later on in the tour, the *Maitland Daily Mercury* of 27 December revealed that Edward Marsden's grandfather was a nephew of the Reverend Samuel Marsden (1764–1838), an evangelist, missionary and early colonist of ambiguous repute. Known as 'the flogging parson' after his arrival in New South Wales in 1794, Marsden accumulated worldly goods but few converts. Eventually, giving up on both the Aborigines and the colonists as candidates for salvation, he went to New Zealand where he accomplished genuinely humane missionary work with the Maoris.

And so, as Prince Kadavu led his team onto the MCG on 25 January 1908, having won the toss but inexplicably chosen to put the Victorians in, his wicket-keeper was actually quite as exotic as any of his teammates but not obviously so. It would have been hard for Marsden to compete, merely by details of lineage and historic associations, with the group that he walked out with. As the *Argus* described it:

> They were all barefooted and all in native costume, except Lieutenant
> E. J. Marsden . . . The two princes [Kadavu and Pope] wore cricketing
> shirts and the native 'sulu', while the rest of the team, with feathers and
> flowers stuck in their hair, wore little more than the generally accepted
> loin cloth and a string of beads. They were decked out with a sort of cape
> of fibrous material, which they took off as they warmed to their work, and
> open work kilts of similar texture. White armbands made from the bark of
> a tree were also worn and these too were removed as occasion demanded.
> Some wore gaudy sashes, but there was nothing of the fancy dress about
> it. It was genuine, and every article of attire had its own significance. As
> play proceeded the ground became littered with the extra impedimenta,

but it was noticeable that during the adjournments for luncheon or tea the players bedecked themselves, and returned to the play in full regalia.

Before taking up their positions, the Fijians formed a tight group and chanted a challenging war song followed by what some assumed to be a national anthem and very well might have been.

The opening attack consisted of Ratu Pope and Joni Siqila; the Victorian opening batsmen were F. Vaughan and G. Healy. Siqila's fast bowler's ritual included laying all his ornamental accoutrements carefully on the ground – strings of coconut shells and other items – before tearing in and hitting the pitch hard, as they say, with genuine pace and, often enough, a good line.

As 'Felix', writing in the *Australasian*, suggested, putting the Victorians in after winning the toss was, 'from a cricket stand point . . . not a sound move', and the opening pair began with some aggression (although later they became cautious). At 0/21, Vaughan smashed a ball through mid-on, where a Fijian fieldsman stopped it with his shin. Long before sound-effects microphones, the resultant rifle-shot *crack* could be heard all over the ground with sickening clarity. But no harm was done, and the game went on. A second stunning blow from Vaughan through cover point had four runs written all over it, when Meleti dived and took a miraculous catch low to the ground. It was, reported the *Herald*, 'a sight for the Gods', and the *Age* rated it 'a catch which would have done credit to any player in a Test Match'.

At the end of the first day, the Victorians left the MCG at 9/372. On the Monday, the last Victorian wicket was quickly disposed of and, in ferocious north-wind heat, the Fijians batted stylishly, Meleti being especially dashing – cutting and driving with an abandon that finally undid him. But 'Pavilion critics,' noted the *Age*, 'including men who have been to England with representative Australian elevens, remarked that these islanders had a quickness of eye and a suppleness of wrist that were pleasant to watch.'

Prince Kadavu and his team were 'greatly pleased' with the MCG, according to 'Felix', who put the crowd on the first day at 'upwards of 9,000'. The whole tour, of which the visit to the famous Melbourne oval was a highlight and certainly one of the MCG's more eccentric 'moments', was a huge success.

As he left the 'G' on that hot Monday evening – the game having been 'prolonged until 6.15', according to the *Age*, 'to give the spectators an equivalent for time lost during showers', Edward Marsden would have been well pleased. He would scarcely have guessed, however, that the Marsdens were not yet done with the MCG. Like the Terminator, he – or at least his son, Marc – would 'be back'.

BUT NOW TOM WILLS waves his baton with irritable force and elaborate circumstance, and the amazing Fijians fade into the spectral gloom while the new Members' Pavilion looms momentarily bright and lit up out of the night. Wills takes his scene back to 1881 (perhaps it was the Fijians' chronological misplacement in his drama that both annoyed and surprised Wills): Prince Albert Victor and Prince George of Wales lay the foundation stone of the new building, which adjoins the original MCC Pavilion. And before the light of 1881 fades from the ghostly oval, Wills points, and two workmen trundle a sightboard on to the ground, the first to be used. It was supplemented in the following year by a marvel of scoreboard technology that showed the batsmen's names, their scores and how they were out – the first ever known or used in the cricket world.

A huge gout of lightning seems to flower from Tom Wills's baton, and the old reversible grandstand, built in 1877, and so called because it allowed patrons to watch cricket from the northern end of the ground or football in the paddock outside, explodes into flames. It burnt down in 1884 and was replaced by the Grandstand, which stood until it made way for the Northern Stand, which quickly became known as the Olympic Stand for Melbourne's 1956 Olympic Games.

IT IS 1949. Memories of the Second World War remain vivid in many forms and guises to Australians. There are the returned men and women, struggling to come to terms with 'civvy' life. There are those who, having spent the war on the 'home front', can now only continue to grieve until grief loses its edge and their loved ones who fell in Europe and New Guinea and the Middle East become more and more distant memories – a revered name on Anzac Day; a vision wrenched momentarily back by the sobbing notes of 'The Last Post'; the object of a special prayer at a special mass.

And there are more urgent, physical reminders of the hard recent past. The government's Department of Post-War Reconstruction, the planning staff of which is headed by H. C. 'Nugget' Coombs, has been for several years devoting itself to the rejigging of postwar Australian society, one in which full employment is a mandatory aim. Government intervention through, among other methods, public works would take up any looming slack in employment – the Snowy Mountains Hydro-Electric Scheme, initiated by the Chifley government in 1949, is the most ambitious and wide-ranging of such enterprises – and a housing scheme would cater for low-income earners. In 1949, the housing position is very difficult, however, and will not ease for another two or three years.

In this partly dynamic and exciting, partly tough and unyielding atmosphere, government funding was under terrific pressure from many directions, not the least from the government's own idealism. One of these arose from Melbourne's having won, in 1949, the right to stage the 1956 Olympic Games. Like all such decisions, especially as the twenti-eth century advanced and the Olympic 'industry' became larger and more stupendously expensive, Melbourne's winning bid was the cause of much rejoicing followed, on the morning after, by growing unease.

Almost immediately, problems arose about funding: what chance was there of government funding amid such acute housing and other pressures? And about the venue: where exactly would these Games be held? On the latter question, some progress was made by the end of 1949, when six possible sites were identified. Granted that there was a strong school of thought that said the main stadium should not be built from the ground up but should be an existing site refurbished, the frontrunners among the six, in no particular order, were the MCG, Olympic Park, the Royal Agricultural Society Showgrounds, Princes Park in Carlton – home of the Carlton Football and Cricket Clubs – and Albert Park, with the St Kilda Football Club's Junction Oval at one end of the lake and the South Melbourne Cricket and Football Clubs' oval at the other.

The MCG seemed a natural venue to many, but there were a sur-prising number of dissenters. Like all cathedrals, the 'G' had spawned factions and cliques within its bureaucratic administration and among its supporters. The main sticking point was that the Trustees, for whom the Melbourne Cricket Club managed the MCG, refused to contem-plate any change to the existing surface of the oval. This led to their offer of the 'G' for the opening and closing ceremonies and for any sport that could be held on the existing surface. Such a stand more or less inevitably ruled out track-and-field events.

A stupendous and labyrinthine series of disputes and argumentation now began among the protagonists and antagonists, better known as the Organising Committee (OC), the Australian Olympic Federation (AOF), the Executive Committee (Ex.C) and the International Olympic Committee (IOC). In these arguments, venues rose into, and fell from, favour like targets at a shooting gallery.

Early in 1951, the Showgrounds seemed signed and sealed, but by the end of that year had fallen from grace, and the MCG was back on the agenda.

By February 1952, a meeting of the Ex.C was told that the MCG was not available as the main stadium. In the following month, a straw poll taken by the Ex.C revealed that choices of the main stadium were, in descending order of preference, Princes Park, Olympic Park, the Showgrounds, Albert Park and – stone motherless last – the MCG (with the 'developed' Olympic Park as a co-venue for track and field).

Only days later – in March 1952 – a premiers' conference, convened in Melbourne by Premier McDonald and attended by the Prime Minister (R. G. Menzies), Lord Mayor Nilsen, various politicians from both sides of the political divide and senior officials connected with the organising of the Games, agreed on guaranteed funding of £1 250 000 for the construction of the main stadium at the Carlton Cricket Ground (Princes Park) and the swimming pool, velodrome and other minor works. The federal government would provide half, and the state government and the Melbourne City Council a quarter each, with their finance ministers representing them on the various Olympic committees.

At last, the squabbling had stopped, projects were starting, moves were being made. But if that were true, there would be no need to go further in an account about the MCG, because the MCG had no part in these plans . . .

In September 1952 an architectural competition, not unlike that which would later produce the designs for the winged Opera House in Sydney, was launched. While at the now-out-of-contention MCG, Fitzroy stole the First Semi-Final by a point, Geelong thrashed Collingwood in the Second, Collingwood held on against Fitzroy in the Preliminary Final and Geelong then repeated the dose on Collingwood to win the 1952 flag, the search for the best design to remodel the Princes Park oval in Carlton as the main stadium gathered pace. In October, a competition winner – architect Frank Heath – was announced, and Carlton recreation ground managers were asked to make the necessary rearrangements of fixtures, and so on, so that work could begin in the following January.

New Zealand stayer Dalray, the top weight and ridden by Bill Williamson, started a 5/1 favourite in the Melbourne Cup and won it while discussions continued on choosing a builder for the Carlton project.

In December 1952, while at the MCG Australia were losing the Second Test to South Africa by 82 runs, a builder was appointed. But on 15 January of the New Year, with the Opening Ceremony of the Games only three years and a few months away, and with surveying, bulldozing and much of the fencing all finished, the premier suspended work on the project as costs began to overrun.

But it was not only costs that had precipitated this – at the time – sensational move. The MCG had languidly raised its familiar profile again in the form of a letter from the secretary of the MCC to Premier John Cain (Sr), made available at a second premiers' conference on 26 January 1953. The Melbourne Cricket Club, said the letter, now supported the MCG as a main stadium venue.

For the past several years the IOC and its irascible president, Avery Brundage, had been watching Melbourne's 'progress' with increasing alarm. Brundage had delivered a number of forthright criticisms of the way Melbourne was going about its Games and had become the *bête noir* of the city's press and cartoonists, not to mention its Olympic Games bureaucracy. Avery Garbage, Avery Grumpage and numerous other stylings in the press, as well as less flattering and less publishable manifestations in bars and among footy crowds and in other more or less disreputable gatherings, dogged his engagements with the city and its Olympic organisers. But Brundage was not easily stared down and just before the January premiers' conference, he delivered his Sunday punch: *If you don't stop squabbling and bickering, you will lose the Games. Four years and still no decision!* He set a deadline of 17 April 1953 after which, if perceptible progress, resolutions and clear directions were not evident, Melbourne's position would be reconsidered by an IOC meeting. This was no idle threat. There was, inevitably, a city in the USA – Philadelphia – that could smoothly take over the whole project and stage the 1956 Olympic Games.

So when Premier Cain, as chair, convened his January premiers' conference, there were so many raging metaphors extant that delegates had to check them in at the door. Melbourne as an Olympic venue *was looking straight down the barrel*; it was *a minute to midnight; the sun was setting on the Olympic dream; Melbourne's shame;* Brundage *ties the noose;* and so on. Without the perceptible progress so beloved of Mr Brundage, the conference was adjourned to 2 February. In the interim, the Ex.C had some intense meetings with the MCC. Sheer urgency drove all their minds and hearts, and when the lobbying was over and the conference resumed, the MCG quickly became the chosen venue for the main stadium with all the earlier funding arrangements intact.

The cancellation of the work at Carlton was immediately confirmed, and the OC braced itself for claims from the architect, the builder and the Carlton ground management. These duly came (£43 637 with a progress payment of £8500 from the architect, and £593 from the builder). The agreement on the payments and all the ramifications raised by them took months of massive, acrimonious disputation to sort out.

So the MCG, which to many observers and insiders had looked from the start an obvious choice, as it had so often done in the past for all kinds of enterprises and events (how smartly Coppin would have claimed it for the Games, for example), would be the main stadium for the Games of the XVI Olympiad. Difficulties arising from the 'G's dual management structure – Trustees and MCC – not to mention the jealously guarded and sternly asserted rights and privileges of the members, the need to upgrade the surface of the arena and the problem of commitments to cricket and football in the interim years before the Opening Ceremony all still had to be dealt with, and none of them was any easier in 1953 than they had been when they had brought negotiations to a standstill in 1949.

But the days of self-indulgent bickering and posturing were over. Since the first proposition involving the MCG in 1949, it had been three years and three months before a decision had been made. It had taken over four years to reach approval of the Heads of Agreement, which allowed tenders to be called for work on the MCG. And it had been five years exactly from November 1949 to the signing of the Final Agreement. Such glacial 'progress' could no longer be tolerated. November 1956 was a mere breath away.

. . . Well, it comes on to early November of 1956, and I am sitting at a desk in Melbourne University's Wilson Hall preparing to grapple with the last question of the last examination of my undergraduate career. 'Design and describe the experiment by means of which you would demonstrate that unconscious prejudice can distort reporting of observed phenomena.' I know the answer to this; I know what has to be said. I'm certain I've done reasonably well in all the other examinations, so I'm twenty-five minutes away from a BA and freedom.

Late-morning November sun streams through the vast windows of the still-new-looking, famous hall. Over the past fifteen or sixteen days, including, as always and to my annual chagrin, Melbourne Cup Day, I had sat in Wilson Hall (it looked new because the splendid original had burnt down some years earlier, not long before my arrival at university, although the two events were unconnected) or in one of the classrooms of the Old Arts Building, writing through some twenty hours of final examinations. Australian History, English Literature and Psychology commanded my entire attention until about the middle of the month when the ordeal ended with this last paper – which happened to be Psychology.

Ray Tynan, by now my inseparable mate, had done different subjects, but we were both Psychology students, and this meant we finished our university courses at the same hour of the same day. Walking exhausted from that last tryst with scholarship (Ray was especially weary because he'd stayed up the entire night before, discovering psychological territory that his year-long attention to snooker and billiards had hidden from him), we contemplated the summer ahead, a vista of freedom that would be interrupted only by exam results and the necessity to find part-time work. We would be back in the following year as trainee teachers to do the Diploma of Education but, essentially, the hard grind was over; if we had passed our finals, we were, as Ray cheerfully put it, into time-on with an unbeatable lead.

My state of mind on that day was a sort of bland, benign torpor as we meandered away from Wilson Hall, carefully observing our rule of conducting no exam post-mortems in case one of us was revealed to have totally misunderstood half the paper (although Ray did remark, with a sort of retrospective amazement that, in furious haste, he had begun his answer to that last question with the words: 'Thuswise would I demonstrate . . .').

But, dynamic as ever, he was not on for torpor. He had plans. First, he said, we should go downtown to Myer's booking office and see if we could get tickets for the Olympic Games. And when we had done that, with whatever success or lack of it, we should go to a pub, Ray said, and 'learn to drink beer'.

Taken aback as so often by his restless casting about for the next interesting move, I was inclined to procrastination. I pointed out that the Opening Ceremony of the Games would take place in less than a week. We would almost certainly not be able to get tickets and, anyway, I didn't feel like trailing down into the city. As for drinking beer, we had both of course had a beer or two at home. In fact, I'd been to a pub. One day in that final year of university, my father said to me, 'Sometime soon you'll be wanting to go to a pub with your friends. I'd like you to have your first pub beer with me.' It was a nice little ceremony that, many years later, I copied with my boys.

But neither Ray nor I had been frequenters of pubs during our undergraduate years. Now, it appeared, this – and several other things – was about to change.

Our chances of getting Olympic Games tickets were slim – even Ray admitted this, as we walked down into the unskyscrapered, tram-choked, self-satisfied 1956 version of Melbourne's central business district. A few months earlier, we had managed to scrounge a couple of tickets to the Grand Final between Melbourne and Collingwood. The MCG had been closed for the first four rounds of that football season when construction of the Olympic grandstand began. For the Grand

Final, in which the Melbourne Football Club was attempting to win a second successive Premiership flag, plans were made to limit the size of the crowd. But, somehow, 115 802 people made it on to the terraces and into the stands and, eventually, around the boundary where they were conducted to ease the congestion. There were figures draped on the cranes that were parked in the construction area and daring groups on roofs and other forbidden high places.

As for Ray and me, we were wedged into an impenetrable swaying mass about halfway around what is now the swooping arc of the Great Southern Stand. It was one of the MCG's less-organised yet great days, during which a rampaging Melbourne slaughtered the hapless 'Woods' by 73 points. I have a memory of a marvellous drama taking place on that wing, and I thought it was in the 1956 Grand Final. Historical evidence, alas, does not support me, and endless conversations with MCG addicts haven't pinned it down.

But what I remember is this: Melbourne's Laurie Mithen made his debut in 1954 as a boom recruit. In his debut game, which happened to be against Collingwood, he received a traditional black-and-white welcome, which left him black and blue, hobbling and unable to continue after three-quarter time. It was a sad and almost ignominious beginning, capped off by Melbourne's being six-goal losers. But Mithen was as good as he'd been cracked up to be. He fought back during the season, became one of Melbourne's key players in the centre of the ground and faced up to his nemesis on Grand Final Day 1955 and again in 1956 with great confidence. Like just about everyone else in the Melbourne team on both those days, Mithen was dominant. As I remember it, some time in the last quarter of the 1956 Grand Final, he delivered the *coup de grâce*. Taking possession of the ball at about the Collingwood half-back flank, he set out on a run around the outer wing with a great open expanse yawning in front of him as Collingwood defenders scrambled to close the gaps. Bouncing the footy, dummying around the couple of desperate opponents who managed to get near him, declining to pass the ball off to a teammate, Mithen ran into the Melbourne forward line and kicked a goal. It was a magnificent, if unnecessary and slightly self-indulgent, solo effort.

Most people in that huge crowd – and certainly the rabid supporters on both sides not to mention his own teammates – knew that Mithen was making a statement, bringing to a triumphant and arrogant conclusion a confrontation that had begun a couple of seasons earlier. It was delicious, high drama – the sort of thing that the MCG seems to encourage by its extraordinary atmosphere and for which it is, somehow, the only proper stage.

I reminded Ray of all this as we walked down to the city. It was the early afternoon of Friday 16 November. The Olympic torch would be carried into the MCG (by Ron Clarke – although no one knew that then) on the following Thursday.

'Remember the Grand Final – it was packed. We won't get in to the Games,' I told Ray. 'We're too late.'

Even to myself I admitted I sounded like Hanrahan warning, 'We'll all be rooned.'

An hour or so later, we had standing-room tickets to every day of the Games except for the opening and closing ceremonies, which we were far too blasé to want to go to, and the day of the 'metric mile' – the 1500 metres, in which the great John Landy was expected to win a gold medal for Australia.

When I remarked to Ray that, despite our triumphant ticket-buying coup, it was a pity we would miss the 1500, he simply said, 'We haven't missed it yet, mate. Let's see how it all goes.'

With the first goal of the mission completed, we repaired to the Mayfair Hotel near the university to get started on part two. We needed to fortify ourselves: we were about to spend two solid weeks at the MCG.

As with so many other Melburnians, our attitude to the MCG was a kind of unthinking and unqualified proprietorial indulgence. If we'd thought about it, we would have conceded that there might be people in Melbourne who were uninfluenced by – even, incredibly, more or less unaware of – the 'G' in their early lives, and perhaps there were some who even managed to maintain this deprived state into advanced maturity. But they would be in a very small minority: even people who were proud of their uninterest in, and total rejection of, all things sporting could be caught out now and then evincing a faint glimmer of pride in the great stadium that erupted into the public consciousness periodically for this or that sensational reason.

And so, although the circumstances were unique for us – it wasn't every day you went off to watch the Olympic Games in Melbourne – it was just like going home really as Ray Tynan and I strode across the footbridge under a warm blue sky on Friday 23 November, our heads fuzzing slightly with what we assumed must be an element of unaccustomed hangover after the previous evening's sortie at the bar; and the 'G' coming into sight below us, seething with queues, decked with colour, purring with suppressed sound like a walled, spired city waking up for the day.

We had been here many, many times. It was just that, *this time*, Melbourne's great secular cathedral had been renovated for perhaps its biggest-ever celebration.

THERE SEEMS NO constraint upon Wills's daring and downright cussed-ness because now, extraordinarily, American baseball teams appear at his behest. Has he made an error? Baseball! On the 'G'? But no, Wills is right again with his summoning baton: an MCC-sponsored team played the first baseball game on the 'G' in 1885 against a team from the American ship *Enterprise*, although not remotely the *Enterprise* that Captain Kirk, Mr Spock and the gorgeous Lieutenant Uhuru piloted through the decades of the recent past – but just as American.

And scarcely have the baseballers moved away, flicking the ball among their mitted hands casually and at great velocity, when bicycles hurtle around the perimeter. It is the Austral Wheel Race, which the versatile MCG hosted in 1886.

Wills is everywhere, glorying in the images and recollections and history and the future all flowering, apparently at his command, from his shiny baton. More hat-tricks (Hugh Trumble, Second Test, MCG, 1902 and then again at the 'G' in 1904, in the Fifth Test and his swan song); the first Victorian Football League Grand Final to be played on the MCG (1902) flits across Wills's phantom stage. Collingwood versus Essendon. Minor premiers Collingwood had won eleven games on end only to lose the Second Semi-Final to Fitzroy. Exercising the new right of challenge available to the minor premiers, Collingwood played reigning premiers Essendon and ran away by 33 points in front of a crowd of 35 202. It was the first Premiership for Collingwood and for the MCG.

ONE HUNDRED YEARS almost to the day after that first Premiership in 1902, Collingwood are back again.

Caterer Michael Birmingham is not feeling especially ceremonial when he arrives at the ground at three on the morning of 28 September – Grand Final Day – 2002. In the black, cold expanses of a rainy Melbourne morning, the 'G' looks at first glance like a city besieged by a ragged army about to make its final assault. Light splashes around the walls of the stadium and beams out from various entrances and doorways and headlamps. Trucks and other vehicles are dotted along the roadway that circles the MCG's walls. Men and women in one official capacity or another and wearing a staggering range of uniforms walk, sometimes jog, or run in purposeful spurts along the path, in and out of the spilling light; and in the car park, tents, swags, makeshift shelters and other innovations cloak the hordes who will descend upon, and eventually breach, the gates of the 'city'. MCC members are there in their hundreds, because they hold reserved but not allocated seats. 'Coffee points' are set up for them while they queue overnight. The Members' gates will open at 8 a.m.

Birmingham, hunching into his coat collar as another squall whips across the park, takes a wander around and through the ground, checking the readiness of marquees, overnight catering staff, staff changeovers, rosters and so on. He is seeing 'how everything is going'.

By 4.30 that Grand Final Day morning, he is ready for a coffee, which he takes to his office where he runs through the paperwork for the day's jobs. As he settles to the task, a distant voice somewhere out in the rainy park beyond the stadium's high walls bellows, 'Go, Pies!' and a wave of shouts echoes or derides this sentiment before a damp calm returns. Birmingham spreads out his material. Each food outlet has its own folder. He needs to be thoroughly familiar with the status quo and then react quickly to the fluctuations of demand. He has to have a grasp of the direction the day will take: this is partly decided for him by the sequence of prematch entertainment and the timing of the quarters once the game starts. He has to know and be ready for those set times during the afternoon when the catering outlets will be *hit* by a huge surge of customers.

He refills his coffee cup, thinking he must cut down a bit on the caffeine. Once he's through the folders, he sets off around the ground again to check with each of the retail outlet supervisors. He doesn't allow himself to be overimpressed by the magnitude of the task but, when he reviews that Grand Final Day of 2002 during the following week, he will discover, with no surprise whatsoever, that the corporate section of the operation – 20 dining rooms and 131 corporate boxes – consumed 6000 plated meals in two hours; 260 dozen bottles of wine; 16 500 litres of beer; 1520 kilos of beef fillets; 160 kilos of lamb; 500 kilos of chicken breasts; 2520 prawns; 150 kilos of smoked salmon; 6400 scones; 11 600 party pies, sausage rolls and pasties; and 200 poached eggs.

Helping all this to happen in their different ways were 200 kitchen staff and 600 front-of-house staff. At the other end of the food chain – out in the grandstands and around those terraces behind the ground-level seats where dyed-in-the-wool standing fans congregate – there were 44 snack outlets, 28 bars and six other sale points. On that day 80 000 plastic cups of beer, 25 000 pies, 12 000 cups of hot chips, 20 000 soft drinks, 6000 hot beverages, 2000 hamburgers and 5000 hot dogs passed through them. Five hundred and ninety sales staff handled these transactions.

That was the catering story of Grand Final Day 2002, but, as he sips his 5.45 a.m. coffee after making his rounds, Michael Birmingham is as yet unaware of these figures, although he could make a fair fist of predicting them. Now he is setting off to the Ponsford Stand – which is on its very last gig – to check on some temporary bars.

The Ponsford Stand has a number of small rooms, not generally much used, that are converted to bars for the members on 'big' days. Birmingham also checks, for the umpteenth time, signage around bars and outlets. Then it's back out into the car park, where queues swelled by overnight campers and early arrivers are lengthening and are being catered for by strolling pie boys. Rain is drifting down again when Birmingham pokes his nose out of the catering office, and his youthful staff are doing a big trade in hot pies but an even bigger trade in white, plastic ponchos. Ponchos and pies, in that order, are the go at 6 a.m. on the day that the amazing underdogs, Collingwood, will play defending Premiers the Brisbane Lions in the 2002 Grand Final at the MCG.

Around half-past six, Michael Birmingham sits down for breakfast in one of the MCC dining rooms. It will be his last chance that day to mix socially and at some leisure with MCC staff. Immediately after breakfast, he checks the roadway outside the catering area to ensure it will remain clear for delivery trucks and buggies. Then, he does something which, if you were watching his every move, would look odd. He takes up position with his back to a pole in front of the Members' gates. It is 7.45. Out in the park, in front of him, the members are poised for the opening of their gates at 8.00. Birmingham, who as a caterer is officiating at his first Grand Final, has been told this is a sight he must see. Old hands call it 'the running of the bulls'. As the gates open on the dot of eight, the members come swarming down the roadway, a ruthless, dog-eat-dog, no-quarter-asked-or-given charge that will be the most physical, dangerous and bruising encounter for the day until the game starts at 2.30.

Michael Birmingham is thankful he has his back to a pole as the tide of grimacing members surges past him like water ripping either side of a rock. Inside the ground, as this influx pours through, the catering outlets are open and ready.

At 8.45 the general public are admitted and by nine the crowd inside the ground is large and growing. Birmingham is on the prowl again, checking staff are where they should be, cross-referencing all areas to ensure the availability of goods, to minimise queue times, work out where the pressures are building and where things are slack and move people around accordingly.

At midday the Grand Final Sprint event is run and at 1.25 the prematch entertainment starts. Birmingham scarcely notices and he will see little of the game itself, as, with his senior and junior colleagues, he keeps all the diverse cogs in the catering machine smoothly meshing for what turns out to be 92 000 people. He does make time, however, for one small pilgrimage. He climbs up into the Ponsford Stand and watches a few minutes of the game from that now-doomed viewpoint, vaguely conscious that when the bulldozers move in on the following day, the MCG will begin a metamorphosis so transforming that it may not ever be quite the same place again.

NOW, ON THAT still fog-tented oval Tom Wills is busy again: Grandstands come and go as he gestures like Mandrake at shapes rising and coalescing in the blackness – the Grey Smith, the Harrison; movies are shown at the MCG to a large, appreciative and marvelling crowd; American gridiron takes over the ground, a remarkable sight so at odds with all expectations of the MCG. Wills is irrepressible. Dear to his own heart, no doubt, the first Australian Rules football carnival (1908) spills across the MCG; now it's lacrosse – the first carnival is held at the 'G' in 1910; soccer in the same year for the first time; rugby in 1914 . . .

The darkened oval, fitfully illuminated at Wills's will, is filling with its ghosts, and Wills is spinning and spreading his arms in hieratic gestures as images stream from his baton and the whole marvellous kaleidoscopic panoply of the MCG's existence over the years rolls by in splashes of fire and light, dark and shade, wild colours and flashing blades, swinging racquets – racquets? yes! Davis Cup tennis in 1912 – and rushing bodies. And every year since that first one in 1902 – the Grand Final.

COLLINGWOOD PLAYED IN and lost the Grand Finals of 1960, '64, '66, '70, '77, '79, '80 and '81, leading to the question-and-answer joke, *What's green, has two wings and eats Magpies? The MCG.*

For all its emerging versatility, the MCG by the eve of the First World War was already becoming known, above all, for one special day and one inimitable event in comparison with which even Test matches against England were battling to compete. The day was, usually, the last Saturday in September. The event was the Grand Final of the Victorian Football League.

The Grand Final is the high mass of the MCG cathedral, the peak and pomp of its many ceremonials. Year after year – even on those reasonably rare occasions when as a contest it fails to live up to its surrounds and the expectations of the crowd – the Grand Final is the climactic event at the 'G', Boxing Day, Queen's Birthday, Anzac Day and assorted 'blockbusters' notwithstanding.

It is 28 September 2002. The last few notes and lyrics of the national anthem have been drowned out by the swelling roar of 92 000 people (always a marvellous, tingling moment at the MCG). The captains have tossed (Michael Voss wins and chooses to kick to the city end). The players have taken up their positions and are already jockeying, niggling and bumping. And Mathew James, at twenty-eight years of age the youngest of the three officiating umpires for the Grand Final of 2002, is about to bounce the ball and start the game.

The first bounce is an anxious enough moment at the best of times. In pouring rain at the start of a Grand Final it is an especially tough task, but James's bounce, in the words of *Age* journalist Geoff McClure, sails 'gun-barrel straight into the air'. Just as well it was good because it was also the last bounce of the game. The rain that had flailed across the predawn queues and campers that morning in Yarra Park and continued in intermittent bursts since, had softened the ground surface to the point where bouncing the ball was very nearly impossible. The umpires decided to start on a high note with a bounce but thereafter to throw the ball up, which they duly did for all stoppages throughout the game.

Collingwood's aim at the beginning of the season was to reach the final eight.

'. . . what I demanded of the players at our guernsey presentation,' explained Collingwood president Eddie McGuire, 'was we must make the finals this year. And, as we all know, once you make the finals, anything is possible.' To go all the way to the Grand Final, winning games as the rankest underdogs on the way, was sheer bonus.

As the characteristically grim-faced Nathan Buckley led his team on to the famous ground on 28 September, all his players knew they had nothing to lose.

'I seriously think that if this team got belted by ten goals, Collingwood supporters would still stand and applaud them,' observed Collingwood club historian Michael Roberts. He considered that the mood of the supporters contemplating Collingwood's amazing run into the Grand Final was one of 'incredulous disbelief'. They had covered themselves with honour before Mathew James triumphantly managed that one bounce of the ball.

And they played like it. Brisbane swept down the ground from the first bounce and Akermanis ran on to the ball nearly in the goal square. Deciding against trying to 'soccer' it through, he bent to scoop it up. He was run down by Ben Johnson, and the ball bounced free and was eventually cleared. It was a small but in some ways significant moment. Nine times out of ten, Akermanis would have expected to gather in the ball quickly enough to squeeze a kick. But today is different. The Woods are here to play, and they have brought no baggage.

If Tom Wills could have watched this game, he would have been stunned at how the rules and manoeuvres on which he had exerted such an influence had developed and ramified. Much of it would have been unrecognisable. And yet: was it the rain? Or Collingwood's nothing-to-lose attitude? Or was it Brisbane's vulnerability through overconfidence? Or the truly massive support for the battling local side (the kind of single-minded partisanship not much seen at Grand Finals in the past decade or so)?

Whatever the contributing factors, this was in some ways an old-fashioned game of footy. It didn't flow all that much; it was, by and large, unspectacular; it was often a ground-level confrontation of players who were simply determined not to be stopped; it was a bit of a slog as rain fell through the early stages and then returned, heavy and dragging in the last quarter; and it was a man-on-man encounter, with both sides desperate to close down any run-on as the final siren neared; and there was never much more than a kick in it.

A low-scoring, rugged, sometimes crude and rarely flowing first quarter would be the kiss of death for the match as a big occasion, you might think. But played out in that amphitheatre that everybody expects so much of in atmosphere and panache, it is absolutely riveting. Another example of how what one can only call *the genius of the place* will lift any contest into another realm.

Keating gets the first hit-out from Mathew James's 'gun-barrel' bounce, and the next ten minutes are frenetic if largely unscientific. There are rolling scrimmages on the boundary after throw-ins and skeleton-rattling tackles, especially by Collingwood, all over the ground. Even the bolters, like Simon Black for Brisbane and Buckley for Collingwood, are finding open space very rare. After ten minutes, not one goal either way.

Collingwood coach Mick Malthouse will be pleased at that, observes commentator Robert Walls, but his colleague, Malcolm Blight, wonders if Leigh Matthews might not also be quite happy to see the opposition going flat out in the first ten minutes and scoreless.

Brisbane's Pike is ranging across the back line, picking up kicks but, from a saving mark, puts the ball out of bounds on the full. Freeborn takes the free kick for Collingwood, finds no one on his mark, runs 30 metres closer to goal and – kicks out of bounds on the full. Minutes later, the normally impeccable Buckley does the same. Nerves, pressure and a slippery ball are combining to produce the tightest Grand Final first-quarter contest anyone has seen in years. The score is 2 behinds each.

Keating stages for a free kick, and the umpire nearest him says, 'Play on' and the umpire 40 metres away awards it. White takes a phenomenal mark in the forward pocket for Brisbane and kicks out of bounds. Every time the 2002 Brownlow Medallist, Simon Black, goes near the ball, he is wrapped in black and white and Akermanis, Brownlow Medallist for 2001, is finding it difficult to get a kick. 'You have to *earn* a kick,' says Blight, marvelling at the tightest game he's seen 'for years'.

A pack gathers on the wing, and the Brisbane captain, Michael Voss, hurtles into it to iron out his opponent, Clement, but succeeds only in nearly knocking himself out. He is down for minutes then, surrounded by trainers, walks gasping to the forward line. As he does so, Brisbane ruckman Beau McDonald, after going for a hit-out, collapses in agony with what turns out to be a dislocated shoulder. He leaves the ground, left arm hanging grotesquely, and will not return. Brisbane are down to one ruckman.

With twenty minutes gone, the score is 3 points apiece. AFL officials don't know whether to be aghast at a goalless quarter or delighted by the tooth-and-claw nature of the encounter. Collingwood are ahead 25 to 10 on tackles, an unsurprising statistic that bears out what has been evident from the start: the Woods are turning on a fierce, physical, take-no-prisoners game designed to bump the fine-tuning out of the champions – and, aided by the rain, they have done just that.

That first goal – still unkicked and waiting its moment – becomes an ever-bigger psychological burden. It will only be *one goal*, after all, but whoever gets it first will find it an inspiration. At the 23-minute mark of the first quarter, Collingwood are 4 points, Brisbane 3. Voss and his opponent, Clement, are the only two players in the Brisbane forward 50 area, and Voss is looking seedy.

Lynch misses a running, angled shot for Brisbane, then McKee takes a free kick and finds Fraser, who passes to Licuria who, after a seemingly interminable hesitation, kicks to Rocca's ever more anguished lead. Rocca marks more than 50 metres out on a tight angle, very carefully lines up his shot, and unleashes a huge kick that, as we always say of such dramatic moments, was still going up when it flew through the goals. Perhaps not – but it's a brilliant goal and, when two minutes later the quarter-time siren goes, the score is Collingwood 1.4

(10), Brisbane 0.4 (4). It has been one of the most remarkable Grand Final first quarters in the history of the game.

A rumbling breath of relief and excitement balloons round the ground as most of the 92 000 people who have just agonised and shouted and laughed and groaned and gasped their way through that extraordinary first quarter prepare to assault Michael Birmingham's 'outlets', flooding through the toilets on their way.

The sky looks greyer and closer. The wind is sharp with flecks of rain. The whole ground is bobbing with white ponchos like wildflowers in the wet spring bush. This is the 'G' – at quarter-time on its famous day of any year, in all weathers, always a theatre beyond prediction and beyond compare.

IN ALL WEATHERS, always a theatre beyond prediction and beyond compare . . .

In the black, foggy paddock of Yarra Park, the MCG rumbles, and its outlines gleam intermittently with the lightning flash of artillery. Wills the circus-master has taken us into the war years and here on the oval is Billy Hughes addressing a pro-conscription rally. Is there no event that the 'G' will baulk at? Is there any character or any controversial gathering that it will not have a go at? Not make a historic moment of?

William Morris 'Billy' Hughes, although he scarcely kicked or hit a ball in anger, could not have been more at home on that field of 'titanic clashes', 'bone-crunching encounters', 'fearless tackles', 'no quarter being asked or given'. Prime Minister of the 1915–16 Labor government, and, after a messy and acrimonious expulsion from the party, Prime Minister of a Nationalist government until 1923. One of the founders of the Australian Labor Party, he became infamous as its betrayer, but 'traitor', harsh word though it is, was only the beginning of the hierarchy of abuse he attracted from his erstwhile colleagues. 'Rat' was further down the scale and the rest of the tirade was easily as bad as any attracted by umpires at the 'G' in the toughest, most brawling moments.

The reason Hughes was expelled from the party was the same reason that brought him to the MCG to address a crowd of 75 000 on 10 December 1917 – conscription. As prime minister, Hughes wanted to introduce conscription of men for the Western Front against the party's wishes and preferences. To escape party protocol, he appealed directly to the electorate in a referendum in 1916. In a bitter campaign, Hughes was strenuously opposed by the Irish-born (and recently arrived from Ireland) Archbishop Mannix, one of the most influential Catholic figures of the century. Hughes was known popularly as a Welshman and when the two squared off in the conscription debates it seemed like a grand Celtic barney was in the offing. He was, however, London born and C of E, which actually made for an even rougher barney. Amid great social and political division, the proposal for conscription was defeated by a narrow margin of 71 549 – about as many as came to hear Hughes at the MCG when he made his second attempt. But in December 1917, conscription was again rejected, this time by 166 688.

The gathering was as rough as any the 'G' would host. As historian (and Hawthorn supporter) Stuart Macintyre put it, 'The Prime Minister had received a warm reception from the members, while in the outer the air was thick with stones and bottles.' Mannix had publicly denounced conscription, and his leadership on this issue was so forthright and confronting that he invigorated and inspired the Australian and particularly the Melbourne Irish community. Hughes, using the secular cathedral of the MCG, and Mannix from his stronghold, St Pat's, slugged it out furiously during the war years. In a sense, Mannix was one of the rare public figures whose own agenda and charisma almost outshone all the history, drama and momentum of great deeds that anyone striding the MCG turf could normally and confidently assume and call upon. Hughes's MCG gathering was dramatic and riotous, but Mannix, from his East Melbourne turf, combined, in Patrick O'Farrell's words, 'the hallowed virtues of religion, and the role of leadership thereby conferred, with the legacy of [Les] Darcy. From the popular Irish Catholic viewpoint . . . he was a fighter, and most of all he was a winner . . . And it was his swinging of Irish pugnacity *away from sport and into politics* that made him so formidable and dangerous to the establishment' (my emphasis). Thus Archbishop Mannix brought politics into the cathedral of God, which in truth was nothing new. And politics likewise came to the cathedral of sport which, despite what many wanted to believe, wasn't unusual either.

The great cathedrals and temples, whether denominational, as most of them are, or secular like the MCG, Lord's and Wembley, can be highly political places. Cathedrals have been the headquarters for profoundly influential state figures – we don't need to go as far away in time or space as Cardinal Richelieu in seventeenth-century Paris for an example; Daniel Mannix of St Pat's, Melbourne, is much closer both to home and to the bone, a man who dominated the Victorian and national political scene from time to time during a long reign as Melbourne's Catholic archbishop.

Likewise, the MCG has a history that is political as much as it is sporting, architectural, social and cultural. It began with a political act – the granting by Governor La Trobe to the Melbourne Cricket Club, founded in 1838, of 10 acres in Yarra Park for the purpose of building a cricket ground. The grant was made in September 1853 and the Metropolitan Cricket Ground, as it was then called, hosted its inaugural first-class game in March 1856. The Metropolitan Ground, which had already been referred to as the Melbourne Cricket Ground, was the subject of an entry in the government gazette for 10 December 1861 which notified that 'it is intended to permanently reserve from sale the Crown Land herein described ['viz., the Metropolitan Cricket Ground formerly designated by the name of the Melbourne Cricket Ground, containing nine acres'] and to convey [this information] to the trustees on condition that the rates of admission to the public be subject to the approval of the government . . .' This important pronouncement safeguarded the public ownership of the MCG and ensured the public's continued access at reasonable prices. Both points would come into acrimonious contention in years to come.

When sportsmen and -women insist that sport and politics don't mix and don't need to mix, what they really mean is: they wish that sport and politics would not cross each other's paths. The truth, of course, is that sport is, or can unpredictably and suddenly become, intensely political and not only at its most sophisticated and international levels.

When I was a green, wide-eyed first-year teacher at a Victorian bush technical school, I copped somewhat reluctantly the job of coaching the school's Under 17 footy team, which played in a Saturday morning competition against teams from neighbouring districts. I was playing football in the town myself and loved the game. My reluctance to coach arose from a disinclination to get sucked into the intensity of that particular competition and the inevitable confrontations with the rural population that supported, coached and advised them – the politics of the game, in short.

Everything went pretty well, however, until about mid-season when, in accordance with our official fixture (to this day I swear I didn't misread or confuse the dates), we turned up for a home game at our own ground and the other side didn't. An enquiry ensued during the following week to decide who was to blame and how, if at all, points should be allocated. I was stunned at, and mystified by, the level of acrimony in this meeting: it was personal, strident, sometimes insulting and unrestrained by an outstandingly biased chairman who, though he represented the football league, was also a member of our opponents' club hierarchy.

We lost the 'case' and the points. I thought my arguments were pretty cogent and I had felt confident until I encountered the atmosphere of the meeting. It was only later I discovered that my known association both with prominent Catholics and the Labor Party branch in my town were much more important and more incendiary strikes against me than anything my team had done or failed to do. Suddenly, by an odd slip in the fixture arrangements, I had exposed my flank. It was duly shafted.

Australian Rules football was the sport in question but, at that 'official enquiry', politics was the game, and the fact that I was an utterly insignificant entity in the labyrinthine network of rural alignments and enmities mattered not at all. Kick where you see a head.

It is a trivial, provincial version of an old story, and utterly unsurprising. The only surprise is that there are still sportspeople who cling to the myth of apolitical sport.

Take the MCG, for example, 'the people's ground'. That very slogan is partly political and invites politicking. How long and how truly does it remain 'the people's ground' if powerful forces in society or government recognise advantages in limiting or in other ways controlling the people's access to it?

In the spirit of the government gazette notification of 1861, the Melbourne Cricket Ground Act of 1933, 'An Act Relating to a Ground Known as the Melbourne Cricket Ground', established the MCG Trust and set in motion a system of MCG governance and management that functioned harmoniously, efficiently and productively until 1998. The MCG Trust administered the Melbourne Cricket Ground, delegating day-to-day management to the Melbourne Cricket Club. Members of the Trust were drawn from both sides of Parliament and from the ranks of prominent citizens with a track record of sporting interests. It was the custom for the premier of the day to be a member. The whole structure operated on the conviction that the MCG in Yarra Park was on land belonging not to the government but to the people.

The Trust as administrator, the MCC as manager and the government of the day saw the great stadium through radical change, the turbulence of wartime and some years of peaceful metamorphosis. The 1956 Olympic Games, with the on-again-off-again crises, the massive and speedy building program and then the two weeks of huge crowds and the world's close and unwavering attention, constituted perhaps the ground's greatest test – from which it and its collaborators emerged with honours. The three-way cooperation between the Trust, the MCC and the government saw the construction of the two-tiered Southern Stand (predecessor of the Great Southern Stand) in 1937, the flattening-out of the ground's slope from east to west (a more than two-metre drop away) in 1955, and building of the Olympic Stand in 1956.

Through the 1980s and early 1990s projects such as the installation of the lights; an overhaul of the toilets (not as dramatic as the explosions of light but just as important); construction of the Great Southern Stand; relocation of the bowling green and its replacement by the practice wickets, thus removing from the oval itself those strips that turned to mud every winter; the introduction of drop-in pitches; renovation of the Punt Road Oval; and much else were all cooperatively planned and carried out by the Trust in collaboration with the MCC and the government of the day. By 1990, planning had begun on the Northern Stand Redevelopment, which would replace the old Olympic Stand.

Behind all policies and proposals for the 'G' was a powerful consensus between the Trust, the MCC and the chief users of the ground, the Victorian Cricket Association (VCA) and the Australian Football League (AFL, formerly VFL), that their overwhelming collective responsibility was to work for maximum use of the ground throughout any given sporting year. The decision to embark on the Great Southern Stand hinged on that consensus. The ground's $140-million investment in the project and the government's guarantee would never have been contemplated had there not been total and unconditional agreement all round on the principle of maximum use. The massive debt could only be managed if the 'G' was buzzing with crowds, whether for football, Test cricket, one-day matches or occasional concerts, or one-off games in other codes such as soccer and rugby.

Many approved of this culture of cooperation between the Trust, the cricket club and the government, but the more corporately inclined characters in the business community regarded it as altogether too cosy and not sufficiently open to the kind of initiatives mostly associated with the market economy and privatisation. In any case, the spirit or culture of cooperation began to erode in the early 1990s under the pressure, above all, of arguments about media access rights; new ground occupancy arrangements with the VCA and the Australian Cricket Board; and ground development, especially the proposed Northern Stand.

These were all important, but the media access rights issue was the most explosive and the most interesting. In July 1998, equipped with legal advice, the Trust and the MCC told the AFL that they would exercise their right to control the transmission from the ground of any electronic signal. In short, they were claiming ownership of the broadcasts – whether by radio or visuals – that were originated within the ground as a result of activities on the ground. It was a matter of intellectual property and, although many thought it remarkable, it did not come without warning.

In the 1930s, the Victoria Racing Club attempted to ban race-calling from Flemington Racecourse. Although they would never have used the term 'intellectual property', the idea behind the ban was that the club 'owned' the call. One result was that colourful maverick race-caller Eric Welch broadcast from a pub on Scotchman's Hill from which distance, incidentally, he correctly called a dead heat.

This bizarre episode contained two pointers for the Trust and the MCC had they been taking any notice of it. First, it demonstrated that there was a real case to be made on the question of intellectual property belonging to sports venues where games or races or other contests are enabled; and second, because the whole thing fizzled out, the Eric Welch incident might have suggested that if such a case could not be made in the relatively simple context of radio broadcasts, it could prove to be tortuous in an age of such complex and sophisticated electronic technology.

Throughout 1997 and 1998 the Trust, on the legal advice of Alan Archibald QC and Neil Young, continued to maintain that the ground managers were entitled to determine who should have access to transmit the signal from the ground, that it was public property. For the AFL, Ross Oakley and Graeme Samuel and for the VCA, Malcolm Gray argued the contrary case. The Trust's eventual capitulation on this matter would set the tone for later negotiations with the AFL.

It was in this atmosphere that pressure began to build to scrap the MCG Trust in its traditional form. Both the VCA and the AFL (with Graeme Samuel being particularly vocal) called for the Trust to be dismantled or at least radically overhauled. The AFL had for years resented the Trust's control over ground admission prices and insisted that football, as the greatest user, should have greater control over ground policies. The media rights issued flared critically when Channel 7 included virtual advertising in its transmission of the Bledisloe Cup rugby in August. Determination to get rid of the Trust was now irresistible.

At the end of 1998, the Kennett government amended the Melbourne Cricket Ground Act, dismantling the MCG Trust and replacing it with a new, smaller and, as far as personnel were concerned, more corporatised membership. This legislative initiative seems to have been Kennett's alone; it did not originate from any minister nor did it emerge from the bureaucracy. He took over the management of the Trust from the Lands Department. The Minister for Lands, Marie Tehan, played little part in the drafting of the legislation. It came out of the premier's office.

During his incumbency as premier, Kennett set up a number of statutory bodies in that style – in philosophy, market-oriented, impatient of, or uninterested in, cultural or traditional imperatives and influences; in structure, comprising small numbers of powerful players from the 'big end of town'.

Essentially, when the original Trust was dismantled and replaced, it was a case of the Kennett style being inflicted on the MCG as it had been, for example, on local government. Replacing the twenty-member old Trust would be a new MCG 'Trust', although the terminology now became ambivalent, because, as former National Party leader Peter Ross-Edwards pointed out, the new Trust was 'really a committee under the direct control of a minister'. It would comprise six members and a chairperson and would be subordinate to the state government which, under the amended act, could give written direction to the new Trust to cover the performance of any or all of its duties and functions. According to Marie Tehan, the Trust would now work 'in accordance with modern business principles', and the new arrangements would allow the Trust to call for tenders to deal with all or part of the ground management.

The 145-year-old role of the MCC as ground manager was thus potentially compromised, to the distress of some and the satisfaction of others who regarded the MCC as fuddy-duddy, smug and tending to see itself as beyond rebuke. The record of those 145 years, however, and especially of the previous fifty or so, stood very strongly in the MCC's managerial favour. The amendment seemed insufficiently thought out and certainly not based on Premier Kennett's personal experience of the Trust and its work because, unlike his predecessors, he had not taken up the membership option and appeared on the trust for the first time in 1997, five years after becoming premier.

The reaction to the state government's proposals and to their subsequent implementation was furious and came from a variety of sources. Former premier Cain wrote to the Melbourne newspaper the *Age* on 28 October 1998:

> The present management [that is, the old Trust] is unique in the strict meaning of the word. It has succeeded over more than sixty-five years. An independent Trust delegates day-to-day management to the long-term occupier, the Melbourne Cricket Club, and stands between the beneficiaries of the land – the people – and the users who put on the show. The sports bodies running Australian football and cricket and other users are more ferociously commercially driven than ever before. They joust for access. Television has become their master. The Trust has ensured no user is dominant. This does not please some.
>
> . . . The Trust must balance . . . sensitive, competing interests, while at the same time listening to the government of the day. Until now,

governments of all persuasions have backed this structure. Victorians should know that the present government proposes radical change.

There is to be a group, not a Trust in any sense, appointed or dismissed at the whim of the government, and subservient to government.

It is to be directed by government ' . . . on the performance, discharge or exercise of any of its functions . . .' and it 'must comply with such direction'.

This is a huge reversal of the independent trust concept. Governments can be driven by short-term, populist considerations and pressures that seem attractive at the time.

The Melbourne Cricket Ground has endured and prospered free from the pragmatism and patronage of any government, and for the long-term benefit of all the people. That should not be cast aside.

Charismatic former 'Invincibles' all-rounder Keith Miller said the proposal was 'a disgrace' and that the MCC had built the stadium into an international symbol of Australia equal to the Sydney Opera House. Miller might have been expected to adopt a broadly 'establishment' view of the affair, but his recognition of the 'G's symbolic status and the kinds of similar monumental buildings with which it might properly be compared is extremely interesting. You could imagine him going on to name a few cathedrals as well.

Former Victorian and Test opening batsman Colin McDonald ridiculed the idea of putting the ground and pitch preparation out to tender, for example. It was a technical procedure, he said. 'You don't call for tenders. You have a staff of three or four people who know precisely what they are doing.' Behind that comment lies an intimate understanding of the fragile art of dealing with the earth and the elements and getting the playing surfaces up to near-perfection in a maelstrom of uncertainties, as well as long acquaintance with those archetypal figures – the head groundsmen – who, at the WACA, the Adelaide Oval, the MCG, the SCG and the 'Gabba, carry out their legendary ministrations to grass and soil, according to knowledge, experience and the kind of eerie prescience about wind and weather, damp and dry, warm and cold that is not subject to scientific evaluation and is equalled only by a water diviner. McDonald could see little sign that the new Trust members had either a grasp of what skills and what kind of person it took to get the ground 'up' for, say, Boxing Day or the last Saturday in September, or that they cared. They had bigger privatised fish to fry.

The interesting common element among the protests was an emphasis not so much on the political and structural aspects of Kennett's MCG coup as on the endangered cultural role of the 'G' which was now, as many saw it, being placed under untoward pressure or simply betrayed. John Cain, joining Vernon Wilcox, Attorney-General in the Bolte and Hamer Liberal governments, and Walter Jona, former Corrections Minister, to comment on the proposal, gave a potent reminder of the central issue, that which perhaps, above all, made the 'G' so important and so distinctive, the characteristic that contributed so profoundly if mysteriously to its unmatchable atmosphere, its aura: 'The public has had its rights to a piece of land preserved and protected by the Trust,' he said. 'It will lose that now. The MCG will become a piece of commercial real estate to be used for short-term returns.'

The new Trust had been functioning, with maximum controversy, for just short of a year when the Kennett government suffered an extraordinary defeat in an 'unlosable' election and was succeeded by the minority Bracks Labor government. Kennett's magisterial arrogance and failure to listen to the electorate were cited as important reasons for this amazing result, and his dominant personal role in the attack on the

MCG Trust was seen as a prime example of that kind of behaviour. But the fall of the government did not mitigate the impact of the Trust that it had engendered, and the new minister, Sherryl Garbutt, was quickly made aware of her inherited problem. Responding in Parliament to the proposition that the growing rift between the Kennett-style Trust and the MCC might 'affect the ground's role as the people's ground and one of the greatest sporting stadiums in the world', she said:

> I have been made aware of a serious deterioration in what has been for many years a harmonious relationship between the Trust and the Club. It seems to stem from the change brought about following amendments to the Act late last year [1998]. I and other then-opposition speakers warned this would happen. Arguably the MCG is the most important piece of public parkland in the state. For over 100 years it was harmoniously controlled and managed and the previous government mucked it up. Like so much else, they wanted their mates in charge . . . The object, it seems, is to run it like another piece of commercial real estate for maximum return. It is not that and never will be . . . Suggestions that the [new] Trust, in early discussions on the new northern stand development, is promoting an option for a new corporate component, with consequent reduction of public seats, alarms me.

Meanwhile, amid bitter personal conflict, the VCA occupancy of the MCG was also laboriously argued out. With the Trust under constant threat of dismissal during 1998, and the new, Kennett-engendered Trust showing its inexperience on assuming office in the following year, many felt that the VCA, led by Malcolm Gray, had exploited the volatile conditions and bullied the new Trust chairman, investment banker John Wylie, with the prospect of inaugurating his incumbency by losing cricket from the MCG forever.

Whatever the case, members of the MCC staff who were involved in the negotiations felt that the chairman had conceded far too much ground to the VCA and had abdicated all claims to media rights in direct contradiction of legal advice. One insider referred to Wylie's concessions as 'catastrophic'.

Whatever the strengths and shortcomings of the original Trust arrangement, the 'culture' of mutual understanding, respect and cooperation that had distinguished the functioning of the Trust, the MCC and the government in concert for so many years was quickly lost after the amendment of the MCG Act and the accession of the new, streamlined Kennett Trust. Relations between the new Trust and the MCC were poor. The latter was, according to some Trust members, anchored in the 1950s, inefficient and hampered by siege mentality. Commissioned studies showed almost exactly the reverse, but the Trust continued to present an aggressive mien, and it was this relentless pressure which, according to sources within the new Trust and the MCC, hastened the retirement of manager Dr John Lill in 1999. When it came to the appointment of his successor, the new Trust actively sought to be involved in the appointment and applied pressure to influence the job specification, to monitor the short list and to reconfigure the position as manager of *both* the club and the ground. Whatever might have been its faults, the old Trust had no record of such interference in its successive manifestations over sixty-odd years and would certainly never have contemplated such actions.

Relationships between the MCC and the new Trust deteriorated rapidly, although recently there may have been some mellowing. The MCC complains that the Trust daily interferes in its management responsibilities and is arrogant and overbearing. Above all, though, the MCC considers that the new Trust does not understand, care for, or have any sensitivity towards the culture of the MCG that has made it such a Melbourne institution for so many years.

The acrimonious atmosphere was also a hindrance to discussions on ground development. The old Trust had already resolved some years earlier to remove and replace the northern (Olympic) stand. It had been hastily put up, had many problems for spectators (with blind spots or impeded views, etc.), and looked shabby. Under pressure from Commonwealth Games proponents, however – for example, Ron Walker – the MCC wilted towards a much larger revamp: the Ponsford, Members' and Olympic stands all to give way to a huge northern equivalent to the Great Southern Stand – but with state-of-the-art features. According to some sources in the MCC, the urgency levered on the decision by the winning for Melbourne of the 2006 Commonwealth Games was phony. No one else wanted the Commonwealth Games, they say.

Moreover, the Games did not need to be on the MCG. The alternative of having the opening and closing ceremonies on the 'G' and putting $20 million into upgrading Olympic Park for the actual events was a real one. Reconstruction of the Northern Stand, argue its opponents, should never have been tied to staging the Games at the 'G'. The same sources regard the chances of the new Northern Stand's being fully completed in time for those Games as extremely slim and they are critical of the necessity to remove eighteen rows of ground-level seating at the Punt Road end to allow for an eight-lane (no longer a six-lane) track at a cost of $18.2 million.

In the end, the Bracks government played a crucial resolving role in all these discussions, as it more or less had to do. The plans for the huge new Northern Stand Redevelopment could not go ahead without the AFL's being locked in. The AFL had sold TV broadcast rights to Channel 7, but there were those on the Trust and in the MCC who maintained that those rights were not the AFL's to sell. There was very good legal advice supporting this. But after this dispute had festered for some time, the Bracks government advised dissidents on the new Trust and on the MCC not to pick a fight with their principal user. The dissidents on the Trust were defeated, and significant concessions were made by the MCC on the intellectual property argument.

Meanwhile, there was a new kid on the block. With the 2000 Sydney Olympics approaching, there would be opportunities for capitals other than Sydney to stage Olympic soccer. Jeff Kennett quickly mobilised his networks and resources for the building of a special stadium for the purpose at Docklands. It would hold 52 000 people and be so designed as to afford the closeness to the action that is the characteristic of soccer stadiums and is made possible by the dimensions of the pitch and the nature of the game. It would have a roof, to ensure that Olympic soccer was not disrupted by Melbourne's dodgy spring weather.

And so what became Colonial Stadium, later the Telstra Dome, rose above the docks as another Kennett plan. When it was not even close to being finished for the Olympic deadline, Channel 7 and the AFL were hastily hauled on board and Docklands became a sort of 'boutique' football ground and, in due course, a financial disaster. Footy followers wondered why the AFL should have planned a stadium that would not hold more than 52 000 (when Essendon and Carlton or Collingwood and Richmond can often attract that many and more during the home-and-away season); why it needed a roof; why viewing conditions had to be so intimate (although many have come to enjoy these refinements); why the oval itself, although perfectly adequate, could not have been larger given they were going to the trouble of making a new one.

They had plenty of time to ponder these questions in the lengthy queues that frequently in Colonial's first season had them still waiting outside the ground beyond quarter-time. The answer, not at all clear at the time, was that the stadium on the docks was never meant for Australian Rules; it *grew into* Australian Rules, and it was always in part a TV studio.

The implications for the MCG were significant. Marie Tehan told the Trust that it should regard the MCG as being in competition with Colonial Stadium. Games allotted to the MCG each year dropped as Colonial's allocation was beefed up. At the same time, yearly attendances at AFL games began to drop and at least three Melbourne clubs were teetering on the edge of extinction. This was a potentially lethal cocktail of developments. The counter-medication was to shift the game more and more towards TV. So fixtures, times and venues came under the influence of the interested TV parties. If you wanted a sign of how these events were butting up against and demolishing 'traditional' league footy, it came on a Saturday afternoon in 2002 when there was not a single game of AFL football on in Melbourne. Tim Lane and his team sat in the studio and discussed issues, interviewed guests, kept an eye on the TV monitor and relayed scores from interstate. There was nothing else to do.

As for the exciting plans at the 'G', there are those who, without wanting to be jeremiahs, wonder if enough attention has been paid to falling attendances at AFL football matches and to the fact that the MCG is being allotted fewer games each year in the AFL fixture. Has the day of the vast stadium passed? Will such stadiums ever be filled again in an age when live-against-the-gate television (a practice indulged in by the AFL and to be continued) turns even the most passionately national or parochial of games into a lounge-room event? Will the 'G' become a vast, never-filled cavern of dreams – not the dreams of footballers, cricketers and athletes, but those of entrepreneurs and market men, who, when the dreams break and fade, leave wreckage and loss in their wake?

Many dire predictions and gloomy pronouncements were made as these wars of words raged. But when you walk into the MCG to watch the footy or international cricket, to what extent, if at all, is there evidence of a decline? Well, not a lot. The atmosphere is as sensational as ever, the facilities are fine, the ground itself, whether with goals at either end, or one-day cricket's centre circle or Test cricket's white-clad figures, is as beautiful, as breathtaking on first sight as ever. Perhaps the most noticeable difference between today's 'G' and that of, say, 1956 is the advertising. It's everywhere, and it offends some though few would expect elite sport in the twenty-first century to function without it.

The one change that almost everybody agrees is loathsome is that you never get a moment's peace at the 'G' any more. It is a cathedral in which the voices of suppliants, worshippers, plaintiffs, eccentrics, partisans, skeptics, aficionados, children are now all drowned by an immense racket issuing from massive speakers and accompanying awful images on the big screens. The instant a break occurs – lunch, half-time, drinks, three-quarter time – this vomit of noise pours from the speakers. Sometimes it is the voice of a ground announcer or a resident clown; sometimes it is recorded advertising. In any of its forms, it is lowest-common-denominator schlock from the schlock bin, vile, silly, intrusive.

Just as the Channel 9 football telecast (following Channel 7's original practice, it must be said) cuts to an advertisement the *instant* a goal is signalled, so that you miss the players' and crowd reactions and the spell is broken – again – in that same style, the ground noise spews out after the siren, or as cricketers leave the ground for lunch or tea, reinforcing the sense that you must *never* be left alone with your thoughts or your quiet enjoyment, or a few reflective words with companions.

Here is one of the unacceptable faces of the entrepreneurial spirit which, in the confident expectation of some observers, will yet reduce the 'G' to just another commercial real-estate opportunity. But it seems unlikely that the Pharisees will be chucked out of this temple . . .

PART TWO

You couldn't ask for more for your first
game, a Saturday afternoon at the 'G'.

Luke Ball, St Kilda Football Club recruit,
The Herald-Sun, Friday 28 March 2003

PHEW! WILLS LOOKS like a magician from whose hat has appeared an elephant and not a rabbit. He called up images of war and Billy Hughes and unleashed a huge political tangle. But that's the way of it when politics and sport intersect as, despite the wishes and hopes of many, they so constantly and routinely do. But Wills is interested in peacetime now: the post-World War I MCG and its doings. He brings into being traditional emblems of peace – hundreds of little children dancing intricate displays for the Prince of Wales in 1920 and then again, although not the same children, for the Duke and Duchess of York, soon to be precipitately King George VI and his Queen, on 26 April 1926 – the same year in which the Victorian state cricket team made a record 1107 runs at the MCG against New South Wales.

But Tom Wills is more interested in the following year on the 'G' and brings into his spotlight the magisterial figure of Bill Ponsford who, on the MCG in 1927, made 437 for Victoria against Queensland. While Ponsford was busy amassing runs, the new Members' Pavilion was planned, its foundation stone set and building begun.

And so the ghosts come and go at the behest of their ghostly master of ceremonies, who now theatrically gestures for a silence into which gradually swells the roar of a crowd. The great Don Bradman is walking to the wicket to face Larwood and Voce in the Melbourne bodyline Test of 1932–33 in front of a then-record crowd on the edge of anger and disruption. It will be a couple of weeks before Australian captain Bill Woodfull delivers his famous summation of the situation to England manager 'Plum' Warner: 'There are two teams out there on the oval. One is playing cricket, the other is not. This game is too good to be spoilt. It is time some people got out of it.'

But passions and tempers are already heated after the Englishmen, under the direction of their captain, Douglas Jardine, make their intentions clear in several games leading up to the Test series. In the First Test at Sydney, the full bodyline armoury is unveiled. Larwood takes 10 wickets for the match, Voce six, and Australia are thrashed. But Stan McCabe plays one of the great innings in Test cricket, hooking and pulling the fast, short-pitched ball to be 187 not out in the first innings. He is lbw to Hammond in the second innings for 32, refusing to succumb to any of the fast 'theory' bowlers.

And so the teams come to Melbourne, with Jardine already the embodiment of all the characteristics that Australians, and Irish Australians, in particular, at that time, loathed in the upper-class Englishman.

NOTHING WOULD SEEM simpler, more innocent, more thoroughly straightforward than a visit to the MCG on one of its big sporting occasions. To this theatre of heroes and dreams, however, as to many another venue in a complex society, people came with mixed and sometimes surprising motives. For example: until very recently, one somehow didn't in any way associate the Irish with the MCG – even despite the distinguished Australian Rules football career of Jim Stynes, an Irishman born and bred and one of the greatest players ever for the Melbourne Football Club, whose home ground is the MCG.

Yet, as we met under the plane trees near the footbridge one autumn morning, looking at the walls of the Great Southern Stand curving around and above Brunton Avenue, my friend Barney Maguire and I recalled our attempt to witness a great Irish moment at the 'G' – Ron Delany's against-the-odds Olympic triumph in the 'metric mile', an event that, had it not been for a much more youthful, larrikin Barney Maguire, I would never have seen. Forty-odd years on from those halcyon days, Maguire and I were on our way to drink some

Guinness at a book launch in the Landy Room of the 'G'. It was 17 March, St Patrick's Day. Cricket, as far as the MCG was concerned, had finished the previous week and the footy would start in earnest at the end of the month. So, for the moment, the great theatre was quiet. Peak hour had passed and the drone of traffic along always-busy Brunton Avenue had lulled to a companionable muttering; birds squabbled and fossicked in the park around us, and from the MCG itself it was as if a palpable silence flowed out to embrace us, a palpable presence of almost unprecedented soundlessness as imposing as the walls of the ground themselves. So rarely at rest, the stadium seemed to rejoice in a silence as massive as the roars and crescendos it was accustomed to. In this almost eerie vacuum, Maguire told me his story of an odd Irish coming to the MCG . . .

'My father, Patrick,' he began, 'came from one of those Irish-Australian families in which the tragic cause of a never-revisited Eire continued to be fought and argued thousands of miles from the emerald turf. Grandfather Gerald Xavier Maguire was born in Waterford in 1881 but came to Australia with his parents and five brothers at the turn of the century. He was completely politicised and detested England and everything to do with it. "The vengeance I seek is the righting of my country's wrong," he would quote resoundingly. "England . . . must be punished; that punishment will, as I believe, come upon her by and through Ireland; and so Ireland will be avenged . . . Punishment of England, then, for the crimes of England – this righteous public vengeance I seek and shall seek . . . for such vengeance I do vehemently thirst and burn." This loud homage to the words of John Mitchel, one of the founders of the Fenian Brotherhood, did not always go down especially well in some of the company on which Gerald recklessly inflicted it. Yet, strangely enough, Gerald was less often in trouble for his views than you might expect. Generalised antipathy towards England and the Poms was quite strong in Australia in the thirties and as often as not Gerald appeared to be simply a more vehement version of what his workmates – Depression victims, like him, of the collapse of the building game – were thinking themselves. In other words, history often connived with Gerald's passion while at the same time affording him the cloak of nonentity.

'The game of cricket, as you might guess, was doubly anathema to Gerald. As an Irishman, he had neither understanding of nor interest in its arcane and devious ways; and, being a Fenian, he loathed it routinely as an invention of the enemy, the Brits. Yet,' said Barney, stopping and gesturing towards the entrances to the Olympic Stand to which our leisurely progress had just that moment fortuitously brought us, 'if you will submit yourself to being transported back to Monday 2 January, 1933, and if you would stand just . . . just over here, you see, and imagine the Outer Ground turnstiles of the Melbourne Cricket Ground clicking away behind you. That's it. Now, keeping out of the way of the queue' – he brought imaginary queues and huddles of people into being with his waving arms and nimble sidestepping – 'cast an eye down the paths leading through the park. You have to look carefully because Australia is batting today with the match up for winning and, barring miracles, Bradman will be out in the middle before very long and that's why there are so many people, hundreds and hundreds, busily heading for the gates. Though they don't know it yet, they will be part of a world-record cricket attendance for one day of a Test match – 69 724. And here come two of those nearly 70 000 people: Gerald Maguire and his seventeen-year-old son, Patrick, my father. Gerald could live very happily without cricket, but he senses not only a victory in this match over the touring ENGLISHMEN, but also controversy as the leg-theory dilemma – bodyline as it came to be more colloquially known – gathers intensity. So here he comes to the MCG, to the Test cricket, concealing his hope of English discomfort and ignominy behind a piously expressed concern that young Patrick should see his country's cricketers and especially the incomparable Bradman.

'The great man duly strides to the wicket at 12.54 and for the next three hours, while his teammates capitulate around him, he ducks and defies the English bodyline bowling, nurses a long and vulnerable-looking Australian "tail" and makes what will turn out to be a match-winning 103 not out. This was how my father was inducted into the game of cricket and the atmosphere of the MCG – a game and a venue he continued to love despite, for him, cricket's ideological burden as a peculiarly antipodean weapon against the perfidious Englishman.

'That perfidy reached one of its peaks – though nothing would have surprised Gerald – a week or so later in the Test match at Adelaide, where Anglo-English relations and Imperial ties were threatened as Bert Oldfield fell to the turf under Larwood's brutal assault and law-abiding, honest Australians began to break down the fence and considered storming the ground. Gerald quoted Bill Woodfull with the same panache and reverence he afforded Mitchel: "There are two teams out there. One of them is playing cricket . . ."; and, Gerald would add – happily allowing subtlety to be sacrificed to absolutely unambiguous clarity – "the one not playing cricket was the bloody Poms."

'So it wasn't all that difficult for Gerald to ride waves that were already there; it was just that no one noticed with what fury he rode them, with what fanatical verve, with what murderous intent.' Maguire, parodying his own grandiloquent utterance, waved his arms extravagantly, spun on his heel and greeted our arrival outside the Members' gate with a mock hieratic gesture.

'Do you remember another Irishman at the G?' he said.

'Well, Tynan's an Irish name,' I said, feigning puzzlement but I knew who he meant.

Ray Tynan, in those days, was a young man of formidable intelligence, sartorial negligence, bohemian inclinations and an addiction to, and brilliant capacity for, a Socratic style of enquiry that often had his interlocutors wanting to administer some mid-twentieth-century equivalent of the hemlock that finished off his role model. He was a disorientatingly lateral thinker long before that term was coined. One afternoon in the university 'caf', for example, several of us, all blokes, were sheltering a while from books and drinking the vile caf coffee as an aid to thought. There had been some talk in the press about UFOs, an early 1950s outbreak of what would in later decades become a worldwide obsession.

'Take a Martian who lands out in the bush somewhere,' said Jack Howe. 'He comes down in a paddock. He might work out that cows are some kind of animal native to the place, but what d'you reckon he'd make of, say, a Southern Cross windmill?'

'He'd work it out,' said Trevor. 'He'd look at the windmill turning, those sail things or whatever you call them going round and round, and he'd see the rod that goes down into the cylinder, see it going . . .'

'In and out, in and out,' came the predictable chorus of the perennially deprived and frustrated.

' . . . see it pumping, and he'd work out that he was looking at a pump. If he'd got from Mars to here, he'd soon work out what a bloody pump was.'

'Why wouldn't he . . .' Ray mused aloud into the ensuing brief pause, 'why wouldn't he conclude that what he was looking at was a cow fan, to keep the cows cool?'

In the stunned silence that followed and before the exasperated chorus of 'Bullshit,' someone said, 'Jesus, Ray, you are a grade-one lunatic.'

It was this grade-one lunatic ('At least I'm grade one,' he'd replied mildly, 'about eighteen grades ahead of you, you dopey bastard'), who, on Friday 30 November 1956 – the last day of spring – turned his mind to what was looming as our biggest problem in those innocent and halcyon days. On the following day, John Landy would be running in the final of the 1500 metres – 'the metric mile'. Besides Landy, four runners in that field had run sub-four-minute miles. And we didn't have a ticket to the 'G' between us. It was the one day we had missed out on.

'Barney Maguire,' says Ray, naming one of our then more larrikin friends and a stalwart at the pub where our beer-drinking classes were well advanced, 'knows a bloke who's a scalper . . .'

'Hang on. We can't afford to pay scalper's prices.'

'No, no, no. Calm down. Maguire tells me he reckons he can get tickets at the face-value price because this bloke's already done so well scalping swimming tickets and anyway he owes Maguire for some reason.'

'It all sounds a bit bloody criminal to me.' I was ever the cautious one, but Ray said it would be all right.

'Anyway,' – the clincher – 'so long as we don't know anything about where he gets 'em from, we're not liable for any trouble. We're innocent parties.' Bush law was another of his interests.

Next morning, there we were, bound on that quintessential Melbourne Saturday journey – across the footbridge and into the trees, and then over to the already desultorily clicking turnstiles of the MCG. True, we were much earlier than the normal football-season time for this excursion, and we would have been judged a little too eager had it been a Test match we were heading to, because it was just after half-past eight when we arrived in the shadow of the 'G'. We were supposed to meet Maguire and retire to some appropriate, shady spot to do our deal.

Of course, it didn't work. Some complication too intricate to follow and, in any case, irrelevant when you got down to it had sub-verted Maguire's relationship with his 'contact'. But, he quickly added as Ray was preparing to be scathing, there was compensation. By means not to be revealed – Maguire emphasised the secrecy by tapping the right side of his generous nose with his right index finger – he had 'come by' a couple of complimentary tickets. These were in the possession of a contact inside the ground who, however, would only hand them over personally to deserving recipients. He would not allow Maguire to get pass outs and take them out of his sight and control.

This was all too much for Ray. 'How the fuck are we going to get them if they're inside the bloody ground?'

'One bit of the fence round behind the Olympic Stand is cyclone wire,' said Maguire. 'We'll pass them through.'

Amazing as it seems now, and reasonably unlikely as it seemed even then, in those days there was a short section of the external wall that was sturdy, very high cyclone. Through it you could see simply the back of the stand and the passing parade of people circulating around the causeway. It was probably a temporary phenomenon left over from the flurry of last-minute activities that brought the MCG to its final Olympic shape.

We found this odd window onto the inner workings of the 'G', where we would meet Maguire and his suspicious mate who, it turned out, had intended his comps to buy him into the favours of two young women of his acquaintance, but they hadn't turned up, and Maguire had convinced him not to waste the tickets by simply hanging on to them. We would buy numerous beers in recompense, we promised.

When we arrived at the cyclone-wire fence, Maguire was waiting on the other side looking anguished. 'The bastard's welshed,' he said. 'The women he was going to give the tickets to came after all. Silly bastard's so excited I can't get any sense out of him.'

'So we're buggered,' I said. 'I knew we'd miss Landy,' I added in my gloomy way.

But Ray and Maguire, from their different sides of the obstacle, were gazing up at the wire fence. There weren't that many people around on our side, and they were all intent on purposeful walking to the gates or somewhere. On Maguire's side it was similarly quiet – a little temporary backwater of the great MCG. It was worth a try. After some theatrical looking-around and massive displays of uninterest and casualness, while Maguire, with equal lashings of melodrama, patrolled his side and suddenly signalled us to go, we ran at the fence and clawed and dug and toe-kicked and scrambled up and over. Too keen not to be caught *in flagrante*, I let go early and fell a long way – I remember noticing from the top how unexpectedly high it was – twisting my ankle on landing, despite Maguire's steadying hand.

Ray landed straight after, more judiciously. He dusted himself off. 'You all right?' he said.

I nodded, though I wasn't. My ankle was hurting, but that would pass. 'I might have to scratch from the 1500,' I said.

'Well, Landy'll be relieved,' said Maguire.

Watched by a small knot of amazed onlookers who had lingered for a moment on both sides of the fence, we strode off towards the causeway, looking as if dropping painfully from the sky to fall sprawling into the 'G' was the standard method of entry compared with which coming in through the turnstiles was the height of eccentricity.

And so, we were in, and a few bounding leaps, or in my case limps up the steps from the causeway, revealed yet again the sunlit arena, its multitudinous ghosts from the past temporarily laid by the bustling urgencies and strivings of all the nations.

What a different world it was in 1956 – a world in which you could climb into the MCG or, choosing your moment, just walk in, unannounced and unhindered by protocols, bureaucracy or anything as petty as requiring a ticket. Veteran ABC sports broadcaster Norman 'Gold! Gold! Gold!' May recalled that, as a young beginner on radio, of no seniority whatsoever, he was disappointed to be assigned to cover a surf carnival at Torquay during the early days of the Games. Coming up to Melbourne eventually, having seen nothing of the venue or the epochal events unfolding there each day, he went to a party at a house not far from the 'G'. At about eleven o'clock, suitably emboldened, he and a few of his mates walked down to the ground and found a way in. Jumping the fence, they circled around the running track, chased each other over 100 yards, had a shot at the long jump then walked out again and rejoined their party.

The finalists for the 1500 began to hover and stretch around the start a little after four o'clock. John Landy, the hometown hero, had been the focus of anxiety and puzzlement for some days. He had qualified right enough, but unconvincingly in a very rough race. Some, like his compatriot and fellow 1500 metres finalist, Merv Lincoln, felt Landy had held much in reserve and had done just enough to make the cut. Ron Clarke, the young torchbearer, agreed. But others, including newspaper pundits, thought Landy had struggled to make the pace and lacked his famous kick into high gear that had taken him round many a field and into the lead. Landy himself sat down after his heat and put his head in his hands, the picture of a man unhappy with his performance.

But at least Landy was there. Pre-race favourite Rozsavolgyi and star performers Waern (Sweden), Salsola (Finland) and Hermann (Germany) were all out of the race. Three Englishmen known for their grim doggedness – Boyd, Wood and Hewson – were still in, as was Merv Lincoln, the fastest qualifier, two dark-horse New Zealanders, Scott and Halberg, the Irishman, Ron Delany, and Richtzenhain (Germany).

The general opinion as the runners lined up was that a world-record time might be necessary to win.

Near enough to 100 000 people saw this great race, few of them had eyes for anyone else but Landy, and only those who had flown in that morning from outer space or at least Siberia didn't know that he was carrying an injury. The starter's gun cracked in an amazing, cathedral-like silence, releasing a throaty acclamation from the crowd that would continue unabated to the finish.

Landy immediately looked sluggish, adrift, and at the end of the first lap he was last. After the second lap, he was at the tail of the field. As the bell rang for the last lap, Landy, in a sudden rediscovery of his old ways, slid around the outside, gathering in twelve runners, graceful, straight-backed, exciting, and the noise went up a notch or two.

But the challenges were stern when they came. Landy wasn't long for the front, with Hewson, Hungary's Tabori and Richtzenhain all making moves. The race grew willing, with bumps and buffets handed out and reciprocated. Landy himself was knocked off the pace, picked up again and, as he did, Delany of Ireland broke from the pack and arrowed at the line. Landy chased him. It was his last throw, and he was bidding for second but would not have run down Delany when the line loomed and he came in a close third.

After he crossed the line, Delany seemed to collapse on the track and, characteristically, Landy stopped and bent over him in some concern. But Delany was saying a prayer in thanksgiving, though he was as grateful to Landy as to God.

'Before I met John, I was just another mile runner,' he said. 'He told me I could run faster and he showed me my capabilities. He taught me how to relax and cut five or six seconds off my time for the mile.'

Not for the first time, the pupil had outshone the mentor. And the Irish had arrived at the 'G', although there would be a long hiatus before they returned – with very different skills and to a transformed MCG.

. . . In 1999 the Irish arrived at the MCG in earnest, a smiling, engaging group but meaning business. Undistracted by ancient enmities or the burdens of history, they trod the MCG turf with the flair and dash associated with the Irish, although in general they left their charm in the dressing-room on the correct assumption that it would be redundant in their meeting with the Australians. These encounters under 'modified rules', a cross between Gaelic football and Australian Rules but with a round ball and the scoring system of goals and 'overs', leaning heavily to the Irish model, were stirring, often brutal affairs, played with a take-no-prisoners intensity that seemed to suggest Australia was the old enemy. As if Cromwell had been a Victorian squatter and the Irish had waited all these years to wreak a legitimate revenge on their country's scourge.

Australian Rules football, the one sport at home on the MCG that had no international dimension, at last took on the world in the shape of the lads from Ireland. It was almost more than the Aussies bargained for.

The pervasive and durable assumption that Australian Rules football must have evolved from the Gaelic game which, although it uses a round ball, has some similarities with Australian Rules, has been conclusively rebutted by the historian Geoffrey Blainey. Aussie Rules was, he maintains, 'a game of our own', explicitly turning away from existing football codes, and was more likely to have been influenced, through Tom Wills, by Aboriginal models than by anything from the other hemisphere – although that too is the subject of great dispute.

The idea of an Irish connection persisted, however, and it

became powerfully linked with another durable talking point about the Australian game, namely its parochialism. Australian footballers would never stride the international sporting arenas because no one else in the whole world played anything like Aussie Rules. Well, no one except . . . the Irish.

The similarities between the two codes impressed themselves on former VFL umpire Harry Beitzel when he watched a live telecast of the All-Ireland final in his hotel room while on a business trip to London. Beitzel had umpired the 1955 Melbourne–Collingwood Grand Final, among many other games, and, following retirement as an umpire, continued to be influential and involved in Australian football. With lukewarm reaction from the VFL, Beitzel decided to organise his own team and tour. 'The Galahs', as Beitzel christened his team, were born, and, captained by Ron Barassi, they took the field at Croke Park, Dublin, against County Meath in October 1967. As journalist Mick Dunne recalled it:

> Those who were there at the beginning recalled that they appeared to be colossally oversized giants of men, all rippling muscles and bulging pectorals, as they trotted confidently, brazenly out from under the old Cusack Stand on that murky day in late October 1967. Those sleeveless, dark green guernseys . . . and tight, hip-hugging shorts accentuated the imposing physique of the pioneering squad of Australian Rules footballers . . . When these cocky, brawny superb specimens of athleticism proceeded to outrun, outmanoeuvre, even humiliate Meath, our recently crowned All-Ireland champions, 23,419 of us flabbergasted onlookers readily acknowledged that Croke Park had never seen anything like it.

The Australians were applauded off the field after this showing and 28 000 turned up on the following Saturday in the hope of seeing

Connacht champions County Mayo take the game up to the antipodean visitors. They did, but still lost a close one to 'the super-fit Aussies'.

With some momentum and interest established in both countries, games were played in Ireland in 1968 and in Australia in 1970, when Kerry toured triumphantly. There were further encounters in 1978 (in Ireland) and in 1981. In 1984, 'Compromise Rules' were introduced which successfully combined features of the Gaelic Athletic Association code and Australian Rules. With contests taking place in 1984 (Ireland), 1986 (Australia), 1987 (Ireland), 1990 (Australia) and 1998 (Ireland), the Australian game had at last achieved a *kind* of international standing.

All of this was a long way from the MCG because even when the hybrid game came to Melbourne, as it regularly did, it was played at VFL (later AFL) Park, Waverley. But on the night of Friday 8 October 1999, the Irish arrived to play Australia at the MCG and 64 326 people came to watch them. They saw a close, bruising spectacle in which the characteristic skills of the Australian footballers ensured that they were always in the game, but they were much less precise with the round ball than their opponents. Without scoring a goal (while Ireland scored two) they ran the Irish team ragged in the later stages of the match but lost by eight points. Nathan Buckley and Stephen Silvagni were outstanding for Australia.

The 'G' looked as stunning as ever under lights and, just as was the case when the Socceroos played Iran on the MCG in front of 90 000 people, the stadium seemed to embrace the new code – different lines, different goals, different dimensions – as if it had been custom-built for the occasion. The fear that such codes as the Irish game, soccer and even rugby might be dwarfed in the vast spaces of the 'G' and too distanced from spectators proved groundless. As with every other performance deposited on its expanses of green grass in front of its cavernous and lofty stands and its huge circle of ground-level seats – from popes to proselytisers, from singers to dancers, from parachutists to sprinters – the 'G' coped beautifully.

The Irish returned to the MCG on Saturday 13 October 2001. In front of a crowd of 49 121, Australia outplayed Ireland to be six points in front at half-time, but the Irish staged a terrific second-half revival and snatched the game by six points. Craig Bradley was brilliant for the Australians who, however, had their usual trouble scoring goals under the modified rules. The game was, also as usual with these encounters, extremely willing and ended sensationally when the Australian umpire, Brett Allen, allowed Stuart Maxfield to have a shot at goal after the final siren. Unheard-of under Gaelic Association rules, this is common practice in the Australian game. The result was not affected, but the Irish coach, Brian McEniff, was furious with Allen, and it was said that he and some of his staff actually manhandled the umpire after the incident. There were also what was becoming the customary array of protests and complaints about the Australian style of tackling. This game was a true MCG event – packed with drama, pretty well patronised by fans and controversial to the end.

TO THE CROWDS that Tom Wills has already conjured up on the oval are now added waves of women – athletes at the Victorian Women's Centennial Sports Carnival in 1934, the year in which yet another dutifully interested royal visitor (Duke of Gloucester) sees yet another MCG children's display. In the following year, Australia's women Test cricketers take to the 'G's wide spaces to play the England women's Test team, 18–21 January 1935.

Suddenly Wills is sweeping his baton in huge circles, encompassing all parts of the ground. In his first arc appears the new Southern Stand of 1936 and then, a *pièce de résistance*, huge crowds materialise beneath blue, sunny skies, packing the stands and terraces – 350 534 at the six-day Third Test, 1–7 January 1937, when Fingleton and Bradman make 136 and 270 respectively in the second innings – and 30 837 on New Year's Day 1940, at the Sheffield Shield encounter between Victoria and South Australia.

A hush falls over Wills's phantasmagoric MCG. The crowds of filmy onlookers seem to melt into the gloom. Outside, the fog settles denser and clinging, the city sleeps in a blur of lost outlines, wan feeble globes and layers of greyness. The 'G' is silent, Wills's baton is by his side, his head is bowed, his manic energy seemingly exhausted. Dimly perceptible are military figures, airmen, equipment. The Second World War has banished football, cricket and everything else from the oval. The Americans are there – pilots and marines. And then the Australians – the RAAF.

The MCG goes into a long, wartime hibernation. The lights go out in Europe and then in Australia. Wills stands motionless in the centre of the oval. His ghosts stir restlessly.

The MCG fills with troops, among them 3600 American marines from the horrors of the Battle of Guadalcanal. For them, as they remembered it ever after, the MCG was 'heaven'. They froze in the blasts of wind round the 'G's stands and concourses but, overwhelmingly, their memory was of feeling safe, of being among friends. The silent stadium accommodated them as it had accommodated so many others and when the emergency was over . . .

Slowly Wills looks up, points to the boundary. The Melbourne and Hawthorn football teams burst on to the ground. It is 17 August 1946. Footy returns triumphantly to the 'G' after the long wartime hiatus. After a dead-even first half, Melbourne come from a couple of goals behind at three-quarter time to win running away, 18.15 (123) to Hawthorn's 13.8 (86), a result not entirely unexpected as Melbourne were in the middle of a winning streak that would take them all the way to the Grand Final, which they lost to Essendon by 10 goals, while Hawthorn came last, with three wins for the season.

From somewhere, at a sign from Wills, light floods the ground and its crowding historical ghosts. Now it is summer, 1947–48. The team that will by and large constitute 'The Invincibles' are hosts to the Indian Test team's first visit to the 'G'. Here, obedient to Wills's summoning gestures, are Sid Barnes and Arthur Morris, making not many runs, and then Bradman and Lindsay Hassett putting on 167, followed next day by a sensational cameo innings from Keith Miller.

Does Wills linger a little over this reincarnation of a long-ago Miller innings? Because if there was a latter-day Tom Wills it was perhaps Keith Miller in his flamboyant prime. It is not Wills's moodiness and taciturnity that is the reminder here, but his panache, unconventionality, healthy anti-authoritarianism, a volatile catch-me-if-you-can confidence in prodigious personal gifts.

Miller was a devastating all-rounder, punishing, and a match-winner with bat or ball. Like Wills, Miller played Australian Rules football with distinction. He was a dashing full-back for St Kilda before making the decision to go to Sydney and to concentrate on cricket. And he was visually arresting. Tall, athletic and with a great mop of black hair, which he frequently brushed back with his hand, Miller commanded attention whether with his 'slinging' bowling action, which generated frightening speed and bounce, his extraordinary close-in catching, or his blazing batting.

The 1870 W. Handcock portrait of Tom Wills shows him as tall – looking tall, anyway – leaning on his bat, slightly spivvish with his bow tie and coloured belt, confidence radiating from his bearing, which is embellished by a stylishly worn cap and trimmed moustache and beard. Just as distinctive, as individual and as carefree of convention as the later great Miller. And, like Miller, Wills could bat brilliantly and bowl very fast, using his much criticised 'round-armer' that worked up great speed. On top of all that, he was probably the best footballer of his age.

If Wills's baton wavers a little to give Miller centre stage for just a fraction longer, who can blame him?

But Miller must depart, like all Wills's shades, to give way to the next scene, which is epochal.

Enter Bradman. Later that year (1948), Bradman will have his unforgettable testimonial game at the famous ground, and some will have their first, last and only chance to see a Bradman century.

Wills is parading a kind of panoply of nostalgia, small boys and girls walking out of their childhood, walking away from wartime disruptions and fear and uncertainty – a generation that will grow up, in Melbourne at least, 'owning' the MCG as it enters the second half of the twentieth century and some of the stadium's greatest times, spectacles, triumphs and dramas.

On his murky stage on a fogbound ghost-ridden night at the Melbourne Cricket Ground, Tom Wills 'magically' floods the oval with sunlight to reveal Queen Elizabeth II and her consort, the Duke of Edinburgh, viewing a gathering of ex-service men and women and then – yes! a children's display. How the royals must have pined to return to the children's displays at the MCG.

And, then, Wills is backing away towards the boundary, self-effacing and, for the moment, conceding to a greater attraction. It is 1956. The MCG is on the eve of one of its many 'finest hours': the Olympic torch is near the end of its long journey. Young distance runner Ron Clarke, ignoring the showers of sparks and embers that are burning his arms, is about to enter the stadium, holding the torch aloft. Any minute now, another historic moment for the MCG will tick over as the Olympic flame bursts into life and the Games of the XVI Olympiad begin on Melbourne's matchless oval . . .

Bill Tickner, Secretary of the Melbourne University Sports Union, was as excited as anyone about the Olympic Games – more so, most likely, given his professional interest and involvement in sport and sports administration. Nevertheless, his lively interest did not prepare him for being contacted by the Organising Committee of the Melbourne Games, not much more than six months before the Opening Ceremony, with a request that he should arrange the transfer of the torch from its first Australian landfall – which was to be Cairns – through to the MCG.

To twenty-first-century ears, this sounds like an extraordinarily hit-and-miss way of going about what has become a highly coordinated, massive and sophisticated operation (culminating in ever more tricky and amazing ways of actually getting the Olympic flame to light up). Tickner, suspecting he was on the brink of a very complicated and demanding task, called in the aid of Marc Marsden, an academic in the Melbourne University Geology Department and a fine sports administrator who had played various roles in many of the university's sporting events and competitions. Perhaps Tickner felt that Marsden, a geologist, would be better able to manage the geographical complexities that were a part of getting the torch from Cairns through certain mandatory places en route and down to the MCG.

The bearing of the torch across seas and continents to its Olympic destination was by no means an established procedure at the time. The Berlin Games of 1936 seem to have inaugurated the practice, and the journey of that torch has been immortalised in Leni Riefenstahl's famous film. The 1948 London Games continued the torchbearing 'tradition', which was not all that difficult given the relatively short distance involved. The same was true for Helsinki in 1952, but a torch procession from Athens to Melbourne? To many, it seemed out of the question and far more trouble and expense than it would be worth, unlike bearing the torch to European destinations. Much the same vacillation dogged this question as had afflicted the arguments about the main stadium venue, with the result that no decision was taken until quite late and when that decision was in favour of a torch procession across the world and then through extensive parts of Australia, time was short.

This was the mission that landed on Bill Tickner's desk and thence on Marc Marsden's. But Marsden had good pedigree for running trans-territorial sporting endeavours. His father was Edward, the onlie true begetter of the Fijian cricket tour of 1907–08.

Marsden's task and subsequent adventures put his father's Fijian tour in the shade somewhat. They included a long drive to Cairns to plan the torch's return route on the run and during which one of the cars was written off. In Cairns, the torch nearly didn't land because wild storms raging through the area looked like forcing the aircraft to turn away. Floods cut off roads they had planned to use and when, in desperation, they put torch and runners on railway flatcars for a short stretch as the only means of getting them across swollen rivers, the

Herald smelt a story and suggested they were cheating.

In Sydney, standing alongside the Lord Mayor on the steps of the Sydney Town Hall, Marsden was stunned to see not one of the chosen runners approaching with the flame but one of his old mates from Melbourne University, now a postgraduate student at Sydney University. We'll call him Bill Lenehan.

Bill Lenehan had gone to Sydney to do Veterinary Science. He was a brilliant, charismatic and delightful character, a university and intervarsity footballer of great ability, a great mate of other noted university sportsmen of the time – Jack Clancy and Marc Marsden. Lenehan was inclined to larrikin behaviour in the best sense of the word and, as practising larrikins ourselves at the time, but with much to learn, Ray Tynan and I found him irresistible.

In Sydney, and ignorant of Marsden's role in the Olympic torch saga, he casually accepted the job of organising a hoax torchbearer to salute the mayor ten minutes or so before the genuine article arrived. The 'torch' was a broomstick-like rod with a plum-jam can mounted on it, stuffed full of kerosene-soaked rags. Lenehan and his team positioned themselves near the end of the route and the phony runner, dressed in white shorts and singlet, with white running shoes, would take off as the real torch was heard approaching. It was easy to know this, because the applause and general noise of the watching crowd increased in volume as the runner was heard to be coming nearer.

At the crucial moment, however, the stand-in torchbearer went to water and refused to budge. Grabbing the torch, Lenehan, despite being wrongly dressed for the occasion (in particular he was wearing ordinary street shoes), set off between the columns of cheering onlookers. It was, no doubt, a great demonstration of how people's expectations will simply override contrary evidence. The spectators were there to see the torchbearer and so they bloody well saw him – ignoring, indeed denying, at least for the time being, the tin can, the shoddy stick, the outlandish-looking runner.

The mayor did likewise and was launched into his speech as Lenehan mounted the Town Hall steps to be greeted by a stupefied, aghast Marc Marsden. 'Here's the torch, Mayor,' Lenehan said, and bolted.

Marsden had still not managed to get a word out, but eventually helped the mayor to attribute this unfortunate episode to irresponsible students, by which time, anyway, the real torch had arrived. Which was just as well. Lenehan's memory of the last few minutes of his time on the mayoral dais was that the crowd's mood had changed, and he might easily get roughed up if he stayed around.

After various other adventures, although none so exotic as that one, the Olympic torch arrived in Melbourne and was triumphantly borne by the singed Ron Clarke into the MCG.

Marc Marsden was one of the group of officials who, with great relief, saw it arrive and saw the flame lit. Bill Lenehan was nowhere to be seen, but the Marsdens had returned to the MCG.

IN ITS CAPACITY to live on into and through new ages, changing demands, fickle fashions and yet still seem utterly at home, the MCG is like a great work of art. Along with only a very few other sites and presences in the city, among them the two other cathedrals, the 'G' has remained unaffected by the rush of colour and sound and fury that is the accompaniment of the kaleidoscoping centuries' unstoppable rolling through time. Shakespeare's play *Julius Caesar* is set in 44 BC, but it has been powerfully used down the centuries by lateral-thinking theatre directors to represent other and much later regimes wracked by power-mongering, politico-moral ambiguity and descent into chaos: fascist Italy and Hitler's Germany are two notable and favourite examples. Arthur Miller's *The Crucible* is about the Salem witchcraft trials of 1692, but its oblique, pungent reference to McCarthyite America and to other intolerant, ideology-driven legislators has made it more than the brilliant representation of a moment in the distant and ignorant past. Leonardo da Vinci's *Mona Lisa* continues to fascinate people and attract analysis and explication according to the age in which it is viewed; it lives on, enigmatic, teasing, timeless.

Likewise the MCG. From its days as a broad, open, parklike expanse in the 1860s, surrounded by trees and grass and tents and flags, through its enrolment in 'Marvellous Melbourne'-style grandiloquence with the building of the elegant 1881 Members' Pavilion, to the early 1900s oval where could be seen the beginnings, including the iron picket fence and grandstands, of its later incarnation as a true 'stadium', the MCG has always been afloat and vibrant in the flood of events and never in any danger of being sunk by them. Like all great buildings that become landmarks and symbols of a city, and like the other two cathedrals, the 'G' brings its history and the ghosts of its former self with it into another and an amazing age and, like them, combines past and present into a timeless, always comforting, always welcoming shape.

And so, when Ray and I, surrendering our standing-room tickets for Day One, clicked through the familiar turnstiles, crossed the concourse and climbed the stairs for our first view of the ground in its Olympic garb, there burst upon our sight something that was both old and new. There was the oval – the broad wings, the goal-to-goal line; easy to see where the Test match and Sheffield Shield wickets would be in summer; and simple to work out where the actual goalposts normally were; and Bay 13 . . .

Yet all was changed as well. The red-ochre, white-line-striped running track slashed in a brilliant circle round the boundary; the jumps pits; the throwers and heavers warming up in the inner circle of the green carpet; the paraphernalia for judging and measuring; the officials running out tapes, clustering at finish lines, adjusting equipment – all under a fluffy blue sky in 'humid and changeable' conditions, as the weather bureau put it.

As it so often had in the past, even if more modestly according to the times, and as it surely would again in the future, the MCG was putting on a show.

Ray and I squeezed in on the fence down in front of the Olympic Stand at about 9.30 on that pleasant, warm Friday and settled into our standing-room niche to wait for the athletics to start at ten.

We were lucky in four ways on the MCG's first Olympic day, no doubt about that.

To get tickets at all and therefore be on hand at the 'G' for some of its most distinguished moments – like idly wandering into a church in Vienna to have a look around and hearing the Vienna Boys' Choir practising Bach's Mass in B minor.

To watch with intensifying fascination Czech Olga Fikotova – a mere student – gradually creep up on the opposition, which included the formidable favourite, Nina Ponomareva, and win the Olympic women's discus title with a record-breaking throw.

To see the phenomenal Vladimir Kuts wear down and then destroy the best 10 000-metre runners in the world, taking a stunning 31.4 seconds off Emil Zatopek's 1952 record.

And perhaps, above all, to see the sun set on the MCG, because there was no Ponsford Stand in the way in 1956, and between us and that sunset there unfolded, over nearly nine riveting hours, one of the MCG's most magnificent, most characteristic dramas.

Not everyone was happy with the 'G' that day. Many athletes complained about the running track, which cut up badly during some races. Kuts was especially critical, matching action to words by running a lane wide for the entire race because of the 'very poor condition' of the track, but it seemed to stop worrying him after a few laps (and how many more seconds would he have shaved off the record if he'd gone by the shortest way).

Englishman Gordon Pirie, perhaps Kuts's most obvious challenger, was concerned not with the state of the earth at his feet but with more brutally practical matters.

'He murdered me,' he said, 'that's all there was to it. I don't think I could ever beat Kuts over 10 000 metres.'

Another unhappy athlete was the 'Flying Milko'. Flamboyant would-be Melbourne legend Dave Stephens had carved out a substantial record for himself as a distance runner and had become a local marvel as he trained on his milk run around the suburbs. He came to the 'G' on that Friday with some high expectations, but Kuts burnt them up. Stephens was lapped (appropriate, no doubt, for a milko but not what he was intending), looked badly out of his class and, in the words of *Age* sports reporter Bruce Welch, 'finished a weary, worried runner, just crossing the line in third-last place as Kuts was completing his lap of honour'.

The 'Flying Milko' was not the first nor would he be remotely the last performer to discover that, despite the vastness of the MCG arena and no matter that it was crowded not just with two footy teams this time but with perhaps sixty-odd figures doing one thing or another, there was nowhere to hide if you failed. Drop a catch in the outfield, run into an open goal and miss, be lapped by the power runners and limp in late – and you might just as well have gone out there naked and playing the bagpipes. Eighty-five thousand people are glaring at you and tendering a remarkably unified line of advice.

All of this was happening while, noticed only occasionally, as one might tune in briefly to get the latest score on the radio, the high jumpers cleared or failed to clear the ever-ascending bar.

High jumping is a deceptively leisurely, philosophical interlude punctuated by moments of spectacular flight and energy. It is leisurely by rule, because each jumper is allowed three attempts at given heights so it can take often a long time just to get through one round of jumps during which, eventually, every competitor might qualify to continue. And it is leisurely in spirit. High jumping is a long, lonely business.

Each jumper sets up a sort of small camp of rugs, drinks, tracksuit and other apparel and gear, and there he or she sits, often covered and cowled from head to toe, in a state of either contemplative torpor or apparent frank uninterest in the surrounding world – including the opposition.

If you are in the crowd watching, say, Vladimir Kuts grimacing his way into the eighteenth of twenty-one laps, and you glance across to see what's happening with the high jump, chances are nothing will be happening. It may look as if all the competitors have given it their best and gone home, or have clustered somewhere to watch Kuts. But more dedicated scrutiny will discover one of them unwinding slowly and deliberately from his chrysalis of gear to begin a long stretching, bending and jogging routine that takes him in good time and with luck up and over, after which – with a glance over the shoulder at the possibly trembling bar – he walks very slowly back to his 'camp' where he subsides into the earth till called forth again like a bud in the warmth of spring.

The high jump that day began at 10 a.m. with elimination rounds sharing an initially desultory stage with Olga Fikotova's discus event. The latter commanded more attention. Slim, youthful and, as the day wore on, ever more sexy, the Czech girl had it all over the rather more blocky Nina Ponomareva and her Russian colleagues when it came to charisma and presence. All she had to do to round off her near-perfect debut at the 'G' was throw the discus further, and this she did, gradually drawing the entire stadium's gaze, cranking up the tension as she went closer and closer to bringing off that result most beloved of the sports pages, *an early upset*.

By contrast, the high jump looked a bit scrappy and indecipherable. But who cared? Who *would* care, with a whole day in warm sun (predicted showers not arriving) deep within the vast nave of the 'G'.

For incense there was the heady smell of the green shaved grass on which the mowers had been circling and snaking past obstacles only an hour or so ago; for litany there was the Gregorian rise and fall of nearly 90 000 voices engaged in anything from idle chat to stentorian outburst; for display and ceremony there were the national colours of the athletes fanning across the oval beneath the whip and snap of flags high above the curve of grandstands.

This was the ritual of the 'G' – so familiar to anyone who had been to a Grand Final or a Test match, yet now so renewed, invested with mystery and *gravitas* beneath the huge guttering candle of the Olympic flame.

At half-past two the qualifiers set up their camps for the final rounds of the high jump. Three and a half hours later, as Vladimir Kuts and the other competitors took their marks for the start of the 10 000 metres final, Charles Dumas (USA) – the only man at the time ever to have cleared 7 feet – Charles 'Chilla' Porter (Australia) and Igor Kashkarov (USSR) were still jumping as the bar edged up to 6 feet 9 inches. While Kuts carted the 10 000 metres field through lap after lap, spreading dismay and distress among them, the attention of the watchers switched agonisingly from his metronomic stride to the small group around the high jump where, in the most fitful and apparently casual way imaginable, a huge drama was taking shape. Twenty-eight minutes and 45.6 seconds after he set off, Kuts rampaged through the tape. His stunning, world-record victory was one of the greatest feats of athleticism ever witnessed at the 'G'. The applause rolled on through his lap of honour, but many who clapped and whistled also glanced elsewhere – to the high jump, where Dumas, Porter and Kashkarov were still jumping.

After more than eight hours, the high jump now had the undivided attention of the 40 000 people who stayed on. Shadows lanced across the oval, the stands darkened, the 'G' began to dissolve in the spectacular long, slanting light of the setting sun. Like wraiths or ghosts in ethereal light, Dumas, Porter and Kashkarov defied each other, drifting into the dusty sunset air, falling again, surviving.

With the bar at 6 feet 9⅞ inches, Chilla Porter hit it on his first jump. So did Dumas. So did Kashkarov. With agonising slowness, each athlete returned to his 'camp', climbed into a tracksuit and disappeared under a blanket to contemplate the challenge. The sun inched lower and the 'G' took on its evensong look – shafts of moted afternoon light gradually capitulating to the advancing deep shadows, like the last light of day battling through stained glass. The 40 000-strong congregation (what any cleric would give for such a turnout) sat in silent, tense awe at the unfolding ceremonial (even Ray and I were gratefully sitting by now, having appropriated a couple of empty seats as the crowd thinned).

Disengaging his lanky frame from its swaddling clothes, Chilla Porter took a long look at the bar as if he had only just then noticed it, bounced up and down a few times, bent low, loped along his curving approach and – flew over. A gusty roar of relief and appreciation rolled round the 'G' even before he had floated back to earth. Now, Dumas, seeming suddenly to want to settle the issue once and for all, briskly went through his preparations, glided up to the bar and drifted over as if the jump were an afterthought, a footnote to the oiled, muscle-rippling run that brought him to his take-off. With the pressure abruptly on him, not to mention the unremitting gaze of thousands of spectators, Kashkarov, grim, tense, hit the bar, which quivered, quivered again – and fell off. While Dumas and Porter relaxed, distinguishable only as reclining mounds of clothing among the green shadows, Kashkarov prepared himself for what might be his last jump in the 1956 Olympic Games. Some flexing and bending and nimble hopping were followed by several deep breaths and then he was running at the bar – which he flicked, with shorts or an elbow, and it fell off. Vast disappointment breathed out across the ground as Kashkarov – inconsolable despite the sympathy of the crowd and his opponents – wrung his hands, bowed his head and began the long walk back to collect his gear and leave the arena.

Now there were two. The sun had dropped so low that you had to squint to see the action that seemed to be taking place in a golden bowl of fire. The bar stood at 6 feet 10½ inches – higher than the sun.

Seeming unhurried, even disinclined to get on with it, Dumas and Porter relax as the light drains away and the first chill begins to gather round the feet of the crowd. Then Dumas is up and jumping and the bar falls. Chilla leaps and fails. And they dress again and lie down and cover up. Minutes pass amid that buzz of suppressed expectation that passes for silence at the 'G'. After all, 40 000 would be getting towards a reasonable footy crowd, so all of us know, from years of tight games and desperate finals, that we are capable of making an immense noise. But for now, nothing could be less apt. It is a time for the odd, strained observation, the side-of-the-mouth comment as Dumas strides into his second jump and knocks the bar to the ground. A roar rises as he does but becomes a gasp of – what? No one knows whether to be disappointed or triumphant. The tension creaks in the air. A silence following Dumas's quizzical moment of contemplation as he regards the fallen bar is broken by a very Australian voice shouting, 'Go, Chilla.' The crowd erupts as if for a brilliant running goal in the last seconds of a close game or a huge six hit over square leg to bring up someone's century, and Chilla, having gone through his routine, rides this tide of genial patriotism right up to the bar, jumps – and hits it.

Charlie Dumas slowly stands, swings his long arms a couple of times, bends and straightens, sets off on his wide curving approach, seems to unwind himself in midair, to stream out like a rope that loops itself up at the bar, and he is over. Tumultuous cheering sounds almost hysterical, and it is true that, watching this extraordinary contest, we feel as if we are part of some contrived play: life, real life, real games, don't go like this. It is too much to expect.

Now Chilla facing, as Kashkarov had done an hour or so ago, what might be his very last move in the Games, sets off on a short jog, still wearing his Australian green tracksuit, swinging his arms, raising his knees to an exaggerated height, hands loose at the wrists. Then, back he comes, peels off the tracksuit, takes three deep breaths, runs at the jump and lifts on a sighing surge of anxiety from the crowd. He is flying, levitating, trapezing above the rays of the sun when his trailing arm flicks the bar. It shivers as he lands, seems to bounce along its whole length, stays on. As both jumpers go into reclusion again, officials raise the bar to 6 feet 11¼.

No one knows what to do, what to say. It's like a drawn game of Australian Rules football – a result easily rare enough to have players on both sides standing round in disbelief, a time when disappointment is an overreaction and triumph is out of place.

I look at Ray.

'Jesus!' he says.

As he is not given to overt religiosity, I take this to be an expression of awed incredulity.

Dumas leaps at the 6 feet 11¼ bar up there in the fading light and misses. Porter misses. Dumas brings the bar down about his feet with his second jump but only after it has hovered and shimmied and shaken for an age. Porter misses again and so, more than nine hours after they first walked on to the arena to begin their event and in light that has softened to a mere afterglow, Charlie Dumas and Chilla Porter come to their moment of truth.

Dumas looks, assesses, flexes, breathes in and out. His approach seems slow, too slow, without the usual momentum. At the bottom of the jump he seems to coil, buckling almost into a crouch and then he is rising through the last light, a lithe uncanny silhouette that wafts up and up – and over.

Chilla Porter joins in the clapping and congratulation and then becomes part of the vast silence of the 'G' as it prepares to host one of its great moments. He takes seven minutes to ready himself for this crucial jump. He walks around, sits down, gets up, rubs his legs (how weary both athletes must be after hours and hours of mental tension and physical strain), swings his arms, looks up into the blackening vault of the sky, exchanges a brief word with a boy scout standing nearby in some official capacity or other, strolls away again head bowed, then, back at his mark, he runs in and jumps. The bar trembles and falls, and it is all over.

At 7.35 the three exhausted high jumpers ascend the victory dais to receive their medals. The crowd, many of whom can scarcely see the distant figures through the thickening night air, salutes them before at last fanning out into the surrounding parklands, heading for the footbridge, the pubs, the trams and trains, the distant suburbs.

Behind them, wisped with rising mist, becoming almost fantastic-looking in keeping with the events it has borne witness to throughout the day, the 'G' melts into the darkness.

IN THE MELT of darkness and fog, Wills's insubstantial pageant, conjured out of the ghosts swirling in that fog and darkness, is continuing, daring to resume even after such an apparent crescendo as the Olympic Games. It is, remember, dark night and deepest winter. Melbourne winter, as it used to be years ago when fogs rolled through June and July (and, by way of balancing the picture, dust storms columned into hot, smoky skies in January).

Ray and I once more are heading for the 'G' which, although slightly less formidable (the Southern Stand is a shadow of what it will become and there is no Ponsford Stand), would have been perfectly recognisable to Michael Birmingham, Jason Edmonds and Tony Ware. They would have especially appreciated it on the Saturday just past when 100 000 people watched the United States track-and-field team win four of the five gold medals on offer. The US total is now five from a possible eight. Russia has the other three.

No stranger to tensions of various kinds, the MCG on these sunny Olympic days is the venue for much pleasure and innocent enjoyment, but there is a sombre international subtext, which is rarely far below the surface. The brutal suppression of the Hungarian uprising is still fresh news and raw in many memories, and occasionally there is a partisan edge to the applause and roars that sweep these huge crowds.

In the same Monday newspapers that covered America's Saturday triumphs in blow-by-blow detail, a small item from Reuters' Berlin correspondent reported that Imre Nagy, the former Hungarian leader, had been kidnapped by Soviet security and, according to reliable rumours murmuring through diplomatic circles and clamorous in the bars of West Berlin, had been taken to Moscow to stand trial for high treason.

Like most students in that turbulent year, Ray and I had followed the Hungarian crisis closely and had devoted endless hours to arguments and discussion about it and the British invasion of Suez. In those days there were not many avenues for public protest, although we had joined one small demonstration against the Soviet invasion.

Curiously, the Olympic Games – benign, sporting and good-willed though they were – provided a sort of acceptable forum for the oblique or half-repressed expression of views, prejudices, loyalties and anxieties arising from a political crisis of unprecedented peacetime severity in the Eastern Bloc and the Middle East. Was it only our imagination or were Hungarian athletes attracting especially hearty cheers and support? This *was* Melbourne, after all, and we were at the MCG, home of the most uncompromising partisanship and shrine of the underdog every Saturday in winter. (For reasons partly ideological, partly base and inexcusable, Ray and I went to a great deal of trouble to get tickets to the Hungary/Russia water polo match. There was blood in the water, literally. It was one of the most violent and brutal sporting encounters most of us had ever seen.)

But, happily, while such feelings were detectable at the 'G' now and then, they were never anywhere near naked, and they did not become so strong as to hijack sporting rivalries and competitiveness and turn them into something more dangerous.

After the intense dramas of Friday – the high jump, Kuts's 10000 metres, Fikotova's triumph – it seemed almost certain that Saturday would be something of a let-down. But, as so often, the MCG itself provided an atmosphere so undeniable, so heady and so exhilarating that even a corpse would be stirred. When 100 000 people cram into that stadium, all gazing down from their multicoloured ranks on to the brilliant green oval beneath a blue-and-white gusty sky, collective excitement and passionate expectation follow as a matter of course. The MCG is itself an event.

Despite the American heroics, the highlight of Saturday at the 'G' – remembering that in those days you would generally expect to end up at the 'G' on most Saturdays – was New Zealander Norman Read's win in the 50-kilometre walk. Read was utterly unheralded: he had an unmemorable name; he came from New Zealand, an unmemorable place, as far as Australians were concerned; and he was competing in an event that entailed leaving the stadium at about half-past one in the afternoon and returning, in his case, at 6 p.m. The marathon, of course, worked in a similar way, but it was quicker (under three hours), famous and dramatic, and it was a *run*, not a walk.

Norman Read's return to the MCG after a four-and-a-half-hour absence, two minutes ahead of his nearest rival, the Russian, Maskinskov, was, like 1956 marathon winner Mimoun's re-entry, a wonderful demonstration of the charisma of the stadium. Merely breasting a tape would have amounted to little. It was the business of bursting back on to that famous arena through a gateway open to few (into the 'G' through the tunnel from Brunton Avenue) that lent both achievements, but perhaps especially Read's as he had walked to Springvale, an outer suburb, and back, a special quality: extraordinary determination and endurance mitigating some vague suggestion of the ludicrous.

Read's gait was faintly hilarious; Mimoun looked like he should have been wearing a beret and drinking pastis. But, lone figures that they were, as they emerged from that tunnel to a Grand Final-style roar of intoxication, they were transformed by the stadium. It did all the work for them. They had been gone for hours. They were nearly forgotten. But they returned – down there! look! here he comes! – making an entry as dramatic and as triumphant as any into the Colosseum.

After he had broken the tape, Norman Read made a wildly eccentric lap of honour, jumping, pirouetting, greeting spectators at the fence. Probably his antics were as much occasioned by relief at being freed from the awkward physical and mental disciplines of the walk – surely one of the least natural, the most unspontaneous array of movements of any track-and-field challenge – as by any sense of achievement. But he was a star turn, the kind of thing you only see at the 'G'.

Ray and I were by now well advanced on our accelerated beer-drinking course and regarded ourselves as having passed undergraduate level. With the temperature up around 90 degrees Fahrenheit on that Saturday, we were heading for the pub as soon as Norman returned, but there was a straw in the wind that made us look forward to the Monday. Two Australian young women, Marlene Mathews and Betty Cuthbert, had earlier that afternoon qualified for the final of the 100 metres. Both looked likely, with the German, Christa Stubnick, the big danger and the pundits' choice.

So back we went on the Monday, taking up our more or less habitual possie close to the fence in front of the Olympic Stand, and saw records fall all over the place – javelin, 800 metres final, pole vault – until, at about 5.15 p.m., the runners appeared for the women's 100 metres final. Just on 100 000 people watched in as much of a silence as such a huge gathering could attain, while the women laced their running spikes and limbered up. Nearing the track, walking to the starting blocks, Betty Cuthbert appeared to trip slightly and a weirdly stifled gasp drifted out of the stands. She had been visibly nervous in the semi-final, in which she had run second to Stubnick after having beaten her in their heat. Now the entire crowd was nervous on her behalf – she was, after all, only eighteen – while at twenty-two, Marlene Mathews, sharing favouritism with Stubnick, also twenty-two, continued cool and unruffled.

The crack of the starter's pistol actually had a brief echo, so breathlessly silent was the crowd, and then a continuous roar accompanied Cuthbert's charge straight down the middle of the track to the tape. Stubnick second, Mathews third, the time equalling the Olympic record.

It was romantic and emotional and exciting: a lump-in-the-throat experience even for moderately cynical – or so we thought – young students like Ray and me.

On three successive days, we had seen the gamut of what you came to expect at the 'G', no matter what particular game or spectacle was involved. Norman Read, the archetypal underdog, Mr Nobody; Betty Cuthbert, youth and beauty claiming what we all at some time in our lives convince ourselves is its just reward.

As with Grand Finals and big feature games and Test-match sixes and blinding catches and brilliant running goals, you could hear the roar back in Melbourne's business heart, because the 'G' is so close to the city on the Yarra, geographically and spiritually. Look, you can see it from here! and here! and up there! And listen, listen to that crowd – someone's out! Or it's a goal! Or Betty Cuthbert's won gold!

MIKE GATTING, CAPTAIN of what his own countrymen were describing as the weakest Test team ever to leave England – 'Can't bat, can't bowl . . . can't field,' said one scribe, unwittingly previewing a famous controversy in Australian cricket fourteen years later – won the toss on Boxing Day 1986 and decided to put Australia in. Undoubtedly, he thought the wicket might do a bit early. And he was right. Australia were bowled out for 141, England replied with 349 and won in three days by an innings and 14 runs. Whatever Gatting saw in the wicket, he would have looked with some interest at the oval.

Only a few weeks earlier, ground staff had used special heating to encourage grass growth on the wicket square in preparation for the touring England side's game against Victoria, and the oval, in general, clearly showed the signs of heavy-duty football seasons. From 1985 Melbourne, Richmond and North Melbourne shared the MCG for home games and the arena surface could not cope, especially if the effects of constant use were exacerbated by wet weather.

The England–Victoria match had taken place on the easternmost pitch of the square. Elsewhere, not only the ravages of the football season but also the lingering evidence of a papal mass held on the 'G' at the end of November were unmistakable and occasionally produced eccentric bounce or a wavering line when the ball sped across the grass. (Gatting would also have remembered this game because he slept in and arrived late at the ground.) By Boxing Day, the surface was in better nick, the oval beautifully mown in the long, parallel corridors characteristic of the MCG (in contrast to the concentric circles of some grounds) and smooth to the eye – no more than the visiting captain would have expected. Which, given his experience in the match against Victoria, might have surprised Gatting. Had he been standing in the middle at the end of November, however, he would have been even more amazed to see the arena up to scratch by Boxing Day.

On the evening of Thursday 27 November, 100 000 people poured through Richmond and Jolimont stations or spilled with relief from packed trams or bumper-to-bumpered their way into the car park, or streamed across the footbridge or flooded in waves through Yarra Park. There were no queues for tickets and at turnstiles and gates the people surged unchecked into the famous stadium, many of them for the very first time, and actually *on* to the oval in places. There were picnic hampers and some footy scarves but very few Eskies and no cans.

You might have thought these were MCG initiates, wise in the ways and charms and diversity of the stadium, taking some extraordinary opportunity to get in free. But this was no traditional 'clash' they were going to – or, on second thoughts, maybe it was. The Saints versus the Demons; Good versus Evil; Peace versus Strife, various manifestations of the oldest, most durable and dogged of antagonists – and in God's corner, His Holiness Pope John Paul II.

The patient crowd, long since settled in, roared as images of the papal procession nearing the city from the airport rose on the scoreboard screen. It might as well have been a tight final score: the sound was almost the same. Then, at about eight o'clock, on to the ground came the powerful, one-man team of the Good: Pope John Paul II. This was the first time in history a pope had been to the 'G'.

John Paul was appropriately dressed – in red and white, the colours of the old Blood Stained Angels, now fallen and fled four years earlier to the fleshpots of Sydney where, as a result some said of a pact with the forces of darkness, they had been transformed into swans. White cassock and red cape glowed in the waning light, but as the Popemobile eased up to the podium and the pope alighted and raised his arms to the throng, the MCG's lights – only a year old and the subject of disputes as bitter and corrosive as those between Lucifer and God himself – came on in their six towers, at first soft and lambent but quickly blazing into a vast effulgence, the way a choir reaches its crescendo of 'Amen'.

Hundreds of disabled and elderly were specially provided for in the stadium. Some, wheelchair-bound, with multiple sclerosis or spina bifida, were pushed to the front as the pope arrived, in the hope of a blessing or even, as one man said, a *miracle*.

Fair enough. Any MCG veteran could have told them that it was the place of miracles – the 1970 Grand Final between Carlton and Collingwood, for example; or the 70-run last-wicket partnership between Allan Border and Jeff Thomson in the Fourth Test, 1982, which took Australia to within three runs of victory; and then the catch that ended it – snicked by Thommo, fumbled and dropped by Tavaré, but gathered up on the rebound just above the grass by Miller; and . . . any number of other miracles, not to mention canonisings and demonisings aplenty.

Italians, Vietnamese, Poles, Greeks, Poms, Turks, Lebanese, Maltese, native-born Melburnians and Victorians made up a huge audience of a kind rarely seen even at the 'G', often enough a melting pot of one kind or another and sometimes a cauldron. Children and many adults fluttered their yellow papal flags. Picnic gear was squeezed into narrow seat spaces in the stands. Tartan rugs were spread here and there. A gasp and a ripple, as people stood all round the ground, greeted the entrance of Herb Elliott dressed in a white tracksuit and carrying a torch from St Paul's – from one cathedral to another.

The pope, greeted with a standing ovation as he rose to speak, invoked ideas of unity, peace and reconciliation. From one point of view, it might be said that such virtues had been rarely enshrined or sought on that 'hallowed turf' where contest, competitiveness and elite confrontation were mostly the order of the years. But looked at another way, even the most intense and uncompromising of the 'G's historic moments of rivalry, triumph, loss, despair, joyful achievement, sensation, hard-won victory were expressions of a society peaceful and unified enough to build, expand, value, patronise and stage spectacles at a stadium like the MCG.

The ecumenical ceremony had 'an atmosphere as good as a Grand Final' in the opinion of the more heathen of his congregation. It was 'immensely moving', 'exciting', 'memorable', 'uplifting', said others. As emotional as a final quarter of tough footy and a win after the siren on the 'G'. When the ecumenical siren sounded, lifting through the stands and across the ground, not with the familiar adrenaline-stirring blare but in the form of a resounding amen, the pope left, in a limo this time and not the Popemobile, because he was going back to the presbytery at St Pat's where he would spend the night.

The amiable and now-blessed crowd trickled away across the oval and out to the park and the trains and trams as fans from no matter what holy and ecumenical ceremony at the 'G' have been doing for more than a century.

In spending the night at St Pat's, Pope John Paul ensured that he would visit all three of Melbourne's cathedrals, because earlier that same evening, before arriving at the MCG, he had made a historic appearance at St Paul's . . .

'If the Pope's infallible,' says a bloke in the crush of people waiting outside St Paul's, 'how come he wouldn't know that it'll be too crowded for anyone to get in to see him?'

'Infallible doesn't mean that,' says a young woman bobbing a mass of blonde curls as she turns towards him. 'It doesn't mean you predict things, tell the future or something.'

'What does it mean, then?' says the bloke, whose belligerent manner and tendency to fall sideways unless leaning on the crowd suggest that he's come straight across Swanston Street from Young & Jackson's.

'It means he doesn't tell lies,' says another voice. The curly-headed blonde turns away with a sigh of exasperation and someone nearby says, 'Jesus Christ!'

'No,' comes a prim voice of uncertain gender, 'he's not and he doesn't claim to be.'

The members of the 'Neo-Catechumenical Community' stand grim-faced under their large, gnomic banner. Slightly revivalist hymns drift out from somewhere near or just inside the cathedral entrance, making heavy weather of it against St Paul's thirteen bells, three years short of their 100th birthday and still in fine voice. PRINCE OF DARKNESS proclaims another banner. UNITY THAT IS FALSEHOOD IS TREASON NOT STRENGTH.

'Pope's a fuckin' eyetie. Don' want any more fuckin' eyeties round here,' says another expat from Young & Jackson's, picking unerringly on the one non-Italian pontiff since 1552. He is unfazed by his error, which a few brave souls point out, but it doesn't matter because the police seem to be more interested in his inaccuracy than anyone else, and they take him off for a philosophical discussion.

Most of the thousands waiting, however, are respectful, curious, even excited. There are cheers and clapping when the pope arrives and is welcomed into the cathedral by the Anglican archbishop of Melbourne, Dr David Penman. It is only the third time in 400 years that a pope has been inside an Anglican cathedral.

A few minutes later, the dramatically white-clad figure of Herb Elliott emerges from the doors, flaming torch held high. He sets off up Flinders Street towards the 'G' with two young kids flanking him. Soon the pope reappears. History has run its course, and the famously divided denominations have had their amazing moment of temporary but resounding reconciliation. Elliott by this time is nearing the 'G'. The pope must follow.

The pope's roll-up of around 100 000 people was impressive, but it was not by any means the biggest attendance, even for a non-sporting event. There have been a few of these, and the religious ones figure prominently on the list. The third-biggest crowd in the history of the MCG, for example, was the finale of the 40th Eucharistic Congress in February 1973, which attracted 120 000 presumably devout communicants. The Opening Ceremony of the 1956 Olympic Games drew the 23rd-biggest crowd of 107 700, the Closing Ceremony came in 29th with 104 700 and concerts by Paul McCartney, Madonna, the Rolling Stones, the Three Tenors and Elton John, while well attended, did not disturb the top 50. But number one, with the biggest turnout ever in the history of the 'G', was the Billy Graham Crusade on 15 March 1959.

Like many another 'star' commanding a huge audience at the 'G', William Franklin (Billy) Graham was at the height of his powers and popularity when he gazed around that stadium that he had scarcely even heard about until it was booked for his Melbourne appearance.

Ordained a minister of the Southern Baptist Church in the United States in 1940 at the age of twenty-two, Billy Graham rose from obscurity as a small-town, small-church evangelist to become the world leader of Christian fundamentalism. A natural orator, he impressed and communicated profoundly with large groups of people by virtue of his sincerity and the sense he conveyed that his own energy in the cause of Christ, which seemed boundless, could be duplicated in those who chose to follow his teachings. At the end of the Second World War he became the charismatic figure in the 'Youth for Christ' movement in America, Canada and Western Europe.

His tour of Australia in 1959, however, is generally reckoned to be one of the most successful, astonishing and intriguing of all his evangelical campaigns. In America when he began his career, Graham had offered some hope and solace at a time of crisis in Europe followed by the American entry into the war after the Japanese attack on Pearl Harbor. He continued to appeal powerfully to people engulfed by post-war bleakness and loss; this was particularly the case with his rallies in Britain. In general, however, these explanations do not apply to 1959 Australian society. What seemed to operate more powerfully in this country was the combination of revivalist, evangelical promise, held out to a population in which traditional, denominational religion was beginning what would be an irresistible decline, and Graham's meeting Australians' increasing, insatiable desire for things American.

The MCG took its place in this phenomenon as naturally as it had become the site for so many other moments of sporting, social and cultural history, and with hundreds of thousands of chanting acolytes out in front of him, Billy Graham entered the pantheon of MCG record-breakers.

Although the attendance that day is officially recorded as 130 000 – in any case the biggest crowd for any event ever at the 'G' –

the then secretary of the MCC, former Test bowler and captain Ian Johnson, announced the number as 143 750, 'the largest attendance on any cricket ground in any part of the world'. People packed on to the arena and 4000 had to be content to listen to the evangelist over loud-speakers outside the ground. The gravity and importance of the occasion can be measured by the fact that women were allowed into the Members' Stand – a rare occurrence, which could only be explained by the close connection of these proceedings with a power higher than the MCC. The best attendance at any of Billy Graham's previous meetings had been 120 000 for his Greater London crusade, so this MCG gathering massively rewrote his own record books.

At the end of the meeting he said, 'I feel very humble. I feel I am just a spectator. I didn't do it. It was the Lord's doing and I am only His messenger.'

As this was Dr Graham's first visit to the 'G' and as he could not possibly have had time to immerse himself in its culture, his comments were remarkable for their conformity to an end-of-hard-fought-contest formula familiar to all MCG initiates: 'It was a great team effort and not only a win for us. Footy/cricket/God was the winner here today/tonight/this arvo . . .'

Four thousand one hundred and seven people made decisions during the meeting but as these decisions were 'for God' there was no attempt to compare the number statistically with the decision rate of the MCC and its committees during the previous decade.

God had come to the MCG.

THERE IS AN air of urgency now subverting Wills's panache and theatricality as if he senses that he has gone far, far beyond that fatal day in May 1880 when he joined the realms of these ghosts of events and people he now conjures. And so here is Don Bradman presenting the inaugural Frank Worrell Trophy to Richie Benaud after that sensational series against the West Indies, which included the tied Test and a second-day crowd at the 'G' of 90 800 for the Fifth Test.

And up goes the Western Stand – later to be known as the Ponsford – in 1967 and here, as Wills points yet again to teams running on to the oval, is the first Sunday football match on the 'G' between Richmond and the doomed Fitzroy watched by, among many others, the Queen, the Duke of Edinburgh, the Prince of Wales and Princess Anne – but as a result, no doubt, of some massive oversight, no one has organised a children's display.

And now Wills rushes us to September – the year is 1970 – when the MCG fills with the record Grand Final crowd of 121 696 and what many regard as the greatest Grand Final ever is fought out between

Carlton and Collingwood. Legend has it that, with Carlton 44 points down at half-time and looking beaten, Barassi asked if anyone had 'any ideas'. Legendarily, his own and only suggestion was to 'handball' – at every opportunity. Carlton were still 15 points adrift at three-quarter time, but Collingwood's McKenna, who had kicked five goals in the first half, and Des Tuddenham, who had led the Magpies' surges into their forward line, were both injured after a collision. With 44 hand-balls in the second half of the game, Carlton hit the front in time-on and Jesaulenko – who had taken one of the greatest marks of all time in the second quarter to give the Blues a sniff of inspiration – sealed the game at the death.

Rain curtains across Wills's MCG, and it is 1971; a year otherwise anonymous marches into cricket history because of the weather . . .

HAD HANRAHAN BEEN around as the rain began to fall early in the New Year of 1971, he would have been tuning up his famous lament.

– down came the rain
And all the afternoon
On iron roof and window pane
It drummed a homely tune.

And through the night it pattered still,
And lightsome, gladsome elves
On dripping spout and window sill
Kept talking to themselves.

It pelted, pelted all day long,
A-singing at its work,
Till every heart took up the song
Way out to Back-o'-Bourke.

And every creek a banker ran,

And dams filled overtop;

'We'll all be rooned,' said Hanrahan,

'If this rain doesn't stop.'

Possibly the news of Melbourne's weather didn't get as far as
Back-o'-Bourke in the first days of January 1971, and perhaps the
downpour that engulfed the city and its nearby stadium and hinterland
of suburbs was not as solid as the one that so exercised Hanrahan. Still,
it was the kind of drenching that would have had Noah nodding with
gloomy and resigned recognition and reaching for his adze and mallet.
When the sun at last glimmered through a sky scudding with rainy
remnants on Tuesday 5 January, not a ball had been bowled in the
Third Ashes Test at the MCG.

To rescue something from the sodden wreckage of the Third
Test, both teams agreed to play a forty-overs-a-side match, weather and
pitch permitting, on the Tuesday.

The weather permitted – it was warm and cloudy. The pitch permitted: it was judged to be 'good'. And so the first one-day, 'knockout'
match (as the Melbourne *Herald* called it) took place on the MCG
which, yet again, revealed its uncanny knack of rubbing shoulders with
history. The 45 006 people who paid an MCC budget-rescuing $33 984
to see this game would no doubt have scoffed at any suggestion that
they were, along with the players in the middle, midwives to a cricket
revolution that day. Although some onlookers perhaps had a glimmer of
an idea, and these included writer Steven Carroll's mates who, as
described in his marvellous piece in the *Age* on 25 January, called 'The
Don and the Day It All Began', saw the possibilities of the one-day
game and proposed them to Bradman, despite being hampered by the
ingestion of vast amounts of alcohol.

So many of the characteristics of one-day cricket with which we are now so familiar, and some which we may be tiring of after massive exposure over the past twenty years, were on show in that first hastily organised game. The big hitting, as demonstrated by Stacky, Ian Chappell and Doug Walters. The importance of precision fielding – as when Ian Chappell's brilliant return ran out D'Oliveira by inches. The different selection criteria – as when the Australian selectors surprised people by dropping star spinner Johnny Gleeson in favour of Ashley Mallett (although this could have been a ploy to prevent the English batsmen from seeing too much of Gleeson early in the series).

The dramatic way some players (and some surprise selections) can turn a one-day game – as when Mallett had the plum wickets of Fletcher, Hampshire and Edrich, finishing with 3/34 off eight overs. And so on.

It is all so familiar now, when the one-day game has long since gone beyond the swinging-from-the-arse stage to become a carefully calculated assault on time, overs and the nerved-up capacities of fieldsmen under great pressure. It can be intolerably suspenseful, almost at times unwatchable, it is so tense, yet overall it is also now predictable and alarmingly forgettable. And, in gradually identifying and attracting a different audience from the core of Test-match watchers, the one-day internationals have become the haunt of the larrikin – a much less endearing version of the species than used to inhabit the old Bay 13 – and the Mexican Wave which, as the long days and the long season wear on, evolves from ebullience through tiresome repetition to, often, violent assault by various chucked objects and liquids.

. . . England made 190 in just under their forty eight-ball overs on that famous occasion, having been put in by Australian captain Bill Lawry, with a great innings of 82 from Edrich and promising aggressive starts by Fletcher, D'Oliveira and Hampshire. But the loss of 7/46 in an hour unravelled a potentially substantial score. Ian Chappell (60) and Doug Walters (41) in particular saw Australia home – 5/191 in 34.6 overs.

As is usually the case in the early, raw stages of any significant process, before experience, accrued expertise, fine-tuning of rules and honing of strategies have taken place, that first one-day international had its crudities in comparison with the slick version that has lasted into the twenty-first century.

When fearsome and highly accomplished English fast bowler John Snow sent down the first ball of the Australian innings to Lawry, it ballooned uncontrollably down the off side. Snow turned to umpire Brooks and ruefully conceded the wide by actually signalling it. When Brooks didn't react, Lawry too signalled wide. After another perceptible lull, Brooks appeared to be impressed by the weight of evidence and also signalled wide!

It was a far cry from the hair-trigger sensitivity of the 'wide' rule in the contemporary one-day game. Again, when Stackpole, who opened with Lawry and was batting with characteristic aggression despite an injured leg, on-drove Snow, Lawry bolted down the wicket for a quick single. Stackpole, perhaps hampered by consciousness of his injury, sent him back. Stranded three-quarters of the way down the pitch, Lawry turned to watch Underwood run in and underarm the ball at the bowler's-end stumps from a few feet away – and miss. Shades of the stumps-crunching, flat fast throws from all parts of the field that are such a customary but always dramatic part of the modern one-day game.

It was all great fun, a fine recompense for crowds who had watched nothing but rain for three days, and it was a tight, satisfying encounter. Not many realised what a huge boulder had been thrown into the placid pool of international cricket and how far-reaching and how potent would be the ripples.

BUT NOW WILLS is hurrying. It may be that there is the barest pale hint of watery light etching a fog-softened outline here and there. Perhaps dawn, the bane of phantoms, is near. Can it be that there is a family in Jolimont that keeps chooks? Was that a rooster that crowed backyards distant – the angry-eyed, preposterous chaunticleer who drove off even the armoured and monumental ghost of Hamlet's father? Whose mad, hopeful first-light shout frightens even vampires with its promise of day returning? Wills, anyway, is hurrying.

He batons into existence a rush of concerts – David Bowie, Linda Ronstadt, the Melbourne Military Tattoo (another first). And soccer matches – Manchester United, Glasgow Rangers, Nottingham Forest, Juventus and Iraklis retrace in phantom form their World Series Soccer encounters of 1984 on the 'G'.

And then there is light everywhere. Wills's slight figure casts a six-pointed shadow as he recalls on to the ground the Australian and English limited-overs teams for the first sporting event of any kind to be played under lights at the MCG since that famous evening in 1879 when the Collingwood Rifles football team played the East Melbourne Artillery. And there is a positive splurge of night sports as the new light towers take the MCG into unfamiliar territory – which it negotiates with its customary ease. Even Wills looks startled as the black night sky seems held just above the roofs of the stands by a dome of brightness.

The 'G' becomes North Melbourne's home ground in 1985, and they play Collingwood under lights in Round 1. The Woods spoil the party, however, with a winning seven-goal last quarter. More light shows as international soccer teams Vasco da Gama (Brazil), Udinese (Italy), Tottenham Hotspur and Australia turn on a glittering double-header in May.

Wills's glinting baton, however, is drawing the years down like bolts of lightning: 1989 strikes with a shower of sparks, and here are 91 960 people to watch a coruscating State of Origin match between Victoria and South Australia. Another jagged spear of light strikes the old Southern Stand, which is roofless for Collingwood's first Grand Final win in thirty-two years and then, almost as soon as the last fan has left the ground, down it comes to make way for what will be the Great Southern Stand.

It is 25 March 1992 and Wills is bringing to life the opening of that stand by Dr Don Cordner, president of the MCC, former champion Melbourne footballer and still the only one to win a Brownlow Medal as an amateur (1946). The stand is ready for the World Cup cricket final between Pakistan and England. Eighty-seven thousand one hundred and eighty-two people see Pakistan win and then it is the footy season and the Great Southern Stand faces up to bigger tests, week after week . . .

IT IS MIDDAY of the Queen's Birthday Monday in 1992, and there are about 3000 people waiting around the bottom of the old footbridge on the MCG side, all stamping in the cold, damp air, and craning and peering, and glancing at wristwatches in the ever-intensifying expectation of the other three or four thousand who have arranged to meet them there.

Behind us (for I am one of this throng) rise the curves and glass and postmodern flying buttresses of the new Great Southern Stand, at the bottom of which there are already long, curling queues.

'Plugger's playing,' says a man near me to a woman who might be his wife.

'No,' she says, 'only if he passes a fitness test.'

Sadly, I could tell them that the big man, St Kilda's champion full-forward Tony 'Plugger' Lockett, has failed the test and is out, but the two of them move quickly on.

'Bloody State of Origin,' says someone else, steaming past. Any listener knows what he means without interpretation: Tony Lockett was injured playing for Victoria midweek. That's why he can't line up today. Bloody State of Origin indeed. The clock ticks on.

Theoretically there's plenty of time, yet there's a crackle in the air, a sort of light-hearted, tightening anxiety, flickering through the crushes of people like an invisible St Elmo's fire; and all those who've arranged to meet at the footbridge become grumpy with latecomers who are scarcely late at all. As battalions of troops wearing the field uniforms of Collingwood black and white or St Kilda red, white and black march endlessly over the bridge, ragged platoons of supporters, meeting up at last with their allies, detach themselves from the mob and storm the gates.

The footbridge is part of the MCG's mystique. Although a new, swooping and elegant footbridge now connects the 'G' with the Rod Laver Arena, the 'old' footbridge is the true pedestrian landmark. It is one of the important sites from which your journey to the 'G' might begin. It leaps the railway and Brunton Avenue, allowing the hurrying spectator to drop down into the park under the plane trees with great expedition and reasonable comfort – although these days it can become packed and slow-moving.

When you're on the footbridge heading for the 'G', you're in a crowd that buzzes and hums. People shuffle but would run if they could, and they spill out gratefully at the other end, collecting friends and raising heads towards the turnstiles like dogs sniffing distant game. On the way back, the crowd is as tight but the mood divided. Some sing and would dance if they could; others plod, the funereal pace suited to the taste of defeat souring their mouths and banishing their smiles.

Arriving at the ground is always exciting. When you have run the gauntlet of turnstiles and grey concrete concourses and the impossibly green, white-painted field of play appears, against all the odds, you enter for a while another world. As I did a decade ago to watch Chelsea play Middlesbrough on a freezing April day at Stamford Bridge.

. . . The teams walk sedately on to the pitch (as the Poms call their footy grounds), and I helpfully point out that Chelsea are wearing 'the blue strip'. My two companions to whom I have revealed this useful hint are immediately scathing about what they regard as my hollow show of expertise, pointing out that our *Official Matchday Magazine* is headed CHELSEA and is two shades of deep blue. Not to mention that the grandstands, fences and most other immovables surrounding us are also blue. This sort of thing is wounding, of course, but you don't usually have to wait long for sports tyros to expose the depths of ignorance from which their disdain invariably emanates. It is only a matter of minutes before a small voice on my right enquires tentatively, 'How many are there in a team?' while from my left comes the crucial observation, 'God, their shorts are baggy!'

We are in the front (and most exposed) row of the West Stand at Stamford Bridge for Chelsea's home clash with Middlesbrough. Not a flash fixture: Chelsea are sitting fourteenth on the Premier League Table and Middlesbrough, absolutely last after having won two of their previous seventeen games, are hoping to pull 'the coal from the relegation fire' as the *Matchday Mag* unbeatably puts it. We were originally bound for Wembley and the Sheffield derby, but our network of ludicrously confident amateur string-pullers and inexpert lobbyists had failed to come up with a ticket for the FA Cup Semi at Wembley. So, here we are at Stamford Bridge, with what feels like bits of the North Sea blowing straight down the ground — a dead-set five-goal breeze (if it wasn't for the offside rule) or I never turned my collar up against one.

Modestly famous for my misestimates of crowd numbers, I guess we're sharing the spectacle with maybe 3000 other refrigerated, sleet-spattered aficionados, but one of my companions insists it is six, and the other loyally agrees with her. Even at the inflated figure, the ratio of cops to fans remains high.

They're everywhere, distributed along the back of the stands in pairs, thick round the fence and among the crowd on both terraces. Most off-putting of all, they're ranged out the front of the ground when we arrive, mounted on quadrupeds of such massive and fiery aspect that only a very good memory and a determination not to panic could connect them to what is commonly known as the 'horse'.

As we thread our way through this stamping, snuffling barricade of broncos, I remember that I had meant to have a punt on the Grand National due to start around kick-off time, but my enthusiasm for horses is waning by the minute. Down there among that forest of equine legs restlessly shifting and bracing, it's like being a pedestrian in a joust.

When we finally win through to the West Stand entrance, more cops! This time, it's a body-search. Well versed in queuing, I absent-mindedly fall into line behind my female accomplices only to elicit a glare from the policewoman who construes my thoughtless manoeuvre as a desire to have her run her judicial digits over me. I cross queues and get done by a bloke and, at last, circling through the turnstiles, we top a small concrete rise and there it is: THE PITCH.

The first glimpse is rather exciting, like the first sight of any footy field, straight and circling white lines printed on the rich green, the white posts at either end. And then the red and white of the Middlesbrough lads and Chelsea in their regal blue, which prompts me to explain helpfully to my companions that Chelsea are the ones in the . . .

As for the game. Well, Chelsea start as if they've all got hang-overs, and 'Brough, with the wind, do everything but score, then Chelsea pick up the pace and play the best football of the day for the last twenty minutes of the first half, thwarted only by some sensational saves and, when the ref blows the half-time whistle, it's . . . nil-all! You have to wonder about the timekeeping incidentally. It seems very casual, this business of the referee snatching endless glances at his watch, calculating injury time, and all the while trying to watch the play. The sort of thing the English justify by calling it 'very English' – like the way they start the Grand National.

'What won the National?' shouts one of the yobbos near us to a mate up the back.

'Void,' says his mate, waving his arms in the traditional gestures of defeat and mystification at the perfidy of fate.

I had studied the field and couldn't remember a horse called Void, so I was pleased I had failed to get on.

That sad saga of how the 1993 Grand National didn't ever start – the horses brushed aside the piece of string used as a starting gate (how very English) and bolted causing the race to be declared 'Void' – ran through the marvelling crowd as Chelsea slammed on four goals in an un-soccerlike spree that delighted those of us who, brought up on one of the only two football codes without an offside rule, are used to seeing lots of scoring and electrifying dashes into an open goal.

My assessment of the five-goal breeze was close enough. Chelsea kicked four. They were against the wind, unfortunately, but you can't get it right all the time.

That was in another, colder hemisphere and, besides, the Stamford Bridge pitch, beautiful though it was on first sight, was not the nave of the 'G'.

But back to the Queen's Birthday, 1992. In the very shadow of the Great Southern Stand, a disembodied voice delivered instructions over the sound system. If you are a Collingwood member or a concessional Collingwood member, you go to the left of Gate 7 as you face the ground, unless you're an AFL member, in which case you go to

Gate 8, except if your AFL membership card is blue or if you're under 5 foot 6 tall and you're convinced Plugger is playing, in which case you try Gate 7, or preferably give up and go round to the Ponsford Stand which you can't get into from inside the Southern Stand and anyway the Southern Stand is nearly full so you might as well go around now unless your St Kilda membership ticket is numbered between 4138 and 7035, in which case try the small gateway to the right of Gate 7 as you face the ground . . . Well, that's how it sounded to people desperately trying to work out which enormous queue not to waste their time in; that's what it might as well have said, for all the good it was.

That was how it was that Queen's Birthday as we tried to get into the Great Southern Stand to see Collingwood play St Kilda.

My three sons and I, and a few friends, had arranged to meet at 12.00; we actually met at 12.05 (some people are just incapable of being on time) and, having tackled with only moderate success the intellectual challenge of how and where to actually get into the ground, we were inside and ensconced in standing room at Section M13–14 by 12.45. For those who still like to watch footy (and cricket, for that matter) standing and with room to move around a little, these covert niches on the ground level of the Great Southern Stand are a godsend. Some of them, including M13–14, are also very handy to a bar.

By and large, standing at the footy is now a thing of the past. But it was not necessarily a decision taken by the supporters. Thousands and thousands of fans – and not only the blokes – prefer to stand. Standing at a footy match means moving around a bit, shrugging the tackles, getting on tiptoe for the high marks, tensing for the shirtfront, hugging anyone handy when the siren seals the one-point win, having room to signal 'BALL' when the opposition is so clearly caught and to wave derision when the same decision goes against you. Few if any of these manoeuvres can be satisfactorily managed while sitting. It might reasonably be argued that it is unnatural to sit at a footy match unless advanced age or declining health dictate the sedentary option. (As my old man said to me many years ago when, as a smallish boy, I complained I couldn't see, 'Don't worry, mate. Everyone moves miles at a footy match.' He was right. Test it out if it's still possible to stand at your favourite ground. Line yourself up on two or three reference points next time you lob in your preferred spot and see where you've moved to by the time the final siren puts you out of your agony of suspense and disputation. Don't bother if you're in a seat, of course. The odds are you'll have gone nowhere.)

But you probably won't be able to test it out, because standers are a dying race at all the significant grounds. When the notorious VFL Park was still being seen as eventual competitor for, and conqueror of, the MCG, special structures designed to cut off the view were put in place to prevent diehard standers from lining the walkway immediately behind the seats, a position in which they were impeding no one – a marvellous example of the AFL sniffing the wind and getting exactly the wrong scent. Could it be that some people actually want to stand?

I saw every Grand Final from 1954 to 1966, all of them except for 1965 as a standing punter, and there were thousands like me.

When Young & Jackson's, one of Melbourne's most famous pubs, was renovated in 2000–01 and reopened with flash, timbered bars, pop music and seemingly every kind of beer in the known fermented world on tap under ritzy, phallic handles, a demographic event occurred of some interest, although it was entirely neglected by other than rank-amateur observers like me and those with whom I was accustomed to raise a glass. Where had Young & Jackson's original clientele gone? Entry to the old bar on the corner of Flinders and Swanston streets used to be either by tattoo or production of a derro card. So if they'd stayed on and frequented the new bars after the renovation, for example, their presence would have been noted, at least for as long as they lasted before being asked to leave.

For the second half of the twentieth century, Young & Jackson's was one of the meeting points – one of the less salubrious, admittedly – for pilgrims heading to the temple down the road. The more feral of supporters from Richmond, Collingwood and Fitzroy found it one of several useful prematch havens. The question is, where have all those original patrons, who gave Young & Jackson's its particular, well, not charm but atmosphere in every sense of the word – where have they gone? To other, less upmarket pubs, I suppose, which would also be less central. They have been driven closer to the margins.

And where have all those people gone who used to love to stand at the footy? To the corporate boxes? Very unlikely. To the reserved seats? Some of them, certainly. To any part of the ground where you can still stand without being chivvied and abused by Security? Quite a few. To their own lounge room to watch it on TV?

Who knows how many, but it's becoming a statistic of greater interest as Aussie Rules begins to follow the examples of rugby league and, in America, gridiron and baseball, to become a television game.

Those of us determined to keep watching the game at the grounds shuffled into seats inexorably as the years wore on because there was nowhere left to stand – except, as I say, for these magic little corners of the Great Southern.

Being early on this Queen's Birthday of which I speak, we command the whole of the fence separating us from a block of Collingwood reserved seats, and we can look straight out to the ground. Because of the low overhang of the Great Southern's first tier, the sight we get is a long green slash from goal to goal – a bit like the narrow image band that cinemascope films turn into on telly. Very high kicks disappear from sight for an instant, but it's still a class spot to be in. Of course, prematch entertainment can be somewhat obscured too, especially if, as was the case on this Queen's Birthday, the entertainment happens to be parachutists.

But, no worries. As we all stand around listening to the hysterical description over the public address system of the jumpers plummeting from their aircraft, one of the yobbos nearby stares up intently at the grey concrete ceiling a mere metre or two above our heads, and, like McMurphy calling the baseball game from a blank TV screen in *One Flew Over the Cuckoo's Nest*, he says, 'Yes, here they come. Jesus, look how high they are. And there's a red parachute opening now . . . '

He points excitedly at the stolid grey overhang. 'Smoke! Look, they've got fuckin' smoke bombs or somethin' attached to their feet.'

Everyone is staring up at a thousand tonnes of impenetrable roof.

'Yair,' says someone, and 'Here comes another one – a green 'chute,' says someone else. So that element of the congregation stuck behind pillars or grotted away in angular chapels out of sight of choir and altar amuse themselves as they wait their hour at the people's ground.

Meanwhile, the loudspeaker bloke was telling everyone urgently that the Southern Stand was now full and people must go to the Ponsford Stand (which you couldn't do from inside the ground) while, outside, unbeknown to us at the time, thousands of people were being locked out.

At about 1.15 a stocky young man standing nearby confides miserably to us that he'd persuaded his mates to drive down from Deniliquin to see the Magpies. They did; they've arrived – and they're locked out. In Deniliquin they might at least have seen the game on the box.

From our vantage point, we have a broad, clear view of the ground surface, on which grassy bits glowing green under the grey, threatening overcast are intersected by long sandy strips that look like they've been trucked in from a local nursery and spread by the part-time bloke who comes in on Saturday mornings. The centre square is a mat of black hair gel, and at various spots around the boundary the surface lifts and clings lovingly to a running boot like mozzarella cheese stringing off a sloppy pizza.

In short, the MCG, about to be played on for the fourth successive day of a rainy long weekend, is just a bit uncharacteristically tatty at the edges. It has been well and truly 'rationalised'. This was the policy whereby games were to be concentrated at a few main venues – the MCG, Princes Park (now Optus Oval), the ill-fated VFL Park at Waverley – in order to phase out the old suburban grounds at Windy Hill, Arden Street, Moorabbin, Victoria Park.

The condition of the playing surface precludes a curtain-raiser, so there's not a lot to do in the hour and a quarter's wait that our fortunate zeal has lumbered us with. We drink a bit, carting the MCG's plastic cups back and forth, but not as much as the young bloke next to me who is sucking on a straw protruding from a black-and-white-striped, thermoslike container.

'That's a cunning way of handling these bloody plastic cups,' I tell him amiably.

He looks stunned. 'S'pose y'right,' he says after reflecting a bit, 'but ackshully, this bastard's full of Scotch.' And it's only one o'clock!

Confusion multiplies around us. A stout, middle-aged man in a grey dustcoat is stationed at the entrance to the seating area reserved for Collingwood members. Over and over he tells wandering, bemused fans why they either can or cannot enter this area.

Two o'clock approaches and news of the lockout has spread through the crowd: everywhere there is a hum of tension like the thrumming of a tightening wire; the banners are unfolded as cold gusts of sleet roll across the ground. Things are getting tough for the man in grey: more and more people are disinclined to take any notice of his patient litany. Although, as always with Australian footy crowds, the mood is amiable and ironic.

As the teams burst through the ballooning banners, 'Plugger's not there,' cries the agonised voice of someone who has apparently only just that instant emerged from a week in a soundproof, windowless room. 'Bewdy,' says a voice from the Collingwood camp in front of us. And then – all disputation is forgotten, nomadic wanderings cease, the bars empty, the causeways clear as the central umpire, pausing perceptibly to allow Channel 7 to rip in five or six ads, advances into the black glue and throws up the ball.

It's on. Collingwood versus St Kilda at the MCG on the Queen's Birthday Monday, 1992, in front of 80 000 people and in the hearing of about 10 000 others milling angrily outside the closed gates.

The game is a blinder. After the first quarter, in which St Kilda have thrashed the Woods but kicked 2.9 from twelve shots, the burly phantom of Plugger strides across the mind's eye. If only he were there, moan the Saints supporters, as another shot is sprayed across the goal front. We can practically see him – fending off two opponents and marking one-handed; putting the ball down deliberately to pull up his socks; looking up at the goals; looking down at the ball; crouching low before starting his run in; banging it through. YES! roars the crowd YES! as the goal umpy YES! doesn't move an inch. And YES! it's all so familiar. But Plugger's not there. Still, the idea of him, the dream of him dominates: 'Thank Christ he's out,' says a Collingwood fan fervently, wincing at the first-quarter blitz. If only he were there, moan the Saints.

Not that the commentators all necessarily agree. When Lockett kicked 15 against the Swans, one expert complained that he didn't handball enough! The same pundit explained that he didn't give Lockett a single vote when he'd kicked 12 because the passes to him were all on the chest and too easy. (Quite right too. As we know, any full-forward will kick 12 or 15 if he gets enough chest marks; it's happening in game after game.) And every year, the instant Lockett faltered, the chorus of 'too fat, too slow and too heavy' would rise enthusiastically from what are often referred to as 'sections of the media'. During one of these tirades, Lockett was second on the goal-kicking list, was averaging five or so a game and got 10 the following week. If only he was playing well.

So he's not there and yet he's present, the big fella, as one of the games of the year unfolds. Tony Shaw and Stewart Loewe have a serious exchange of basic philosophies as the quarter-time siren sounds and, in true Socratic spirit, the other thirty-four players join in.

Gavin Brown dismembers St Kilda during the third quarter and the Saints fight back in the last. With minutes left Devonport, who has already been dragged once and given a blazing talking-to by coach Ken Sheldon, who was pop-eyed with rage, runs around the flank, ignores Craven on his own in the goal square, and threads through a brilliant goal.

The Saints are one point in front, and we are dying a thousand deaths when a bloke appears from behind a nearby column and says, 'You've won it.' We are about to chastise him for overconfidence and putting the mozz on, and so on, when he points out to us that there's a TV set mounted on the other side of the column and it's showing thirty-five seconds left with the ball deep in the St Kilda forward line. So the Saints get in by a point. Without Lockett – as the pundits immediately note.

All that was a decade ago. The MCG, with its formidable Southern Stand, its penumbra of bright light after dark, its leafy bracelet of parks and the surrounding orchestration of traffic and trains stands as solid as ever. Much has changed and yet has not changed. Back then, the VFL/AFL, after years of intensifying qualms about the future and adequacy of its Waverley ground, was beginning a long process of consultation and evaluation that would see Waverley abandoned and sold. But the MCG, the home of footy, the home of cricket, repository of sporting history and legends, the site of Melbourne's only and memorable Olympic Games, could not be nailed down. A decade on from that Queen's Birthday, the AFL had already built its own stadium and was grappling with lockouts, confusion and customer resistance on a scale and of a durability never encountered at the MCG, even during those first faltering days of the Great Southern Stand.

The Docklands stadium, slick, roofed, state-of-the-art although much of it is, will never displace the 'G' in the imagination of Melbourne. You can start life as a parish church and evolve into a cathedral – by and large, the story of St Pat's, St Paul's and the 'G'. But Docklands started as a soccer stadium, didn't make it in time for Olympic Soccer in 2000, became a bit of a joke and, throwing off that stigma, evolved as an ever more amiably regarded oddity, even in certain ways a wonder, but always eminently dismissible. Just as, on that Queen's Birthday, the haunting, imagined vision of Tony Lockett belied his physical absence, so the MCG remains a potent *presence* in the Melbourne psyche in a way that only places of mystique, ceremonial and awe can be.

WILLS TURNS TO LOOK down the ground and the Great Southern Stand seems to fill again to capacity as a crowd of 83 262 comes to watch Collingwood, in their centenary year, play Carlton. But, as one journalist put it, despite the brilliance of Kernahan and Silvagni for Carlton and Daicos for Collingwood, three votes went to the Great Southern Stand. Just as the MCG, with its history, atmosphere and sheer class, is an event in itself, so the Great Southern Stand is an event within an event.

And now there are more concerts. The ghostly Wills summons images of Paul McCartney, U2, Madonna, Michael Jackson, the Three Tenors, Elton John, Billy Joel . . . These phantasms of the living tunefully join his evanescent throng, among whom now, however, there are mutterings and movements. Have they too heard a rooster crow? The fog and dark lighten into a glowing grey. Dawn is near. The music of the singers rises around Wills by some magical process . . .

THE PAUL MCCARTNEY CONCERT came as something of a surprise to the Trustees of the MCG. Early in 1992, concert promoter and entrepreneur Paul Dainty had raised with the MCC the general proposition of using the 'G' for a 'big' concert by an internationally famous pop star. The preferred time would be in the summer of 1993.

When the 1992–93 cricket fixtures for the MCG had been finalised, the MCC approached Dainty again to suggest that there would be a good opportunity to put on a concert in early March, subject to further discussions on financial details, logistical considerations, and so on, before the venture could be approved.

Dainty, however, construed this conditional reopening of discussions as constituting the go-ahead. So, he went ahead, arranging the entire Australian tour of Paul McCartney with a two-night MCG concert as its centrepiece. At the same time, he engaged BASS to begin ticket sales in mid-December and set ticket prices.

Early in December, to its great surprise and then consternation, the MCC received a request from BASS for a box plan for the 'concert at the MCG on 9 March'. This was the first the club had heard of the plan since what it regarded as tentative early feelers earlier in 1992. Dainty had to be told that the concert was not to go on because it had not been approved by the Trustees. But when Paul Dainty heard of this decision, he rushed to the MCG to consult Dr John Lill, the MCC secretary. It became clear that cancellation would look very bad for the MCC and that, in any case, such a concert would be a great event for the ground and for Melbourne.

Instead of pulling out, the MCC talked some turkey with Dainty, and the concerts were arranged. In an explanatory memorandum to the Trustees, the secretary of the Melbourne Cricket Ground Trust, Bryce Thomas, regretted 'that circumstances prevented a normal application to the Trust for approval of the staging of the concert on two nights, 9th and 10th March, and for approval of the uniform seat price of $53 before the concert became public'.

Trustees inclined to be irascible about this breach of due process could take comfort in the deal that would bring a 'net return to the Trust from two concerts . . . in the order of $300 000 whilst satisfactory booking arrangements were negotiated for corporate lessees and MCC members'. A further disincentive for Trustees to become needlessly picky about the manner of the deal was that '. . . two complimentary reserved seats are available for each trustee, and if additional reserved seat tickets are required by trustees, they may be purchased from the Trust secretary at $53 each.'

In this way, Paul McCartney joined that vast and heterogeneous throng who, by virtue of whatever amazing talents and unparalleled achievements in any one of hundreds of endeavours, contests and entertainments, strode the turf of the mighty 'G' and did their stuff.

He was a knockout.

AS THEY CAME, so now do Wills's phantom players troop from the arena and fade through the turnstiles into Yarra Park where trees pour with foggy moisture and outlines are slowly emerging. Soon, only Wills is left, standing in the centre of the ground. He raises his baton into the vestigial light seeping through the stadium as if about to command some new wonders from the arena on which he was himself such an extraordinary performer. But what we have thought all along to be a baton is now, we see, glinting in his hand, not a baton but a pair of slender-bladed scissors. He raises them above his head, blades pointing down, as a sickly daylight fingers the tops of the light towers and slides slowly along the ridges of the stands . . .

TOM WILLS PLAYED his last game of cricket in February 1876 against New South Wales and in the same year he played his last game of football – aged forty-one. In the next four years the alcoholism that had already affected his life and sporting prowess intensified. Who knows what demons plagued him in the dark nights? His miraculous escape from the massacre all those years ago may have left him with a guilt that festered rather than waned, that returned in graphic reruns of those events once his crowded, often spectacular life was settling into mundanity.

'. . . Some of the blacks – the younger men and boys – were against the murder, but the elder men threatened to kill them if they divulged their plans . . . The boy . . . showed my brother, Horace, and me where the young blacks had spent the night previous to the murder. I asked this boy whether, if my father and the bullock driver had got together and shot one or two blacks, the others would have bolted. He replied, "Carra." (No) The blacks were in their hundreds . . . It makes my blood boil when I start on this subject . . .'

Perhaps if, like his brother, Tom had allowed his blood to boil, had recounted the ghastly narrative in which luck saw him spared while some of his family died in fear and suffering; perhaps if he had thus released it from the tortures of mind and memory, he would have survived its ravaging of his dark nights, its predatory incursions into his solitudes. And thus not have come to that terrible day, that last afternoon. Perhaps, like Horatio, Wills was haunted by a presaging image that, finally, he could not ignore.

'My father had a presentiment of something having happened or being about to happen,' Cedric wrote at the end of his article in the Rockhampton *Record*. 'In his last letter to my mother he asked if anything had happened at home, as "his lady in white had appeared to him" twice previously. This "lady in white" had appeared to him just before something serious had happened.'

Perhaps Wills's equivalent of 'the lady in white' was the emptiness, the horror that faces the champion athlete if he or she is not ready for the silences and the anonymity that come with retirement, with the waning at last of those great and inexplicable powers of movement, eye, hand, muscle, coordination, quick intuitive and strategic mind.

Because he had in the past threatened suicide, he was looked after at his Heidelberg home by male attendants. But on 2 May 1880 – a Sunday – Wills briefly eluded his guards and stabbed himself in the chest three times with a pair of scissors. He was forty-four years old.

PART THREE

The football stadium is one of the few really large constructions that turns its wrong side out. The oval bowl excludes the world, reserves its mystery or initiates. The TV cannot violate it, cannot even begin to catch it. It's a place of collective obsession, of exaltation . . . communal delirium.

Tim Parks, *A Season with Verona*

. . . at 11 a.m. today, the atmosphere will be as thick with expectations as it always is. Only at the MCG does it happen quite like this. [The MCG] should be called the true cathedral of the game in Australia.

Ron Reed, *The Herald-Sun*, December 1996, Third Test, Australia v. West Indies

AND SO WILLS is gone. For one fogbound Melbourne night in the twenty-first century he has unravelled so many of the multitudinous and multicoloured strands of the MCG's dynamic life before re-enacting his own self-destruction when personal history became too much to bear. Since the 'baton' that produced his magic was revealed in the end as the makeshift dagger that he plunged into himself, there is, at last, an idea of peace and reconciliation for that tortured soul, a peace found by invoking the panoply and achievement, the displays of prowess and style, the sheer wonder of the life of the MCG at the heart of the city of Melbourne.

It is a wan, sad, foggy morning and deepest winter. The first traffic begins to growl on the bridges and along Brunton Avenue; the first trains rattle among fog-wisped red and green signals; the first joggers appear in Yarra Park masked by their own puffing breath; the first dog owners unclip their panting, straining friends who initiate nearby tree trunks with the first one for the day. The 'G' looms in the normal mist as cars and trucks arrive sporadically, and cleaners and caterers and groundspeople and office staff thread their way across the park and filter through towards the security entrance at the Members' area. Life is going on.

And Wills, who left this life in sadness on that May Sunday afternoon in 1880, but who has during the past night of ghosts and dreams reclaimed something from that long-ago defeat, has gone.

But there is more. Not even Wills's magic could plumb the riches of the MCG, for it is more than history, more than the games and contests to which it lends such miraculous ceremony, atmosphere, *élan*. Like all great cathedrals in great cities, it is central to more than the spiritual, or sporting, life of the people. The 'G' is, for example, a good place to, well, just meet, no matter what great feat of athletic or other endeavour is providing the backdrop . . .

THE QUEUE, FOR the invention of which the English are usually given the credit, does not derive, as many think, from an innate desire for orderliness but rather from the strong puritanical streak in English Protestantism. The essential idea of the queue was not originally to impose order but to defer gratification. Whatever it is you want, hope to buy or intend to negotiate over, standing in a queue to do it will put off the moment of climax, the point of relief or resolution. From such frenzies of deferral one emerged, so the theory went, a better person. That queuing also happened, by its very nature, to organise quite large masses of people into manageable lines to be dealt with one by one was simply a bonus, a spin-off from the higher purpose.

The English became exponents par excellence of the queue because it originally involved ideological or religious overtones. Like many another religious observance in modern life, for example, Christmas and Easter, the queue is now an organisational remnant of a much more serious, profound and meaningful ritual.

But it is a strong and persistent remnant in its country of origin.

At a conference I ran in London some years ago it took some ingenuity and persistence to stop the predominantly English conferees queuing at one urn for morning tea, even though four were available. Once three or four had formed a line in front of the first urn they came to, the rest followed and would not be swayed from their purpose. This meant that, on the opening day, before we twigged to what was happening, the tea queue was about 200 metres long, and some people would still have been waiting halfway through the next session.

When you combine this behaviour with the English attitude that sentient life cannot be continued without a midmorning infusion of tannin, you have a problem on your hands of significant proportions.

The word 'queue' is itself a queue. The quaintest, least biddable letter in the alphabet is railroaded into line by a string of bullying, repetitious vowels. As for the act of queuing itself, it is passive, accepting, knuckling under. This probably explains why the English, having been trained for centuries in the art and necessity of queues, are so stoic in adversity.

Paradoxically, however, there is no rage to equal that which a whole queue of seasoned queuers will turn on a 'queuejumper'. Once at Heathrow Airport, in the home country of the queue, I inadvertently joined a huge queue halfway along, mistaking what was a temporary gap for the end of the line. I was abused and vilified by two stylish women and a civil-service-looking bloke, who waved his rolled-up umbrella at me as if chastising a lazy punkah wallah. Only when I skulked off to the real end of the queue did their diatribe cease, but even then they kept craning to look back at me, as if, once clear of their recriminatory stares, I would make another break for the front and destroy civilisation as we knew it.

Queuing, like the novel, is a Protestant invention. In Catholic countries they don't queue. Take Italy, for instance. Italians, following decades of close contact with England and the English, are fully aware of the theory and practice of queuing. And in their cities these days they will even form a rough, straggly sort of line while waiting for gates to open, or ticket outlets to begin sales, or even for the church doors to swing wide for the morning congregation. But the barest squeak of a hinge, the scrape or quiver of a ticket window as an unseen hand prepares to raise it, the arrival of the teller in his niche in the bank – any one of these clarion calls will turn an already raffish Italian 'queue' into a roiling human lump fighting its way across the foyer or the piazza or the bank or the post office. Three or four people, not one, will lay claim to the critical territory – the counter, say, in front of the teller or the ticket seller, and all four will lean across each other waving hands, documents, money. The second line, consisting of five or six or seven 'queuers', will lean in on this front row shouting and gesticulating. The shirtfront, which the AFL is seeking to outlaw in Australian football, is alive and thriving once an Italian queue disintegrates and gets down to business. As are the kidney chop, the ankle hack, the trip and the melee.

In the northern Italian city of Trento some years ago, I would regularly catch a six o'clock bus at the bus station. A more or less distinguishable line of passengers, something like a queue, would assemble while the driver leant on his vehicle and had a smoke and a yarn a couple of hundred metres away. The moment he glanced at his watch, flicked his butt to the ground and climbed into the cabin – a sequence covertly watched for by nearly everyone at the bus stop, although many disguised their passionate interest with elaborate shows of indifference – the 'queue' would give a dangerous ripple, casting off a few of the aged or unwary by centrifugal force.

As the bus approached, the line would break out in all directions. The feeble and the unready would change their priorities from catching the bus to ensuring they didn't die under it. Meanwhile, a clog of humanity would jam the doorway. There would be anguished gasps and shouts from the most genteel of lips. *Merda* and *Ma va* and *Muoviti* and *Togliti dai piedi* (Shit, I don't believe it, Hurry up, Get out of the way).

I soon learnt these expressions because I heard them at the same moment every day.

Australians in general are queuers. Given the choice between Mediterranean riot and Anglo-Saxon discipline, we have gone for the straight and narrow. But we are more light-hearted, more ironic in our queues than our British exemplars. And, when it comes to queues at the MCG, it has to be said, the lines may on occasion be long but unlike the mills of God they move fast as well as sure.

. . . Although the famous clocks above the entrance to Melbourne's Flinders Street Station have become unreliable guides to anything that might be contemplated, aspired to, intended or neglected by the now privatised rail systems, they remain a part of Melbourne lore as a place to meet. 'Meet you under the clocks' makes sense to anyone who is even vaguely, adoptively or temporarily a Melbournite. A more limited coterie, but still large, would respond instantly to 'Let's meet at the footbridge', meaning under the plane trees at the MCG end of the old footbridge.

You had to be an MCG stalwart to understand that mixture of geography and lore, but of course thousands did, and the old footbridge on match days is still swarming with people waiting for swarms of other people. If you are doing the waiting, you tend to divide your attention between the masses flowing over the bridge – idly reflecting, no doubt, that you had not known the game had enslaved so many – and the queues forming over at the various visible gates of the Great Southern Stand.

Depending on the day and the game, the ratio of the queue extension to the number of minutes your mate is late appearing can drift alarmingly out of balance. There's probably a formula for it, but no one who goes to the 'G' is ignorant of queues or the psychology of queues. You queue to get in; you queue for beers; you queue for pies; you queue for sauce; and, yes, at big events – any footy final, Boxing Day, the match of the day – you queue for a piss.

The queue was never a place to meet, whether at the 'G' or anywhere else. You had to meet first, then join the queue together. That was the case, anyway, until the arrival of the mobile phone. Even the footbridge – probably under the clocks too, if the truth were known – has been rendered a much less powerful meeting point now that people can simply dial up and tell someone to wave or shout or just say exactly where they are in which queue or grandstand or wherever. This means you can now actually meet *inside* the 'G'. This was certainly possible in the past, and some occasionally managed it, but it was risky. Too often the crowds turned out to be bigger and more crushing and less penetrable than expected, the directions, which seemed so simple outside the ground, became labyrinthine amid the alphabetical and numerical signage – the stairs up to this or the aisle down to that, the levels sealed off, the paths not to be taken.

Not any longer. Nowadays the 'G' trills and pipes and squeaks and shrills to the orchestrations of mobile phones transmitting, among much else, identifications and directions.

'We're in F8 row 13. Where're you? Near *what* sign? The Virgin Blue – oh yeah, I see you. We'll come over . . .'

So, these days, people meet inside the 'G' as a matter of course. They even *arrange* to meet inside the 'G'. It's easy – *just give us a bell*. They probably even meet in queues these days, a development that you would have sworn not even modern technology could have made possible.

Vincent Buckley, poet, intellectual, legendary Melbourne University teacher, and Manning Clark, controversial historian and intellectual, had a famous meeting at the MCG in 1959.

Buckley says, 'We met at a Test match between Australia and England,' raising the exciting possibility that they arranged to meet inside the ground and actually succeeded in doing so.

The 1958–59 Ashes tour of Australia featured two Tests at the MCG, the Second and the Fifth, but internal evidence in Buckley's account places their meeting at the Second Test, which was played on 31 December 1958 and 1, 2, 3 and 5 January 1959.

England won the toss and batted and were all out for a modest 259, mostly falling to the soon-to-be-controversial fast bowling of Ian Meckiff, who took 3/69 in England's first innings and 6/38 in the second.

Meanwhile, the great all-rounder Alan Davidson did more or less the reverse – 6/64 in the first innings and 3/41 in the second. As Davidson and Meckiff, with 18 wickets between them for the match, led the team off ahead of captain Richie Benaud, no one could have predicted the tragic drama soon to unfold, in which Benaud and Meckiff would be the principals and which would end Meckiff's meteoric career.

So, for all sorts of reasons, there was, as usual, plenty of action, tension and high achievement out on the oval at the MCG the day Vincent Buckley and Manning Clark chose it as their meeting place. Recalling what he refers to as an 'inaccessible' quality of Clark's mind at their very earliest meetings, Buckley goes on:

Once, early in 1959, I had a phone call from him. He had just been to Russia and had something of the greatest importance to tell me. An insight to which he was sure I would respond. It concerned the true nature of the mental world of Soviet Man. To understand it was important to the future peace of the world. He would like to meet me and talk about it.

We met at a Test match between Australia and England. There, remembering that Clark had been a keen cricketer in his youth, and trying at the same time to watch Harvey belt Tony Lock all over the field, I followed [Clark's] oscillant movement from one level of the terrace to another, and back again, and he talked and talked. The mental world of Soviet Man was in an odd way a religious one, and he felt some urgency about communicating his sense of this religious vision to McAuley and me [James McAuley: poet, intellectual, sometime editor of *Quadrant*, sometime Professor of English at the University of Tasmania]. For slightly different reasons [Clark felt] we were the two people in Australian cultural life who needed to hear his account. Hence this assignation, so worthy of filmic treatment.

He seemed most agitated, in a state of quite impenetrable anxiety, while saying all this. I listened with sympathy and concern (for I owed him both hospitality and help), but there was so little of pertinent particularity about his speech that I could say nothing of use. The one particular claim he did make was of such patent absurdity, advanced with a kind of innocent exultation, that it embarrassed me . . .

I had known Clark as a man of religious preoccupations, prodigious capacities for work, and a generally worried, if witty demeanour towards the world. I had never thought of him as political . . . Nor did he offer his remarks as having the least political significance. His venture was evangelical, its models biblical; the few just men were to be told a truth especially pertinent to them. He must have been taken aback, and perhaps affronted, by my lack of response. I was appalled.

What Clark was with anguish rehearsing that day for Buckley and McAuley (who also seems to have managed to find them *inside* the ground) would become the central argument of his book *Meeting Soviet Man*, in which Soviet man is seen to have attained a higher state of consciousness despite the regime but to have at the same time been transformed by the invigorating sense of purpose and focus endowed by that same regime. If these ideas are held in tension in the book, they are only some among several balancing acts. Clark's passion that day as he tried to tell his story at the cricket emerges in the one-step-forward-two-steps-back prose of *Meeting Soviet Man* where no proposition, description or speculation is without its corresponding worry, parenthetical subversion or tentative disclaimer.

It must have been an odd scene at the 'G' that day: a conversation that never quite got launched because of the weight of Clark's monologue; the three unmistakably donnish characters pacing the terraces – the leonine, diminutive and intense Vincent Buckley; the tall almost gangling Manning Clark, bearded, dishevelled, distracted; the slightly aloof, ironic but amiable James McAuley.

Buckley was right with his throwaway observation about the scene's filmic qualities. Imagine it. Out in the middle, Neil Harvey busy making what would be a brilliant, flawless 167, with most of his teammates falling around him before the pace and guile of Brian Statham, who took 7/57. With Harvey on the attack and wickets falling at the other end, the stadium thundered with rising and falling roars of shock, approval, admiration, overwrought excitement. Like recitative joining bursts of resonant arias, Clark's hesitant, cultured tones – hard to hear and strangely at odds with the cacophonous surrounds – drew out his intense message. Bending towards each other the better to hear, the three heads would be raised as another Harvey hook or pull or cover drive came ripping across the turf, then down again would go the heads to hear Clark's apocalyptic pronouncements.

To any of the sun-drenched, squinting people in their immediate vicinity, it might have looked as if Clark, a useful cricketer in his day, was analysing the fine points of Harvey's magnificent knock; he might even have been describing the peculiar 'power' of the MCG, the cathedral-like regard in which it was held in and around Melbourne and beyond, and the correspondingly remarkable, sometimes miraculous, deeds that it seemed able to engender with stunning regularity and equally amazing variety.

He *might* have been saying this, but what he in fact was telling his two listeners was, among other things, that on his travels in the Soviet Union one of his companions, who knew no Russian, had been able to speak with ordinary Russians despite their knowing no English. It was, in Clark's opinion, the man's inherent and transparent goodness that enabled him to accomplish this feat, and Clark gave examples of this gift in action. This was the proposition that Buckley found patently absurd and embarrassing.

And so this strange meeting consumed the hot afternoon while Harvey marched on and Lock, as Buckley was able to glimpse from time to time, was carted all over the famous 'park', finishing with 0/54.

Most likely Clark had suggested the venue for their meeting. He was an avid cricket lover and had been a very good player himself as a young man both in Australia and at Oxford University. The historian Geoffrey Serle remembered Clark as a talented cricketer and wondered why he had given the game away so early. In his cups, a youthful Clark would boast of having hit Hedley Verity for six, although Serle, as a second-grade district wicket-keeper, remembered a match in which he caught Clark for a duck.

Buckley was a highly rational but implacably loyal supporter of the Collingwood Football Club who rarely went to matches. Likewise, he delighted in cricket but was not a frequent attender. He may have been slightly surprised to find himself at the 'G' in a big crowd and the year scarcely two days old. And if he was surprised, McAuley may also have been somewhat bemused: *days in the sun* was not his style.

Yet, as all three would have recognised, meeting at the MCG was much like meeting on the steps or in the booming nave of one of

Melbourne's other two cathedrals. Some important conversations had been conducted in cathedrals, some portentous plans had been hatched and fates decided. So, the MCG was a proper setting for the strange discussion that proved to be a blueprint for the quirky, controversial, euphoric *Meeting Soviet Man*.

Clark chose the sunlit MCG at one of its characteristic high points of drama and popular pressure to intimate his intuition that 'Soviet man was different from Western man, different not only in tastes, clothes, leisure, hobbies, but at the very heart'. Obscurely but unquestionably, he saw a great appropriateness in delivering his message to what he hoped were like minds at 'the people's ground'. His message was about the people, a new people, as he saw them, rightly or wrongly. Wrongly in Buckley's view because, as he later noted: 'Evidence? None. None indeed; for these conclusions are offered as reflections, an "idea" that "darted" on a particular night.'

Nevertheless, it was heady stuff – but the 'G', as always, was up to it and Buckley, at least, craning and glancing between bouts of attentive listening to see 'Neil Harvey belt Tony Lock all over the field', saw no incongruity in their talking against such an archetypal backdrop in such a totemic place.

MEETING AT A PACKED MCG when there is a game on is one thing. To go to the stadium when it is empty and still end up having an encounter as important and as memorable as Buckley's with Clark is quite another matter – and sounds, anyway, contradictory. How do you meet anyone in an empty stadium?

It is very difficult to come upon any of the world's great cathedrals – and this includes St Pat's, St Paul's and the 'G' – when they are empty. For one thing, quite apart from the variety of functions they serve professionally, so to speak, all are tourist attractions, and queues begin forming long before the main doors open. Unless you are one of the acolytes, of whatever exalted or low rank, an opportunity to savour the great interior silences of cathedrals seems unlikely.

But sometimes you can be lucky. Coming early on a winter morning in Venice to Santa Maria della Salute, or even San Marco, you can fluke just a moment or two of a silence that is a rustling memory of echoes and incense more than an absence of sound. And an early start at Melbourne's St Pat's or St Paul's will see you solitary for a few minutes before the first couple of venerable ladies or giggling croco-diles of schoolkids come shuffling in. And at the 'G'?

Well, many paths lead to the 'G', some of them indirect, mean-dering and unsuspected and, having innocently taken one or other of them never realising where it will take you, you just never know who you might run into even when, arriving at that shining green oval and its surrounding tiers of seats and stands, to your great surprise you find them utterly empty.

In 1987 I became president of the Association for the Study of Australian Literature (ASAL). Founded in 1978, ASAL was a bold, direct and irreverent response to the widespread ignoring of the national literature and literary history prevalent at that time in univer-sity English departments (with some honourable exceptions) and their journals and institutional offshoots, such as the Australasian Uni-versities Language and Literature Association, whose record of neglect was considered to be especially grievous.

From the start, ASAL had a larrikin tinge to it. Its inaugural and succeeding conferences were innovative and occasionally off the wall. Some famous and influential academic papers were delivered in the early years that profoundly enhanced and dignified the study of our own literature – but, as well, in moments of relaxation from the serious business of scholarship and discussion, there were the equally famous Parody Competition, the Frank Moorhouse Perpetual Trophy for Ballroom Dancing and the informally archival approach to Australian cultural artefacts and emblems (a Violet Crumble Hunt at the Can-berra Conference of 1979; 'bookies' fielding for the ballroom dancing competitions engendering 'Fine Cotton'-style corruptions; the disap-pearance of the trophy and its eventual rediscovery under a bed in a Gulgong motel; and so on).

It might be said that the ASAL stalwarts – and there were rapidly increasing numbers of them during the 1980s as the association provided at last a dynamic, respectable and exciting outlet for academics in Australian literature and for those Australian writers who did not revile or shun the academy – understood the intimate connections between life and literature and refused to be claimed exclusively by either while wholeheartedly embracing both.

Success brought, as always, complexity, ambition, achievements and problems. ASAL (during my presidency as it happened, but the vital spark and the original idea came from Barry Andrews, literary historian, archivist and innovator) embarked on compiling *The Oxford Literary Guide to Australia*. This was published by Oxford University Press and edited by Peter Pierce, a former Rhodes scholar, a long-time member of ASAL and a significant and respected critic in the field of Australian literature. A few years later he would produce *From Go to Whoa: A Compendium of the Australian Turf* – a perfect illustration of the kind of cultural range and larrikin edge to be found among even the most eminent of ASAL's members and a combination of qualities and tendencies heartily encouraged by the association.

Buoyed by the success of the *Literary Guide*, ASAL went on to further publications and one of these was the *Dictionary of Australian Quotations*, which was to be compiled and edited by ASAL member Stephen Torre. As president, I inherited this project along with the dramas it was trailing in its wake. A book in the same general field as ASAL's proposed dictionary already existed. It was *The Dictionary of Australian Quotations*, published in 1984 and compiled by the then editor of *Overland*, Stephen Murray-Smith.

When he heard of the ASAL venture, Murray-Smith was extremely angry. As a member of ASAL himself and a great supporter (although he did not attend the conferences, which is why this publication plan came as a surprise to him), he saw ASAL's project as a kind of betrayal of his own efforts and interests by people who should have been his mates. The dispute became public and very corrosive.

I knew Stephen Murray-Smith quite well, and I undertook at least to initiate some reconciliatory moves, as in any case I was bound to do in my position. I had no idea whatsoever how I would go about this. A preliminary attempt during a special meeting between Murray-Smith and the ASAL executive was disastrous and only served to reveal the depths of acrimony that underlay the dispute. A man of unwavering and courageous loyalty in many causes and towards an array of friends, acquaintances and colleagues under a variety of pressures, dangers and threats, Murray-Smith was not to be taken lightly when he cried 'treachery'. I was reluctant to attempt anything on the phone, and, living in the Adelaide Hills, it was not easy for me to get to Melbourne to arrange a meeting. But at just this time, he became seriously ill following a heart attack, so all plans and strategies were deferred.

In April 1988, I went to the launch in Melbourne of Ross Fitzgerald and Ken Spillman's anthology *The Greatest Game*, in which I had a piece on bush footy. The launch was held on a Wednesday at the MCG in the Landy Room and was scheduled, I thought, for 10 a.m. It seemed a funny time for a book launch, but I had lost my invitation and couldn't check.

I walked through an eerily unguarded gate, crossed the concourse and wandered up the steps as if going to find a good spot to watch a game. But there was no shouldering, pressing crowd, no fortresslike crenellation of heads in front of me when I reached the top. On that Melbourne April day, blundering around looking for the book launch, I caught the splendid MCG oval unawares. There was not a soul to be seen. The bright blue and red and white blocks of seats shone in the morning sun. It took minutes for me to understand why this sight amazed me: it was because I had scarcely seen it before. Normally these brilliant colours, now on full and unabashed display, were lost in the crush of thousands of seated bodies. The grass itself was a rich green and across it snaked two long hoses, one red, the other blue, one end of each disappearing into a small trapdoor in the ground – that mysterious repository into which disappear various temporarily redundant items during Test matches. A bright-yellow wheelbarrow stood abandoned in the forward pocket. A pile of white rope and two blue buckets lay on the grass in front of a cavernously empty Ponsford Stand. Three hysterical fluttering and darting sparrows brawled for territory with a large, scarcely interested magpie on the Members' Stand wing. The 50-metre arcs had just been repainted and stood out from the turf in a mauvey–red colour. And then there were the white lines of the goal squares and the boundary and the centre square. And not a single soul to be seen. Not a movement.

Standing there, caught in a kind of suspension – of sound, of motion – I was reminded of a strange and haunting experience in London years before. Our friend Philip Hughes, one of England's foremost painters of landscape, was at the time chairman of the Trustees of the National Gallery – the first painter ever to hold that high office.

One night he invited us to have dinner at a restaurant with his wife and some of their family. We would then go on to the gallery for, as I thought, the opening of an exhibition.

We had a pleasant dinner and all set off for Trafalgar Square. The gallery, of course, was closed – it was well after eight o'clock by the time we arrived – but doors opened for us as if by a wave of Philip's arm. With all the lights blazing, corridor after empty corridor of still, silent paintings opened up to our tentative pacing. Some of the world's greatest art treasures glowed on the walls, naked to our gaze. We had been to the gallery before – many times. But now there were no crowds, no shift and scuffle of feet, no bobbing and leaning heads between us and the paintings.

Under normal circumstances, the presence of large crowds gives the works of art themselves a sort of urgency by association. You know they won't just disappear, but there is a constant subliminal anxiety that you might not see them properly, that you might not be able to give them their due. You might be forced to move on by the slow but ineluctable momentum of the crowd. Or perhaps you will fail to see for long enough around heads and shoulders in front of you.

But on this amazing night, long unpeopled canyons, luminous with art, lay before us like a motionless world we had somehow entered by chance or magic. I remember clearly catching a glimpse, from the corner of my eye, of *people* at the far end of a corridor, a long way down to my left, as I crossed it. I went back to check. They were people – life-size, in earnest conversation among dark cypress trees, their robes glowing in the last light. 'They' were figures in a landscape – a painting seen as few of us have the chance to see art. Far from taking us to an 'opening', Philip had given us an amazing gift, an unmatchable experience.

The memory of those empty, well-lit corridors and the rich, waiting life of the art everywhere visible and on offer has haunted me ever since. It was difficult not to feel it was a clandestine experience, somehow illegitimate – getting under Art's guard, behind its scenes. As in Peter Goldsworthy's poem 'Act Six', where, after the curtain has fallen, Romeo does the dishes, Juliet is in the supermarket, and Mr Macbeth goes home on the 8.15. Or, from another point of view, like Keats's 'Grecian Urn', with its world of possibilities always about to happen but never actually breaking into motion.

And that was how it was at the 'G' that day – as if I'd been given a silent, privileged view behind its scenes.

When I found the Landy Room and joined the throng for the

launch, I went immediately to the huge picture window overlooking the ground and stared again at that wondrous sight, this time from higher up.

'Looks like some kind of naive painting, doesn't it?' said a voice at my side. It was Stephen Murray-Smith.

I greeted him with great and genuine enthusiasm and asked about his illness and his recovery.

'It's been bloody rough,' he said. He told me about the shock, the pain, the fear. His gratitude to be coming out 'the other side' of it. Then, staring out over the sunlit, still-empty oval, its stunning green and randomly distributed doodles and splashes of paint that were hoses and wheelbarrows and the strict delineation of boundaries and the surrounding orderliness of coloured seats, he said, as if speaking to himself but allowing me to overhear: 'Heart trouble – I've become an expert on it, of course, as we all do with the illness that might knock us over – affects you in various ways. One of the ways is it induces irritability, bad temper. I think I was an especially crook case. I gave people a hard time – colleagues, the family, above all my wife.'

As he spoke he had continued to stare out the window and so did I. A solitary, blue-overalled figure was now crossing the ground from one wing to the other, trailing the red hose in a long, rapidly flattening arc.

'I said things,' Stephen went on, now looking directly at me, 'that I wish I could unsay, I took stands that weren't worth the effort, that could have been sorted out another way. I was crook, true, but that's not really an excuse. And I'm certainly – certainly sorry for the unpleasantness and, and difficulties that might have – might have resulted.'

We were looking each other straight in the eye. A language was being spoken that was clear enough yet needed some decoding, needed to be correctly interpreted.

'I understand, Stephen,' I said carefully. 'I know what you're saying,

I greatly appreciate it and I'll be happy to, well, report our conversation to our good friends.'

'Thanks, mate.' He returned his gaze to the oval, where several more figures had appeared and were wheeling barrows and folding hoses and stacking equipment, as the rising tumult of laughter, talk and greetings – to which, in the intensity of our moment, we had somehow seemed to become oblivious – now washed over us again.

And that was how Stephen Murray-Smith and ASAL healed a grievous and distressing rift – in one of the chapels of the 'G', overlooking its massive and heaven-vaulted nave.

I formally reported, as I promised I would, our reconciliatory conversation to Stephen's friends at a meeting of the association's executive, making a point of emphasising the exquisite appropriateness to both of us of our surroundings at the time, and the matter was duly and with great relief deemed to have been successfully and amicably closed.

But by the time this happened, only a few months after we had talked while we gazed at the midweek insouciance of that great oval, Stephen was dead. Of a heart attack.

Had we become swept up in the laughter and talk and gossip of the launch as soon as we arrived, Stephen and I would most likely have exchanged little more than greetings. It was because we chose to share contemplation of the great nave of the 'G' – catching it off guard, with its acolytes busy about their daily work in the populated silence of empty cathedrals – that we felt licensed, released, to speak of weighty and personal matters. Of democratic temper and 'offensively Australian', Stephen felt the presence and the influence of the MCG, which had loomed large in his life as in mine, and, despite the oval's looking for the moment like a naive painting, it moved him – as cathedral interiors and resonances and vaulted spaces always do – to as much of prayer as his sturdily non-believing philosophy would tolerate.

THAT MEETING AT the MCG in which Manning Clark rehearsed the substance of what would become his *Meeting Soviet Man* seems to have been rather peripatetic. There is the feeling in Buckley's account that the conversationalists were much on the move. They may have had a beer or two, although all were at one time or another 'on the wagon' (Clark permanently for about the last twenty years of his life) and perhaps this was one of those dry times.

It would be a fair bet, however, that they didn't settle themselves in Bay 13. In those days, Bay 13 was still a place where, by and large, people seriously watched the cricket – or quite a lot of them did. It was assuredly, however, not a place for serious discussion about Soviet man or any other version of man whose social altruism and profound devotion to an ideal inclined him to being teetotal and dismissive of the subtleties of cricket. Let me refer you, Wills-like, to Bay 13 . . .

Now the days are getting long, summer's on its way,

And I can't wait for Christmas time, because the day after is Boxing Day.

And you'll know where to find me, ten rows back at the MCG,

Right behind the bowler's arm.

Paul Kelly, 'Behind the Bowler's Arm'

WHAT I REALLY LIKE about one-day cricket is that good old Mexican Wave. Jeez that's fun. You get a group round about Bay 13 at the 'G' begin counting down: ten – nine – eight – seven – six. And they chant ONE! and they all stand and shout and throw their hands in the air. This is a signal to the next bit of the crowd to carry it on, and then the next, and so on. The wave goes round the packed crowd like a – well, like a wave. Sometimes it takes a few countdowns to let people know a wave is getting started. A bit like starting your old car – it takes a few bursts before it catches. But when it does, the wave goes round the bays of the Great Southern Stand of the MCG and then through the Olympic Stand and on to the Members. Of course, the members don't wave so everyone BOOS! until the wave goes again on the other side of the Members, through the Ponsford Stand, and comes back round to Bay 13, and then it goes on round the Southern Stand and through the Olympic Stand and at the Members it stops, and everyone – yes – BOOS! and then it picks up in the Ponsford and COMES AROUND AGAIN TO BAY 13! and everyone screams with surprise and fun, and then it goes on round through the Great Southern Stand and through the Olympic, and when the members won't wave everyone BOOS! Jeez it's good, and then it comes back to Bay 13 . . . and the bastards reckon that's mindless, they just don't bloody know how to have fun.

If you're holding a beer during the wave, well you throw that too. When it gets a bit later, with the lights on, and everything, you do get a bit muddled, what with the grog and the heat and, if you're coming on a bit aggro, well this is a good time to throw your plastic cups and bottles in the air as well, and if you happen to have a golfball on you, or by sheer chance, a billiard ball – I've lost track of the number of times I've put my hand in my pocket for some change, and there it is! a bloody billiard ball! Talk about pocket billiards! Anyway, whatever you end up with in your hands by the time the lights are going on, you chuck in the air, or at someone when it's your turn to wave, and then the wave goes on to the next section, and they all do the same, and then it goes on round the Southern Stand and into the Olympic Stand, and then the bloody members refuse to wave, and everyone BOOS! – it's so funny, even the fifty-ninth time, and then you drink a lot more booze, and the wave starts again, and LOOK OUT, HERE IT COMES! into the Southern Greater Stand and on to the Limping Stand, and the bloody standing members won't, and round the Pronsdorf, and back to the Greatest Standing whatsaname, and laugh! Shit, I nearly bought me own beer. And then the cops stick their noses in, and we all shout, 'You are a wanker, You are a wanker, You are a wanker, You are a wanker, You are a wanker' and the wave starts again and goes through the Great Big Huge Bloody Southern and into the Olympic Games, or whatever it is, and then the bloody members BOO! and round the Ponting, and back here to the Standest Great South Thing. Jeez, it's good.

Some bastard in the dunny goes, 'The Mexican Wave will destroy one-day cricket. I'd tie five-kilo weights on everyone's wrists at the turnstiles. That'd stop the buggers.'

And so I've gone, 'You are a wanker.' Which was really telling the bastard. Like the Barmy Army. All wankers. They go to the Test cricket as well, though. Sometimes, according to a mate of mine, they watch the game. We Mexican Wavers don't give too much of a shit for the cricket. People at the one-dayers don't even notice the 50 partnership or someone's classic cover drive or any of that shit. And when the Test matches start, you won't see us. Five days! Five fucking days! That's when we stick the surfboards on the rack and head for the coast – great fun with a few cans and the old red 'P' for Panic Plate in the rear window, zipping down the Geelong Road in and out of the lanes, fucking up the old bastards in their Holdens. I reckon those Young Liberal pricks who want to put a 'G' plate on the old bastards' cars have got a point. Anyway, that's us – the Mexican Wavers. We're here to stay, mate, just like one-day cricket and millions of ads on telly after every ball, or whatever. You won't catch us being washed away by the tide of history, like that judge said the other day about the Abos and the Rorta Rorta tribe, or whatever they are. Anyway, what's he know about tides? Y'see, the thing about tides is, when you surf you know these things: tides do wash things away, it's true. But they also wash them back! I reckon I've had an important thought there. I'd better be more careful. Ha! Ha!

That's the voice that has replaced the voices in Bay 13 in the twenty-first century. It was not always so. Before the Great Southern Stand more or less obliterated it, Bay 13 at the 'G' – being pretty much right behind the arm of a bowler running in at the southern end – was the preferred spot of some of the truest cricket buffs, those who watched through binoculars, kept scoresheets and could announce after an over or two on the first morning that there was a little bit of outswing and some early moisture in the wicket. Standing – all day – up behind the ground-level seats in Bay 13, thus being high enough to see over the sightboard, was another favoured position available, by its nature, to only a small group keen enough to get there early.

But true cricket buffs were of various shapes, sizes, ages and temperaments. Because you wanted to be behind the bowler's arm, because you were knowledgeable and observant about what the ball was doing, seen from that vantage point, did not mean that you were of pensionable age, plagued with gout and dying for a cuppa from the thermos. On the contrary, because the seats out in front of the old Southern Stand were exposed and hot, they were less attractive to the aged and aging who, if they were really intent on it, could still be behind the arm but higher up in the stand and in shade most of the day.

The evolution of Bay 13 at the MCG had much to do with what happened to Test cricket in the period following the return home of 'The Invincibles'. Bradman's exploits alone had been for years sufficient to ensure cricket's popularity in Australia. Those who weren't particularly interested in the game were intrigued and often entirely won over by the very idea of the Don's magisterial dominance, especially against the Poms. The Invincibles' rampage through England on the '48 tour, Bradman's testimonial game at the 'G' (and in other states) later that year, the charismatic brilliance of Keith Miller, the youthful genius of Neil Harvey, the newly discovered talents of Bill Johnston, the continued dominance of stars such as Lindsay Hassett, Arthur

Morris and Ray Lindwall all ensured that the cricketing decade of the 1950s made an exciting start.

Almost immediately, intrigue and mystery appeared in the slightly shambling form of spinner Jack Iverson, whose unique method of spinning the ball, using the second and third fingers in a sort of pincer movement, made him one of the outstanding bowlers of the 1950–51 Ashes series in Australia. Australia won 4–1 . . .

Sometime in November 1962, I decided to upgrade my living arrangements from squalid to moderately conventional. I was a teacher at a Melbourne suburban high school so it wasn't easy to find time for looking at likely premises. I spent fruitless evenings and weekends touring an array of overpriced attics, damp, gothic basements and backyard sleep-outs redolent of lust-racked tomcats in St Kilda and environs – my chosen terrain.

Not long after the visiting Poms under 'Lord' Ted Dexter amassed 7/633 at the MCG against an Australian XI but some days before Australia beat them by 70 runs in the First Test at the 'Gabba, I saw an advertisement for a flat in Balaclava. It sounded ideal, but required prompt, weekday action. I had the first part of the morning free of formal teaching so I decided to take a look.

I was greeted at the front door of the flat by the agent, whom I instantly recognised. It was Jack Iverson. Taking up cricket at the age of thirty-one in 1946, Iverson had graduated from Brighton Thirds to Test cricket in four years. He was that archetypal figure – the 'mystery spinner', as intriguing and romantic as the unknown lad from the bush who turns up unannounced for a practice game and belts the cream of the bowling all over the park. In the 1950–51 series against England, Iverson took 21 wickets at 15.24, including 6/27 in the Sydney Test. Then he disappeared – back into the no doubt somewhat anticlimactic territory of real estate.

He was a big bloke, his bulk accentuated by a tweedy-looking sports jacket from the sleeves of which protruded those famous hands. I remember glancing at them: they were as huge as legend suggested. He was pleasant and welcoming. While we chatted – a conversation in which, for my part, I tried to avoid wide-eyed, 'knowing' references to his cricket career (which as a matter of fact I knew intimately) with the same pathological intensity Basil Fawlty brought to not mentioning the war – two more people arrived, a flinty-looking couple in their forties. Iverson then took us on a tour of the flat. It was perfect but, being new to respectable tenancy, I didn't know what was supposed to happen next. It was obvious the fortyish couple were equally pleased. Was I supposed to make a bid?

With an amiable smile and a flicker of amusement behind his eyes, Iverson simply said that he would see us in at the city office in Collins Street. With a great show of nonchalance the three of us farewelled him and headed for our cars. Theirs was shiny and new. Mine was an FX Holden that ran on equal parts of oil and petrol and sounded like a tractor when it was not espousing long periods of Trappist-like silence. It seemed a strange way to manage the negotiations, but as far as I could see the flat would go to whoever arrived at the office first.

Having a lot of luck in the running along narrow, congested High Street, I barrelled into St Kilda Junction, threaded its chaotic crisscross of traffic and settled into a roaring, blue smoky negotiation with St Kilda Road. This route in the reverse direction was one I knew well, because most Friday nights I played snooker and drank beer at the University Club, 100 Collins Street, before heading for home in the early hours. So it was not as if I felt apprehensive about swift passage through city traffic and Collins Street was familiar ground. I steered straight for the office, planning to work outwards from there for a parking spot but, as

I approached, a car pulled out right in front of the door. I was upstairs to the first floor before you could say 'Howzat!' and greeting Jack Iverson across a reception counter (how did *he* get there so fast?).

'I hope you didn't break the speed limit,' he said with a quizzical, irresistible version of that amused look. I reassured him, produced all the necessary credentials, wrote a cheque and we shook on it. My hand disappeared in his.

On the stairs going down I met the couple coming up. She gave me a rancorous glance, and I had the impression that the husband was going to cop some flak for being such an unadventurous driver.

Thinking about all this much later, I concluded that part of the explanation for the rather extraordinary *modus operandi* was that Iverson might have been bored witless by the job and was introducing some spice into it. As well, though, I think he took a bit of a shine to me. Being fair-haired and fair-skinned, I looked about sixteen (I was twenty-five), I was almost embarrassingly transparent and guileless and quite obviously ignorant of the whole rich world of real estate and its protocols. Whereas the competition – the husband-and-wife team – were stony-faced (patently not cricket lovers) and probably a little presumptuous about their chances against such callow opposition.

That's what I like to think, anyway. But maybe I have continued to be haunted by his wan, ghostly smile, by the memory of shaking that 19.4 overs, eight maidens, 6/27 hand, and by the knowledge that, some years after our brief encounter, Iverson walked out to the garage of his suburban home and shot himself . . .

In the 1951–52 season, the West Indies arrived with Worrell, Weekes, Walcott, Ramadhin and Valentine. They won the Fifth Test, just missed in the Fourth when Doug Ring and Bill Johnston edged Australia home by one wicket and were convincingly beaten in the other three, yet their style, attitude and sheer class charmed and excited Australian cricket watchers who saw their own team looking vulnerable for the first time and enjoyed the continuation, following Jack Iverson's revelations, of magnificent spin bowling from Ramadhin and Valentine.

It was a decade that saw players like Harvey and Bill Johnston thoroughly fulfil the promise they had shown on the 1948 tour and come to dominant maturity. The same years saw the emergence of some of Australia's greatest Test cricketers – Richie Benaud, Alan Davidson, Colin McDonald – and a whole generation of players on the very edge of greatness in their different ways – 'Slasher' Mackay, Ian Craig, Ron Archer, Wally Grout, Jim Burke, Peter Burge. And the decade ended with one of the most famous tours ever – the West Indies team under Frank Worrell began its 1960–61 season in Australia with the amazing tied Test in Brisbane and never looked back.

More importantly, as far as Bay 13 was concerned, there were some great Test matches at the MCG: the Second Test in December 1950, in which Iverson took 4/37 and 2/36 and Australia won by 28 runs; the Fourth Test in 1951–52, when Australia won by one wicket after that heart-stopping partnership between Ring and Johnston; 'Tyson's Test' at Melbourne in 1954–55, when he took 2/68 in the first innings then smashed Australia's second innings to pieces with 7/27 off 12 overs; the Fifth Test in 1961 when Wally Grout was involved in a 'fallen bail' incident and was given the benefit of the doubt amid much controversy. Whether through sportsmanship or carelessness he sacrificed his wicket next ball. 'Slasher' Mackay and a nervous Johnny Martin then eked out the few runs required for a win by two wickets.

Throughout the decade there were also some huge crowds at the 'G'. A total of 300 270 people saw the five days of the Third Test ('Tyson's Test') in 1955. The strain on general management, incidentally, proved too much on this occasion and the *Sporting Globe*, affectionately known in Melbourne as 'the pink comic' because of, respectively, its coloured newsprint and, presumably, the quality of its content, launched a furious attack on the MCC, citing substandard toilet facilities, cold pies, warm beer and a general sense that the concept of 'the people's ground' had been lost because the 'people' were being so arrogantly neglected while members and others were seeing the game in great comfort.

Large crowds also attended the Second Test of the 1958–59 Ashes series and, of course, the second-day attendance at the Second Test against the West Indies (December–January 1960–61, following the tied Test) was a record 90 800 and the whole match attracted 274 424 onlookers.

All of this had important implications for the evolution of Bay 13. Cricket was popular, exciting, often dramatic. With that uncanny capacity the 'G' seems to have for becoming the stage for both expected and totally unexpected drama, the famous oval became one of the centres of interest in Meckiff's short and tragic career, hosted several agonisingly close games and, in the extraordinary 1960–61 West Indian visit, provided the sensation of Joe Solomon's hit-wicket decision to stave off any sense of anticlimax after the tied Test (Solomon's cap fell on to the stumps and dislodged a bail; Grout and Benaud appealed, and he was given out, much to the displeasure of the entire crowd – a displeasure aimed especially at Benaud).

Just being there at the 'G' was much to be desired; being behind the wicket and privy to the subtleties was even better; being behind the wicket, having a drink with your mates and keeping a more or less general eye on the subtleties was often sufficient. The only other place in the whole ground where you could do that was at the other end, in the Members, and that was possible for only a privileged few.

I am not often seen in the Members at the MCG – well, not

ever – but I have rubbed shoulders with the quality at Lord's. It is 17 June 1992. Among the jostling, cricket-loving crowd in the Austrade Chalet at the legendary Lord's cricket ground just before the toss – day one of the Second Test – only the women and I are not wearing ties. I'm not wearing a suit or a blazer either, having favoured mole-skins and my old Donegal tweed jacket. My ensemble, which I regard as in itself a concession to my hosts, is topped off rather nattily I think by my neatly rolled collapsible umbrella (from the umbrella shop in Bloomsbury), which I twirl and wave with what feels to me like the nonchalant panache of a bandmaster. Not too many others seem to see it this way, however, and these sartorial deficiencies might have become the object of comment as the day wore on had not English aspirations towards imperial disdain been thoroughly subverted by the Australian top order (Mark Taylor 111, Michael Slater 152, David Boon 164 n.o., Mark Waugh 99) after Allan Border had won the toss.

The Austrade Chalet is one of the hospitality pavilions ranged along two sides of the practice area at the Nursery End. No doubt it was called a 'chalet' to denote certain expectations about the weather and to honour the well-known exploits of the Swiss Test team. Well, how do I know why they called it a chalet?

Anyway, it's a highly civilised way of being at the cricket, although it means that you watch most of the second session on telly because the forty-minute lunch break is scarcely long enough for the invited businessmen and assorted moguls to finish their preprandial drinks, let alone deal with the excellent lunch on offer. Not long enough for a stray academic and writer either, although on day two, when Mark Waugh starts to take the attack apart straight after the break, I excuse myself from my incredulous party and rush out to get the beauty of it live.

'Of course,' says a magnate from some distant county at lunch on the first day, 'the trouble with the English is they still regard it as a *game*, you see. The Australians dropped that idea long ago.' This sort of surrealism is the Poms' way of genteelly accusing us of the ultimate crassness – winning too often and too trenchantly. He was suffering from what Vincent Buckley called, in *Cutting Green Hay*, '. . . that impossible aim of the gentleman, to win without competing'. But his comment also identified him as one whose interest in cricket doesn't go much beyond swanning at the receptions, chalets, buffets and luncheons that dot the team's progress through Britain. A bloke I met at the station who'd come up from Devon with his young son on the off-chance of being able to get into the ground for something a bit less than the house mortgage would have made better use of my luncheon partner's ticket . . .

For aficionados of the MCG, Lord's is a bit of a shock for the first few hours of a sell-out Test match, because it both does and does not measure up to one's febrile anticipations.

When Australia, having made 4 declared for 632, took to the field, Mark Waugh, only a few yards from the bat, collected a crisp, slightly uppish drive square in the tackle. You could hear his shout of agony all round the ground. There were three reasons for this: first, the Poms watch cricket at Lord's in an atmosphere of reverential silence, especially at crucial moments (and I don't mean that nervous buzz of adrenaline-fired excitement that passes for a lull at the MCG, I mean *silence*); second, Lord's is an amazingly intimate ground – no one is very far from the action (members in the front row at the Pavilion End sit right over the boundary); and third, Waugh shouted *very* loudly. This was because, as all the males in the crowd recognised with eye-watering sympathy, he was in truly great pain.

Probably one would have heard Waugh's plight out in St John's Wood Road, not to mention Merv Hughes's exhortation from deep fine leg, 'C'mon, Oz, get the fucking finger out!' There were certainly plenty of people out there to hear. Lord's, which holds only about 20 000, locks so many people *out* every day that it rivals our own twenty-first-century lockout palace, the Docklands Stadium.

When you emerge blinking into the light from the St John's Wood Underground Station, your first task is to navigate the poor buggers who are desperately asking for 'spare tickets'. There are hundreds of them, and you keep on meeting them all the way along Wellington Road as you head for the North Gate. 'Spare ticket, Guv, got a spare ticket?' 'Gotta ticket y'don't need, sport?' Of course, there are touts too – scalpers, as we say ('Orlright, Guv! If y'aven't got forty quid, just give us wot y've got, and it's yours – know wot I mean?').

And that's why Lord's comes as a bit of a surprise to an Australian who is used to, say, the MCG. It's a marvellous ground, a wonderful *place* – but lots of people who would love to get in can't; there is nothing of the stadium about it; and, while you can still take your esky with beer and wine into Lord's, you certainly need to because massive pressure on the relatively few bars and food outlets by compulsively queuing Poms makes starvation and teetotalism attractive options.

Still, if you can actually get in with your well-packed esky or your Austrade Hospitality Chalet pass (I did both at different times), it's all very jolly. With your unbelievably expensive ticket guaranteeing you a spot, you can afford to linger at the famous Nursery End and watch the boys practise.

When I arrive on the Thursday, the Australians are in the nets wheeling down the fast, the slow and the medium amid the pock! pock! pock! of the drive, the cut and the pull; and the Poms are chasing balls hit by one of the batsmen to all corners of the field and picking up smartly on the run.

Well, as the game over the next few days falls more and more under the iron control of the Australians, I grow more expansive and conciliatory, and on Sunday I turn up wearing a suit (in my wardrobe, there is no intermediate outfit between the Donegal tweed and mole-skin ensemble and the 'good grey suit', hence the overkill). Selecting from my range of neckwear, I choose my St Kilda Football Club tie, which I confidently expect to fool any cursory glance and mystify any closer one. Abandoning the umbrella, I even consider my battered and greasy Akubra still smelling of pilchard for the flawless blue-skied day it is, but settle at the last minute for a £5.90 white sunhat with the Australian crest. Thus accoutred in a manner I had never considered at the MCG, and never expect to at any time in the future, I hit the Austrade Chalet at about quarter to eleven with a shine on my new black Hush Puppies and a gleam in my eye.

The effect was gratifying, but things got out of control a bit. After a long lunch (I stayed the distance this time, because the Poms were pinned down and anxious, and everything was quiet for the time being), I set off back to my seat in the Edrich Stand behind the wicket at the Nursery End. Just my luck to run into a dozen or so Australian visitors all wearing shorts and St Kilda football jumpers. This is not a joke; this is documentary truth – a brand of truth of which I'm particularly fond.

Needless to say, they spotted my tie, and a kind of ambiguous camaraderie was established. Ambiguous because their delight at the tie was turned into deep suspicion by the suit that surrounded it. And in their state of insobriety, which exceeded my own, though by how much need not concern us, suspicion easily turned to hostility. I was saved, however, by Shane Warne (among his other attainments, ex-St Kilda Seconds footballer and these days a mate of 2003 Saints captain Aaron Hamill) coming right down to deep fine to field. Practically under our noses. My new friends cheered and waved, and Warney mimed handpasses and drop-punts and absolutely no one around us had the slightest idea what was happening.

Under cover of these celebrations I abandoned my teammates and watched the last session standing up the back, which you were not allowed to do, but the attendant there was a Zimbabwean so entranced with the fine second-innings resistance of his countryman Graeme Hick (c. Taylor b. May 64) that he probably would have let me strip off and do a streak if I'd promised to shake Hick's hand.

The match seemed admirably simple to me and perfectly resolved. It was only when Ted Dexter commented on it all at the post-match press conference that I realised how much I'd missed.

'How long is a piece of string?' he asked profoundly and then, in case the proposition was too much for the honest scribblers, repeated it: 'How long is a piece of string?' Wrapping it up, he added, 'Perhaps Venus was not in juxtaposition with something or other.'

Did he *really* mean to say Venus? Venus the goddess of love, that is, whose 'juxtapositions' scarcely involved the great game of cricket and are probably best not thought about by a team in England's plight. I shudder to think what the luminaries in the Austrade Chalet would make of this – even before lunch.

What about day five, I hear you cry. Well, I didn't have a ticket and couldn't buy one anywhere. But I had a plan: down to St John's Wood I went for the fifth successive day and took up a good position outside the station.

'Any spare tickets, Guv? Got a ticket y'don't need, sport? Spare a ticket anyone?'

It wouldn't happen that way at the 'G'. Talk about riches to rags . . .

Bay 13, anyway, developed its own kind of prestige; its kudos grew: to be there was to appear something of an aficionado, even if you weren't. But, increasingly, it was also just a good place to watch from and a splendid place to gather. The gatherers and the drinkers, young, outspoken, restless, oblivious of sun and exposure, gradually outnumbered, and by their noisy enthusiasms expelled, the more sober and conservative behind-the-wicket devotees. Bay 13 functioned as an acceptably rowdy, mostly amiable, quite often fairly drunken enclave increasingly through that good decade of cricket in the 1950s and on into the sixties.

. . . Neil Harvey is on 198, batting at the Members' End in the Fifth Test against South Africa at the 'G', when a bowling change causes him to request the sightboard to be moved. His raised arm gets no result, nor does a sort of half-wave. The sightboard attendant seems to be dozing, and raucous advice from the crowd doesn't stir him. Harvey, in a desperate attempt to attract the attendant's attention, is now standing in the middle of the pitch waving his bat back and forth like a flag. Suddenly, a drunken voice up the back of Bay 13 screams out in joy and wonder: 'He's seen me! He's seen me!'

Bay 13 is pretty well exclusively a cricket phenomenon. Football crowds are generally too packed, and they don't delineate themselves in any but the broadest ways – Members, Olympic Stand, top deck, M13, and so on. Above all, there is too much happening that they have to concentrate on to allow time for any form of leisurely ruckus, wandering, elaborate thematic abuse, extended byplay with mates or antagonists a few aisles away, and so on. Nevertheless, many football fans used to gravitate automatically to Bay 13, or its environs, driven perhaps by some obscure atavism – a summer memory directing their winter feet.

Ian Turner, historian and originator of the annual Ron Barassi Lecture on aspects of Australian footy, was one of these, as his great friend John McLaren remembers:

Turner took a delight in cricket and on New Year's Day would be found with his mates among the barrackers in Bay 13 . . . doing his best to discomfit the visiting team, particularly if it was the turn of the English. But football awoke his deepest passions. He frequently remarked that Australian football was the only sport in the world that brought together followers from every walk and station in life. The Richmond supporters gave him what he had lost when he left the Communist Party – a group of friends united in a common cause, linked to the people but allowing room for individual thought and judgement. A Saturday afternoon in Bay 13 at the Melbourne Cricket Ground was as close as he came to enjoying the classless socialist utopia that he fought for all his life. Here in the Outer of the MCG was the Marxist ideal, where those who worked at their various pursuits all week came together at the weekend as hunters of victory and gatherers of pride, and went away at the end of the match as poets and philosophers together and apart.

When they were not playing Test or Sheffield Shield cricket, Doug Ring and Bill Johnston both played for Richmond in the district cricket competition. They played on the Punt Road Oval, which is just across Yarra Park from the MCG and, in winter, was the home ground of the Richmond Football Club – the Tigers – before they moved to the MCG.

... In the Fourth Test at the MCG against John Goddard's West Indies, Ring, handy with the bat, has made 16 and Johnston, last man in and a 'rabbit', is a precarious two. Australia need 20 to win. The tortured buzz of excitement around the 'G' quietens to a murmur as each ball is bowled, because each ball, especially against Johnston, looks like being the last. Huge gusts of relief follow a successful defence or a near-miss and a run produces roars and ovations. In one of the 'silences', as Sonny Ramadhin runs in to bowl to Johnston, a bellowing voice booms out from Bay 13: 'Eat 'em alive, Tigers.' The time-honoured football-club rallying call, heard often during the winter at the Punt Road Oval but sensationally exotic in the hot dusk of a desperate, last-wicket run chase, snaps the tension. The crowd is caught between laughing and gasping, Johnston plays, misses, survives. The two 'Tigers' fight on . . .

Although Bay 13 is claimed often as the progenitor of some of the behaviour increasingly characteristic of one-day international crowds at the MCG, the seething broil of drunkenness, beer chucking, random aggravation and Mexican Wave obsession – not to mention the hundreds and hundreds of characters with their backs to the game orchestrating waves and other variations – are not direct descendants of the alcohol-fuelled but amiable, ironic and parodic behaviour of the 'old' Bay 13. Behaviour and general restlessness in Bay 13 were moderately disruptive on occasion in the 1950s and 1960s.

. . . It is the fourth day of the Fifth Test, Australia v. England at the MCG, on 17 February 1959. Having won three and drawn one of the previous four Tests, Australia have regained the Ashes under their new captain, Richie Benaud, and are heading for a big win. A modest crowd is quietly awaiting the start of play. It is that time when players have finished their warm-ups, groundsmen have departed with all their equipment, and the umpires have not yet appeared.

A slight figure vaults the fence in front of Bay 13 and walks without haste towards the wicket. He moves with such assurance that once he gets going, if you didn't see where he came from and how he got on to the ground, you might think he was out there in some official capacity or other. Security in 1959 is nothing like that of the new century, but it does exist, and a policeman on the far side looks up with interest. The lone figure strides to the wicket area and, carefully avoiding trespass on to the pitch itself, circles round the Members' End stumps, stooping at one point close to the popping crease to rub a hand over the turf, like a spin bowler getting some 'rough' on to his fingers. He is well embarked on the stroll back before two policemen have made much move towards him, and by the time he climbs the fence and is absorbed back into the welcoming arms of Bay 13, the coppers simply see him off and return to their spots.

Few notice that, in bending over casually to rub a hand on the turf, he had also deposited an object. When the umpires, Messrs L. Townsend and R. R. Wright, walk out to the wicket, they examine this object with what is obviously – even seen from the boundary fence and the lofty stands – a degree of fastidiousness. This is because the object is, they agree, a large, glistening turd. A dustpan and brush are called for and the offensive matter is ceremonially removed.

In Bay 13 there is uproar and cheering. Mission accomplished (although the item itself was skilfully fabricated, not organic, and this story, although unquestionably true, can somehow never be confidently pinned down to any particular day. It is Bay 13 legend).

But basically Bay 13's denizens were there because they loved, in many cases played, in many other cases were amazingly knowledgeable about, the game of cricket. Larrikin behaviour, booze and massive contempt for bullshit and pomposity were part of the mix, but the game of cricket was the focus for the Bay 13 stalwarts. In any case, they were mostly entertaining, an antidote to cricket's capacity for solemnity. This is a far cry from the rabble in and around what used to be Bay 13 at one-day games.

IN ITS HEYDAY, Bay 13 was not a place in the ground; it was an event. If you had taken the Melbourne Cricket Ground tour in those days before the Great Southern Stand, it is unlikely your guide would have paid Bay 13 much, if any, attention. Perhaps a passing glance, a murmur about yobbos and larrikins. Empty of its players that stage would have been as bare and uninteresting as any other unpeopled and drama-less proscenium arch.

The MCG likewise is an event in itself, is at its stirring best when its poor players are strutting their stuff on either side of the boundary fence. But even bare and quiet and silent it exudes atmosphere and authority. This is the MCG you see when you take the official tour, backstage MCG, so to speak.

Just pay $16.00 and join a guide and a small, random group of fellow enthusiasts on any weekday. The tour is excellent, taking you on a big wander through the 'G's niches and galleries and the exclusive bits and the cricket and football change rooms and the museum. Every now and then you emerge from some concourse or doorway, or pause by this or that window and see a new vista of the ground, a view of the oval you most likely had never encountered or never had the chance to encounter before. Each time it is breathtaking – whether dotted with groundsmen and equipment and bristling with markers where the surface is being attended to, or lacking some or most of its customary lines, shorn for the time being of that sense you get, when you first see it on a match day, that dramatic and irresistible events are going to happen on this expanse.

This is the cathedral midmorning on a weekday, when a vacuum cleaner is whining away in the sacristy, or somewhere out of sight, and a cleric in trainers and tracksuit is replacing candles on a side altar, and an electrician is miles high on a ladder repairing the sound system. There is something about a cathedral at such times, caught with its ceremonials down, that helps the solitary visitor to feel, if not less dwarfed, at least more belonging, less out of place, while still in awe among the reverberant silences.

In the same way, there is something about the way the MCG oval sits among its empty grandstands, beneath a ragged Melbourne weekday sky, with a rainy wind gusting and swirling, that is, for all its size, welcoming, endearing. And this is because, I think, somewhere at the heart of the 'G', beneath its undoubted and proper sophistications and its size and its capacity to inspire awe, there lies some essential Australian footy and cricket ground – but more of that in a minute.

When our tour guide conducts us into the strangely sparse, monastic change rooms shared by the Melbourne and Richmond football clubs, I stroll away from the group, through an open doorway, and find myself gazing down the race at the distant other end of which is a rectangle of green grass and a sliver of grandstand on the opposite wing.

Without looking back at the guide, in case I am not supposed to venture further, I jog down the race and on to the ground! The roar as my feet hit the yielding surface is deafening, a physical as well as an auditory blast. The packed stands seem miles high, leaning over me . . .

Well, we can all dream. In my ears, needless to say, was not that visceral greeting but, as it happened, an endless clink-clink-clink, a sound of whipping and snapping coming from above. It was the stern and persistent wind plucking at the cords and wires and buckles on the flagless poles above the Members' Pavilion.

Around me, seeming boundless, stretched the Melbourne Cricket Ground, the actual oval, the earth. A few metres further around the boundary from where I stood was the 50-metre line, yet from there the goals looked not just distant but unreachable. What a salutary experience for all of us non-playing experts and could-a-beens to be stuck out on that vast paddock, its sheer enveloping size, its loftiness spiralling beyond the stands to the scudding blue sky, forcing us, by its very vastness, the prodigious pressure of its implicit expectations, to admit that it was more than just a crook knee that closed the 'G's doors on our burgeoning talents all those years ago.

The MCG Tour is highly recommended. But there is, of course, a bigger picture, which would need a bigger tour – unmanageable, no doubt, but still interesting to contemplate.

. . . This tour, ladies and gentlemen, boys and girls, would show the MCG as a part of the landscape and the society that evolved with it – not just that society's sporting venue, but a reflection of and creative influence on it.

To begin, therefore, let's remember that the MCG is a kind of template, an archetype of the Australian sports ground. Like any local oval in the bush, the MCG started out on a paddock – the Police Paddock. And like all bush ovals, the paddock was just out of town. This was in September 1853.

As Tom Wills's spectral theatre has shown us in passing parade, the MCG was devoted to cricket, hosting its first match on 30 September 1854, the same year in which a modest pavilion was built.

Football followed in 1858 in the form of the famous, originating game of something recognisable as Australian Rules between Melbourne Grammar School and Scotch College, with Tom Wills as one of the umpires. This match was played not on the MCG but alongside it. The first football match *on* the MCG playing surface was on 12 July 1859 between Melbourne Football Club and South Yarra, after which there was a hiatus as far as football on the 'G' was concerned until the 1870s.

In 1876 Melbourne played Carlton on the MCG but, forbidden from wearing stops or spikes, the players found the wet surface hard to negotiate. The MCC changed its attitude to the playing of football on the youthful but already hallowed turf when it became clear that other cricket clubs were prospering by welcoming the footballers and, in 1879, the Melbourne Football Club played all its home games on the MCG.

The graduation of those early teams to playing their matches on suburban cricket grounds was very significant for the evolution of the game. As Geoffrey Blainey has shown, Australian Rules was originally played on rectangular grounds not unlike soccer or rugby pitches. It adapted to the oval configuration when forced to by the move to cricket grounds.

In 1865 the MCC opened a bowling green next to the pavilion and, in the early 1880s, added two asphalt tennis courts near the bowling green. Thus was completed what would become an archetypal pattern for the most modest and distant of grounds – an oval for football and cricket, a pavilion with change rooms, a scoreboard (enlarged and then further improved in the early 1880s), tennis courts and bowling green. Much more so in the bush than in the city, this pattern would provide a social hub, the heart of small towns.

True to this model, on the near outskirts of any Victorian bush township or provincial centre, you will find the oval. Depending on how big the place is and how things are going generally, it will have some sort of grandstand, a dressing shed, a scoreboard quite often, even if rather basic, and, according to the season, goalposts at either end.

Most likely, you will spot the oval, or the sign to it, as you drive into the township, probably not long after the 80km/h restriction sign. Or, you will see it on the way out, a kilometre or so before the 100km/h *de*restriction sign. Near the oval will be the tennis courts and, where the finances can run to it, the bowling green.

Driving into one of these townships on a Saturday afternoon in winter, you will see white-clad figures serving and volleying and chasing on the tennis courts and larger white-clad figures leaning into the bowls at a more stately pace, and the footy oval will be surrounded by cars and utes, parked nose-in to the boundary fence, with a good mob of supporters in the stand and a knot of experts round the bar.

Aromatic smoke, flavoured by the sizzle of steak and sausage, drifts away from the barbecue in front of the clubrooms and flattens out blue and wispy in the cold air. The players slog it out on the picturesque, well-mown but in places muddy oval, and the home fans greet goals with an orchestration of car and ute horns and roars from the stand, while two small boys push their mathematical capacities to the elastic limits as they grapple with the big, white numbers to hang on nails on the scoreboard.

These bush ovals are the nurturing places for an enduring and endearing Australian sporting myth – the vision of the young, raw country lad, bursting with phenomenal talent, who emerges from some country township somewhere and walks into a city club looking to have a kick or a hit in the nets. Such, give or take a detail or two, were Dougie Walters, Tony Lockett, Don Bradman, Glenn McGrath.

And such also was Bob Rose, one of the greatest players ever to pull on a Collingwood guernsey and later one of the club's great coaches.

Nyah West is a small township 40 kilometres east of Chinkapook and about 30 kilometres north-west of Swan Hill. In 1945 – the first year of the Mid-Murray Football League – Bob Rose, just seventeen, ran on to the oval at Nyah to play for Nyah West in the Grand Final, in front of a crowd of about 2000, most of whom, he wryly points out, were his relatives.

Nyah West won that flag, which was just as well, because they then entered upon one of the great success droughts in country football history, winning their second Premiership in 2001. As if to emphasise that they were really back in business, however, they won again in 2002.

Bob Rose was not part of that drought. In 1946, he went to Collingwood to try his luck in the big league and played his first senior game with three home-and-away matches left in the season.

Almost a year to the day after his triumph at Nyah, Rose ran down the race at the MCG, and the roar of a then-record Second Semi-Final crowd of 77 370 hit him like an explosion. It was a sound that literally made him falter a split second in his stride. But despite the importance and tension of the occasion, he remembers almost chuckling to himself as images of his Nyah West Grand Final irresistibly returned. In the space of one year, between his seventeenth and eighteenth birthdays, 75 000 people had been added to the crowd, and Nyah's pleasant, typical country oval had been replaced by the towering, packed stands and surrounding terraces of the famous MCG.

'What the hell am I doing here?' he muttered as he sprinted into that maelstrom.

What he was doing there was taking the first steps in an illustrious sporting and leadership career with the Magpies, although one also that would bring some bitter disappointments in the form of narrow losses on crucial occasions and that would be associated with personal tragedy.

Although naturally enough he quickly came to know and feel at home in Collingwood's notorious Victoria Park headquarters, Rose was keen to see and dreamed of playing on 'the sacred turf'. But his first visit to the 'G' did not come until halfway through 1946 when he went especially to see the famous ground and to watch Richmond play Melbourne.

His enduring memory of that game was of a 'tall, skinny boy', who had played the previous year for the Lake Boga Air Force team against Nyah West in the Grand Final and who, like Bob Rose himself, had then come to the city to try his luck. He cracked a game with Melbourne and was doing quite well by the time he arrived at the 'G' that day to play Richmond. While his horrified Mid-Murray League colleague watched from the outer, the 'tall, skinny boy' was ironed out by Jack Dyer.

'The poor guy was wide open. They carted him off ten minutes before half-time and apparently he was still unconscious when they came back from the half-time spell. That was my first horrific sight of what League football was all about,' Rose says. 'I made sure I kept out of Jack Dyer's way ever after.'

Little wonder that he remembered that first time at the 'G'.

His other 'horrific sight' was also on the 'G'. In the last quarter of the 1955 Grand Final, after being seven points down at three-quarter time in a low-scoring game (Melbourne 4.13, Collingwood 4.6), the

Magpies were desperately trying to mount a counterattack. Des Healey, along with Rose one of Collingwood's best players on the day, had the ball on the outer wing with the proverbial 'paddock' in front of him and he set off for a run. Keeping pace and just slightly behind him, Rose shouted, 'Go, go.'

As Healey, who was very fast – one of Collingwood's renowned 'little men' – sped round the wing escorted by Rose in the bright sunlight of early spring inducing a continuous roar of mounting tension and excitement, the way a daring riff does in a jazz tune, two incidents were about to combine with catastrophic consequences.

The first was an oddity. For some reason, Melbourne coach Norm Smith had chosen to set up his coach's bench not in front of the Members, where it usually was, but on the outer fence, on the southern side. Here he sat with the nineteenth man, Frank 'Bluey' Adams, the twentieth man, and a handful of other club staff (these were the days before coaches, following the lead of Ron Barassi, took to a higher vantage point and thus required intercom or phone contact with staff at ground level).

The second was that, when a Melbourne player was injured and then taken off in front of the Members, the wave of a towel signalled to Smith across the other side of the ground that he could send on the nineteenth man.

'Bluey' Adams had been sitting for more than three quarters, full of adrenaline, dying to become a part of the Grand Final. When Smith sent him on, he burst off the bench like a runner out of the blocks. Ahead of him on the sunlit wing was Des Healey – with the ball. Healey didn't know what hit him. Neither he nor Rose saw Adams until he shirtfronted Healey, their heads clashed and both fell to the ground unconscious.

'It really frightened me, just the clash of the heads,' Rose says.

'I stopped, the ball spilled to the ground. I really got a fright. And then the ball was picked up and taken up the other end, they kicked a goal, and we lost the game, of course.'

Rose says that he has since heard that Norm Smith's strategy against Collingwood's brilliant and elusive small men – Healey, Merrett, Lou Richards (and Rose himself, although he doesn't say that) – was to 'run straight at them'.

'It's good tactics, I suppose,' he adds in a musing tone.

His great time on the MCG, he reckons after some thought, was the 1953 Grand Final in which Collingwood beat Geelong. Rose, Healey and Merrett were dominant for Collingwood and, when the Cats fought back in the last quarter with Collingwood beginning to tire, Rose remembers a long handpass, unusual for those days, from Ron Richards. In the clear a fair way out from goal, Rose kicked what he himself says was a beautiful torpedo and sealed the game. The handpass was probably 15 yards or so, and Rose had to kick maybe 50 or 55. But, he explains, with the passing of time, Richards usually estimated his handpass at about 30 yards and Rose remembers his kick travelling 80.

Like many other country people, Rose was at Bradman's testimonial game at the MCG in 1948. His great memory of that is rather typical of a man who himself had such phenomenal hand–eye coordination.

At a certain point of the game, Bradman leg-glanced a ball almost to the boundary. The batsmen ran a comfortable two as the fine-leg fieldsman gathered the ball in and sent a huge but slightly wayward throw back. Instead of heading for the wicket-keeper, the ball dropped straight down to Bradman, where he was standing, having easily completed the second run. Bradman caught it on the full – on the face of his bat! Then, having fully brought it under control without ever touching it, flicked it to the keeper.

Bob Rose returned to the 'G' as a coach in 1964 taking a side that had finished ninth, seventh and eighth in the previous three years to the Grand Final and another magnificent MCG encounter, which Melbourne won by four points.

In 1965 he coached Collingwood as far as the Second Semi-Final, which they lost by one point to St Kilda in an electrifying finish, and his 1966 team lost the Grand Final to St Kilda by one point.

In 1970, Collingwood lost the so-called game of the century when, with McKenna (who was 'knocked rotten' by a 'ferocious bump' when he and Tuddenham collided) and Tuddenham injured, Carlton staged their famous handballing comeback.

But, Rose says a little sadly, the MCG was 'kind to us' when his son Robert, playing for Victoria against New Zealand and destined for Test selection until struck down by a tragic car accident, made a brilliant, quick 70, taking champion bowler Richard Hadlee to the cleaners, and later the same season, carting the formidable Dennis Lillee all over the famous paddock. In another game at the 'G', Robert led a last-ditch partnership with number ten batsman Max Walker to score 50-odd runs for victory against South Australia.

'All these things happened on the MCG,' Rose says. 'I absolutely loved it, the MCG, playing and coaching there. Going on to that ground is a sensational feeling that even overseas players seem to experience.'

He speaks of the drum-tight atmosphere as the players run out, and this reminds him again of his first experience of it in 1946. That game, against Essendon, was a draw, so the second Semi-Final had to be replayed the following week. Collingwood lost and so had to play the Preliminary Final against Melbourne, which they also lost. But, having never trodden the MCG in his life, the eighteen-year-old Rose ended up playing three finals there in three weeks.

'Whether I earned it or not,' he laughs. 'But anyway, I did. Sometimes,' he says, 'when you were coming off the ground at the

MCG, someone near the race would call out, "Good on yer, Bill" to Bill Twomey or, "Well played, Bob." But every now and then, a voice would call, "Good on yer, Rob." And that was someone from Nyah West, because at home, to all my friends and family, wife, brothers, everyone, I was Rob. So the MCG just for those few seconds, while I tried to see who had called out and wave to them, became Nyah West. They're sort of all the same oval in some ways, aren't they.'

In summer, on country ovals like Nyah West and Nyah, the latter being the best ground in the country, according to Rose, there may not be as many onlookers, but there is just as much activity on court and green and, on the oval, the crack of the ball on bat, the rise and fall of voices in enthusiastic sledging. Eucalypts in the park and along the roadside fence droop dusty, long leaves in the heat, kids squeal and laugh under a sprinkler near the tennis courts, and in the clubrooms the beer is icy cold.

These scenes are repeated all over the bush on a Saturday. And, allowing for obvious greater sophistication here and there, they are recognisable versions of what happens at the famous stadium just out of town in Yarra Park. They are enactments of a sports ritual that the MCG from its earliest days enshrined. It is in that sense more than any other, perhaps, that it is truly the people's ground – a place that provided the guidelines and blueprint for even the loneliest and dustiest of bush ovals with their tennis courts and bowls loyally alongside.

Like the MCG, the bush oval fulfils many functions. It is on the oval that townspeople congregate when bushfires burn so close that many of them – especially the children – have to evacuate. I have vivid memories still of climbing on to the roof of our house in the Mount Lofties to fill the spouting with water and to catch a glimpse over the tops of the stringybarks of the fire front coming straight at us, with the family safely dispatched to the oval and the fire pump putt-putting near the tanks, and the sprinklers all around the house and along the roof ridge flinging water into the hot, burning air.

During the fierce fires that raged in north-east Victoria in 2003, a resident of Omeo, which had been ringed by fire and threatened for weeks, referred to the local oval as 'the safest place in town'.

Like the MCG, of which they are distant offspring, bush ovals also turn their hand to concerts and performances. When Sir Robert Helpmann toured his dance company into the provinces, he found himself playing to a large audience seated on a township oval with a stage specially and lovingly constructed by local builders and handy-men for the occasion. For dressing-rooms, the corps de ballet would use the football club change rooms. Helpmann, as the star, was allot-ted the umpire's room. Despite the locals' painstaking preparations, no one had thought about make-up. When the starting time for the per-formance had passed by a few minutes, one of Helpmann's party went along to see if all was well. He found Helpmann standing precariously on a chair, which was in turn balanced on a rubbing-down table, with his face up near the 60-watt electric light, applying his make-up with the aid of a small shaving mirror.

'Are you all right, Bobby?' said his slightly taken-aback minder.

'Yes, I'm all right,' Helpmann said, 'but God knows how these fucking umpires manage.'

The show – excerpts from *The Firebird*, hence the importance of make-up – went on and was a huge hit out there on the quiet remote oval under the stars.

Whenever I summon up pleasant memories of those marvellous and distant sporting arenas and their communities and their nearby townships sprawling casually across a wide road, I remember my experi-ences as a learner driver. Because my attempts to get a few driving lessons out in the bush became intimately bound up with country footy, its supporters and the remote townships in which it engendered such corrosive passions.

. . . My father had an assortment of mostly ancient cars before he belatedly entered the modern world and bought the only new car he ever owned, a Volkswagen, so I had at least a vague understanding, as a callow youth, of the internal combustion engine and its associated mysteries. For one thing, my father's pre-Volkswagen cars necessitated much tinkering, replacement of parts, dismantlings and complete stripping down, as well as endless discussions with his brother about timing gear, carbies, torque, universals and other automotive intimacies. So when I started to hanker after driving, I already had some grasp of the theory – which, as every driver knows, does you no good at all when you're behind the wheel for the first time, crunching the gears, trying to counteract what seems to be your car's magnetic attraction towards traffic in the oncoming lane, and coping with the strange phenomenon whereby, the moment you start the motor and let out the clutch, everything seems to happen at around about the speed of light.

My father and my uncle tutored me to the stage of being reasonably proficient at changing gears and steering straight, but their attentions were perfunctory. It was all second nature to them, so they couldn't see much point in going into silly detail.

'Just start the bastard, mate,' my uncle recommended, 'then into first and away y'go. Don't worry if it jumps about a bit. You'll soon get the hang of it.'

Jumping about a bit was his offhand way of describing the series of violent darts, leaps, lunges and then the silence of the stalled that is the first encounter many neophyte drivers have with the joys of motoring.

When I 'went bush', I still couldn't drive well enough to pass a test. A fellow teacher – the proud owner of a trim, two-toned FJ Holden – proposed an interesting learn-to-drive deal. Don was an umpire in one of the minor country footy leagues. This meant he would often drive long distances on Saturday to some isolated bush oval redolent of sizzling sausages, liniment, assorted manures and hay, and encircled by utes and battered sedans. What about I come along for the ride, he suggested, thus making the trips more pleasant for him and allowing for en route driving lessons.

What I didn't realise, and what he of course didn't tell me, was that on his umpiring assignments he suffered not only from the loneliness of the long-distance umpire but also from the irate attentions of the losers, at least as passionate and intense as their city counterparts but a good deal less subtle and refined in their modes of recrimination.

On my first trip, a raucous, close and bad-tempered game was followed by a few tense beers at the local pub before we set off home. This session was interrupted by a bloke who marched into the bar carrying a large wheat bag.

'Where's that fuckin' umpy?' he said.

The locals pointed Don out then backed away like the extras in a Western movie when the mysterious new arrival is accosted at the bar by the town hard man and says, 'You speakin' to me?'

'Well, here's a present for yer,' said the bloke, and up-ending the wheat bag he released an enormous goanna.

The only time I've seen a pub empty more quickly was in Belfast, when an old man dropped his full pint of Guinness on the uncovered wooden floor, making a sound like *whump*. The pub had been bombed three times already, and everyone had his own escape route worked out, which included, in one case, kicking out the imitation plate-glass window.

That goanna flailed and snapped and whacked legs and panicked and spiralled into the air and leapt on to tables amid an eruption of glasses, cigarette packets, keys and form guides and we slipped out in the confusion and hit the road in the FJ – too fast to be bothered about driving lessons.

After the game the following week, skipping the niceties of a few beers, the locals, whose proud footy team had been shellacked, ran 'that fuckin' umpy and his mate' out of town. Once again, the FJ was at warp speed and couldn't be risked in the hands of an amateur.

More or less undaunted and in any case true to my promise, I saddled up for my third trip convinced that no further evils could overtake us and that I might get a few driving hours up. The chances of a second giant goanna interfering with our program seemed remote, even if being again run out of town was not entirely off the agenda as Don's on-field decisions seemed to win scant approval, but I owed some loyalty.

On this trip, Don realised that he wasn't sure how to get to the oval in question. It was somewhere just outside a dot on the map near the state border. So we stopped at a pub in yet another tiny township nestling in the scrub and Don went in to get directions. I waited in the car. So did the ignition keys, which he had left dangling from the dashboard.

We were angle-parked about 200 metres from the pub and the street was absolutely empty. A midday, midwinter torpor enveloped the general store, the service station and the CWA. From the pub came the languid, nasal buzz of voices interwoven with sudden bursts of laughter and the twangy timbre of the race call on the radio. I eyed the ignition keys.

I decided that fate was beckoning. My driving aspirations, thwarted so far by goannas and raging bush footy fans, could now, at last, be realised. I slipped into the driver's seat and started the motor. I put the column gearshift into reverse. As we were angle-parked, I decided I would back straight out, drive down the road as far as the end of town, then return and park in the same spot. I let out the clutch – nervously, jerkily.

The car leapt backwards and, as with many new drivers, my panic resolved itself into a convulsive jab not at the brake or even the clutch, but the accelerator. The FJ executed a huge, exultant swoop out of its parking spot and arrowed straight across the road. As I dragged at the steering wheel, foot still glued to the accelerator, this swoop became a wide handsome backwards curve and then a complete circle. Narrowly missing the opposite kerb and then, on the return lunge, the rear ends of the cars we'd been parked next to, I brought the FJ to a halt adjacent to our parking slot and, after a few deep breaths, manoeuvred it back in. I returned to the passenger seat. The town slept on.

If anyone had witnessed this extraordinary exercise, it must have been from behind a twitching curtain. The blue gums lining the street rustled. Dust lifted and settled. Laughter drifted again from the pub – but not at my expense. Nobody had noticed.

Don returned minutes later. 'Useless bastards,' he said. 'One of the blokes in there was at that pub when they turned the goanna on us. He recognised me. Couldn't get a bloody bit of sense out of them after that. They reckon the mob I'm supposed to umpire'll be better off if I don't get there.' He looked at me. 'What's wrong with you? You're as white as a sheet.'

'Bit of a hangover,' I muttered – an excuse so thoroughly plausible that he didn't pursue the subject further.

Months later, after some laconic but real lessons, I drove Don to the local police station of the country town where I was a new teacher to take my test.

'G'day, Charlie,' says Don to the copper. 'Mate here wants to do his licence.'

'Righto,' says Charlie, hopping into the back seat. 'Take us away, mate,' he says to me, 'we'll go and have a look at the floods.'

I backed carefully and smoothly out of our angle park. 'Taking a look at the floods' entailed a short straight stretch up to the main intersection of the town, a left turn, a straight, flat run of about 15 kilometres (during which we saw one other car), a left turn, a mostly straight, moderate (and utterly solitary) descent to the river, a left turn, then a pleasant 20 or so kilometres of gently winding road following the tortuous route of the Goulburn River, which was indeed in flood.

All this time, Charlie, having rolled a smoke with great attention to line and form, chatted to Don about the footy, the new coach, 'some bastard who got bitten by a goanna in the pub up the way somewhere' (an anecdote at which Don laughed a little too heartily and did not comment on), and the floods.

A left turn at the end of the riverfront road brought us back to the police station, and I parked in exactly the same spot we'd started from. I had accomplished a kind of large-scale, quieter and more successful reprise of my solo effort months earlier.

'Good, Brian,' says Charlie, 'we'll just pop into the office and sign you up.'

About a year later, I bought a car – another Holden – and set about teaching myself to drive.

When bush footy and cricket fans briefly forsake their own teams to come to the 'G', as they do for Boxing Day, Easter and Grand Finals, they know, as they inhale the heady bouquet of hot dogs, pies, chips, doughnuts and hamburgers and shuffle through the turnstiles, that they have arrived at a place both wondrous and strangely familiar.

So, you can see at least the ghostly shape of the 'G', the idea of it, in even the most distant and isolated of bush grounds and visiting a few of them would be, ideally, a good start to the 'big picture' tour of the 'G'. But there are many roads to the MCG.

You can, for example, wind down to the stadium in Yarra Park by following the river that gives the park its name. The original inhabitants certainly made this journey, in many stages and at different times, fishing and hunting their way down to the great gathering place where the MCG and the Punt Road Oval now face each other and where Melbourne settlers, or the denizens of Bearbrass as it was at first memorably called, observed vast Aboriginal gatherings in the late 1830s and early 1840s. Aboriginal sacred ground and Koori sites along the river's course attest to such journeys.

We don't have the time to navigate the whole of the Yarra, even in a 'big picture' tour, but there are some little bits of jigsaw portraiture that we can put in place as we approach the MCG from the distant reaches of the river that finally flows nearby it.

'Big Pat's Creek' might be an evocative place to notice on the 'big picture' MCG tour. About four months after that first game of Australian Rules in August 1858, Pat O'Hannigan left Melbourne with five fellow prospectors. Unlike the Aborigines, 'Big Pat', as he was known, was going upstream where he expected to find river terrain similar to that which had yielded vast amounts of gold in other parts of Victoria. The gold rushes were nearly a decade old at this time. There were 20 000 miners on the Victorian diggings by 1851 and, in the year of the Australian Rules game and Pat O'Hannigan's trip up the Yarra to test his own gold theory, that number had risen to 150 000. At Warburton, then known as Britannia Creek, Pat O'Hannigan struck gold and continued to do so working along the river as far as the creek that bears his name.

O'Hannigan, as the discoverer of gold at Warburton, was given a reward of £200. Although it is unlikely that he knew or cared, as a successful and intrepid goldminer he was one of the many who brought prosperous times to the infant Melbourne Cricket Club.

Sharply rising membership and the availability of more cricketers – as Melbourne, at first denuded of population by the gold rushes, began to thrive in their sumptuous aftermath – swelled the club's coffers. The new pavilion of 1854 was an early indication of these better times, just as the fortunes of Melbourne's other two cathedrals began to flourish around this time for the same pragmatic and secular reasons, even if their clergy were able to identify more spiritual explanations for the windfalls.

As we cross the East Warburton bridge at Big Pat's Creek on our way down to the MCG, spare a thought for Pat O'Hannigan, miner, not a member of the MCC, subsequently imprisoned by the Gold Warden, Mr Warburton Carr, for damming the Yarra and cutting off water for downstream miners and, in 1860, dying by his own hand for reasons unknown.

One of Pat's five fellow prospectors was Maurice O'Shannassy – less rambunctious and more fortunate. He gave his name to a reservoir and then to the bridge over the canal that was to carry the water from the O'Shannassy Reservoir down to the city and its people and its parks. O'Shannassy Aqueduct footbridge crosses the Yarra on the 'Congleton' property in Woori Yallock.

Downstream from Big Pat's Creek, ladies and gentlemen, boys and girls, you will see Bramich Footbridge. It leads to the Warburton footy ground and sports complex – a bit more flash than some you'll see further up the country, but true to the model, it sits just out of the town proper and shows the town's progress and pride in its trim appearance and its range of resources for sportsmen and -women of all ages.

Much further downstream, running into Kew and Abbotsford through Yarra Bend Park and Studley Park, we arrive, ladies and gentlemen, boys and girls, at the confluence of the Yarra and one of its major tributaries, Merri Creek. The two watercourses join just above Dight's Falls and, on Saturdays past, within easy hearing distance of a large, biased and aggressive crowd at Victoria Park, home of the Collingwood Football Club. Victoria Park, now Jock McHale Stadium in honour of the Magpies' most famous coach, was the burial ground of many VFL teams arriving in hope and departing, whipped and despairing, victims of the 'Mighty Magpies' and their legendarily feral supporters.

But times changed, the Magpies' dominance waned and, in 1994, they went down the Yarra to Yarra Park and began playing their home games at the 'G'. In 2003 they leave Victoria Park forever.

Merri Creek rises some 50 kilometres north of Melbourne and flows down through Donnybrook, Craigieburn, Fawkner, Coburg to Abbotsford and the Yarra. Before the white man, Merri Creek was a habitual haunt of the Wurundjeri – for fishing, water and food-gathering – and evidence of their camps can be detected even now, despite the degradation of the creek to such an extent that it was threatened with becoming a freeway route and required the efforts of environmentalist groups and 'friends of the creek' to save it.

As early as the 1850s, Merri Creek soil was 'mined' close in to the city and was the staple soil for cricket pitch (turf wicket) construction through most of Victoria and certainly for the square on the MCG. Its superior quality for the purpose led to its being transported also to grounds in Brisbane, Sydney and Perth, including the 'Gabba, the SCG and the WACA. Suburban sprawl forced soil-gathering operations to be moved ever outwards and in more recent times Craigieburn (about 30 kilometres north of Melbourne) became the preferred site, although the quality of the Merri Creek soil at that point is regarded by many as inferior to the earlier samples.

Seeing where Merri Creek flows into the Yarra – from where they both begin their journey down to the river flats, the MCG, the city at Princes Bridge, the new Docklands, where cranes and gantries and masts are being dwarfed by high, bland apartments – reminds us, ladies and gentlemen, boys and girls, that for all the considered virtues of Merri Creek soil, the MCG wicket area has had a very patchy history, if you'll excuse the expression. Indeed, you might say it has been, from time to time and surprisingly, the 'G's least successful feature.

Do I hear gasps of disbelief, objection? Well, I'll refrain from giving you a lecture on the matter of the MCG wickets but . . .

Let's reflect for a moment on big scores. During the 1920s, MCG pitches were hard and not fast. It was an era of huge scores at the 'G': Victoria amassed 1059 against Tasmania in 1922–23, of which Ponsford made 429; in the 1924–25 season, the Second Test ran for seven days, and the pitch was rock hard and virtually unmarked at the end of the game. In 1926–27 Victoria eclipsed its own previous performance, setting a first-class record for a team innings that still stands, with 1107 against New South Wales. Ponsford was again a beneficiary of the long innings making 352, only to enter upon his *annus mirabilis* in the following season with scores at the MCG of 437 against Queensland (Victoria: 793), 336 against South Australia in a team score of 637, and 202 against New South Wales out of 355. That it was an era of great batsmen does not wholly explain these run feasts, which were not so marked or so consistent on other first-class grounds.

By the early 1930s the MCG wicket square was increasingly regarded as inadequate for elite national and international competition. Plans were made to re-lay the square and upgrade the drainage system, the latter especially in view of its growing reputation as a 'sticky' wicket. The hitherto assumed virtues of Merri Creek soil were now called into question. Pitch controversies continued during the 1970s and 1980s. Greg Chappell questioned whether the MCG wicket was up to standard for international cricket given the extraordinary difficulties of teams facing even modest fourth-innings targets. While Sheffield Shield games were transferred at various times in the 1980s to other venues – the Junction Oval at St Kilda and Kardinia Park, Geelong – further work and investigations resulted in removal of deep, impacted layers of Merri Creek soil and re-laying of shallower strips with sub-surface heating cables added.

But in the late nineties came the next and perhaps most remarkable development in the up-and-down story of the 'G's wicket square – 'drop-in pitches'. Suddenly, the gluepot in the middle of the MCG during the football season was a thing of the past. Football and cricket, after more than 100 years of not always harmonious cohabitation on the oval, were now reconciled – at least as far as the earth was concerned, even if not in other more political ways . . .

Well, as I said, I won't give you a lecture on the MCG wicket square, ladies and gentlemen, boys and girls, but recommend you read its story in any one of a number of accounts, such as Richard Christen's excellent book called *Some Grounds to Appeal: The Australian Venues for First-Class Cricket*.

And so we glide down into the city, grateful that Mark Kershaw's description of the Lower Yarra in the vicinity of the 'G' in 1886 is no longer wholly accurate: 'In its lower courses, where it winds across the flat marshy ground which divides Melbourne from the sea, it ought hardly to be called a river. Other rivers might object. It is as sinuous as a snake in spasms. Its banks are of mud, and its stagnant waters a mixture of sludge and filth.'

But long before the dockland flats, the familiar high points of the 'G' – the light towers, the flagpoles, the high roof of the Great Southern Stand, will soon come into view.

Now, for a completely different but still 'big picture' approach to the MCG, let's assemble at Young & Jackson's, opposite St Paul's

Cathedral. This was the preferred starting point for many footy fans en route to the ground on Saturday mornings of football match days. John Batman bought the land on the corner of what became Flinders and Swanston streets for £100 in 1837. A girls' school later occupied the block, after which a hotel was built there in 1853 and added to over the years.

As with so many other buildings in Melbourne, including St Paul's, gold influenced the destiny of the site. Two men who had found fortune on the New Zealand goldfields – Messrs Young and Jackson – became the most serious and successful of a string of owners. Young and Jackson took their goldfields luck, gingered up, no doubt, by a certain amount of acumen and opportunism, into business in Melbourne.

Their hotel's destiny became fortuitously entangled with that of a famous contemporary painting – *Chloë* by Chevalier Jules Lefebvre. Shown in 1880 at the Exhibition Building and transferred to the gallery in 1881, *Chloë*'s curvaceously svelte body and not wholly mysterious loins were too much for Victorian society. Banned from the salacious gaze of gallery goers, *Chloë* was rescued from obscurity by Young and Jackson, who hung her squarely above the bar of their hotel for the edification of their suddenly increased clientele.

Not only because of *Chloë* – although of course in her demurely erotic way she helped – Young & Jackson's became a meeting place to rival 'under the clocks' at Flinders Street Station opposite. During two world wars, Australian diggers made arrangements to meet 'back home' at Y & J's. Everyone knew where you meant.

From here, however, it is just a step to the Duke of Wellington, a long-established launching pad for calm, swift or even last-minute visits to the 'G'. From the Duke you can walk or jump a tram to the Hilton Hotel stop. Coming up from the Punt Road side, you might want to linger in the Cricketers Arms to meet your mates or study the racing form. Like the 'big picture' tour, all roads, however far away, however devious, however prone to distraction and temptation, lead to the 'G' . . .

It's any Saturday afternoon during the Melbourne winter. For one reason or another, you're not at the footy. It may be that your team, in these progressive days of national competitions, is playing in Brisbane or Perth or Adelaide. You might be planning to watch them that night, or on Sunday at noon, or at whatever time best suits the TV channels and their sponsors. You'll go along with the timing as best you can – although it may engender domestic tensions, coldnesses and even crises.

But on this Saturday afternoon, anyway, you're pottering round in the shed doing some long-put-off jobs, or cleaning this or that, or taking something apart or, even worse, doggedly trying to put something back together. On the bench is the radio tuned to ABC 'Grandstand'. Tim Lane, Dwayne Russell, Stan Alves, Mark Maclure and Caroline Wilson are in the ABC broadcast box at the MCG where Hawthorn are soon to play Richmond. They are chatting to Kevin Sheedy, who is putting his always trenchant and often lateral views on the question of rule changes. Wills would have been at home with Sheeds in the ABC box because Wills was always provocative, sometimes prescient, sometimes simply wrong-headed about the rules of the game on which he had such a huge impact. You pick up part of the carburettor you're trying to clean and reassemble, thinking how good it would be to have that view of the ground from the broadcasting box at the 'G', to hit the microphone with, 'And there's the bounce of the ball to start Season 2003 . . .'

Dear Brian

There will be an MCC pass waiting for you at the window at Gate 1 on Sunday. After entering at that point, turn right and walk to the red Food Court sign which hangs overhead (only 30 metres or so from memory). Go up the stairs (on your right) to the first level and the Media Centre will be immediately in front of you. The man patrolling the door will have your name on his list and will point you to our box. Feel free to turn up any time between noon and match time.

Just to put me at ease, could you pop me a confirmation that you've received (and understood) all of this. I look forward to seeing you there to witness another triumph of the rapidly rising tyros in Blue!

Regards

Tim

This welcome email from Tim Lane, the finest sports caller in Australia, arrived on Friday 30 August 2002 and was the latest of several such communications stretching back over nearly ten years. Tim was as always extremely forbearing, which was just as well because I was invariably the initiator of such contacts usually in some hour of need.

In 1993, as head of the Menzies Centre for Australian Studies at London University, I decided to run a cricket conference on the eve of the Lord's Test, and I wrote to Tim at ABC Sport in Melbourne to see who was coming over from the ABC, with a view to pirating some of them for the conference.

It was a slightly cheeky thing to do and could have been justifiably regarded as intrusive. We had met only once – years before in the foyer of the old ABC building in William Street. I was there to be interviewed by the Coodabeen Champions about my then recently published book, *Oval Dreams: Larrikin Essays on Sport and Low Culture*. As I hurried into the building clutching my copy, Tim Lane was hurrying out – also clutching a copy. He was taking it home to read before his weekend program commitments. So we met, briefly and for the first time, over a book. It was on that sketchy basis that I wrote to him from London.

My hope that Tim himself would be covering the tour was dashed when he told me that Neville Oliver was doing the honours, but he was tremendously helpful about various others who would be available and worth asking and in the end a rather stellar line-up of visiting Australians, including Neville Oliver, Pommy writers, journalists, pundits and assorted cricket-mad academics assembled for the two-day conference and the keynote address by former Australian Test batsman Paul Sheehan.

Years later, Tim Lane and I sort of met again – over another book. Towards the end of 2000, I had the idea of inviting him to the launch of my new book, *A Fine and Private Place*, because it is, among other things, about football in the life of Melbourne and the spectacularly fluctuating fortunes of the St Kilda Football Club, in particular. The sort of thing a complacent Blues supporter needs to be reminded of every now and then. Olympic Games duties in Sydney ruled him out of that, but I gave him a copy anyway, which he took with him on a post-Games recuperative trip to Tasmania.

On the basis of such fugitive connections, I wrote to him again in July 2002 to see if he would have time for a yarn about his own considerable experience of the 'G' and, pushing my luck to the limit,

I wondered if there would be a chance for me to join him and his team in the ABC broadcasting box during one of their calls.

He replied that he 'would love to sit down and have a chat . . . about the famous temple down the road' and that he was sure a visit to the box could be organised.

I was almost as delighted with his spontaneous reference to the MCG as a 'temple' (given my own cathedral imagery, which I had already written) as I was with his generous response to my letter.

And so it was arranged. We met in the ABC cafeteria and swapped yarns and memories of the football and cricket past and views on the tumultuous present. His team, Carlton – those 'rapidly rising tyros in Blue' – were heading for their first-ever 'wooden spoon', the mythical trophy for coming last, and my team, St Kilda, were second-last and had more wooden spoons than any other team by a cool margin.

Tim's boyhood was spent in Tasmania, and he was a young man before he saw much Melbourne footy, let alone a Grand Final at the MCG. He recalled how, in 1966, although already by then true blue, he was barracking passionately for Collingwood in their 1966 Grand Final against St Kilda. This was because, with so many famous Tasmanians playing for the Saints that day, or having played for them in the past – Jim Ross, John Bingley, Verdun Howell, Darrel Baldock, to name a few – St Kilda were the fashionable side and everyone, especially the kids, wanted to boast of supporting them.

This was an extremely novel story for me; the idea of St Kilda ever being so popular as to engender some backlash hatred – like Collingwood! – seemed outlandish.

Tim recalled snippets of his Catholic boyhood: battling up a long, arduous hill to mass on Sunday morning, covertly reading his *Footy Record* in church, trailing back down the hill afterwards. We speculated on how many games over the years had been replayed in someone's mind's eye at mass.

I remember my father remarking that his concentration on the sermon of the eloquent and voluble Father John Ashe at St Finbar's East Brighton had been devastated one Sunday morning by St Kilda's centreman of the day, Jack McDonald, flashing on to the screen of his mind and delivering one of his trademark, long, raking left-foot drop kicks to Peter Bennett at full-forward. My father and I had watched McDonald play a blinder as St Kilda beat Richmond the day before in an upset at Punt Road.

We resolved to pursue the conversation further after Tim had had a chance to think about his career with the 'G'. But our conversation lingers on long enough for him to tell me the story of a former BBC cricket commentator, the late Brian Johnston, and his first-ever twenty-minute stint calling cricket in Australia. It was the Second Test in 1958–59, in the days when the broadcasting position was on the top deck of the Members. Johnston came on to broadcast about twenty minutes after the start of play.

During Johnston's first over on air, Australian all-rounder Alan Davidson took three wickets (Richardson caught behind 3; Watson bowled 0; Graveney lbw 0). With England at 3/7, Johnston leaned back to catch his breath and a seagull crapped on his head. Soon after, and with enormous relief, he surrendered the microphone to the next caller. Immediately, it seemed, the ubiquitous circling seagulls found somewhere else of interest and less than immediately, but with great style and calm in the crisis, Peter May, the English captain, made 113.

Talking of seagulls – and pigeons too, whose aim is as unerring and whose ammunition tends to be more fulsome and flowing – leads us to consider the famous buildings around and above which the 'G's resident birds glide and swoop, as their compatriots and fellows do around the more venerable walls of cathedrals everywhere.

The model for the sweeping new development of the MCG – which will see the demolition of the Ponsford, Members' and Olympic stands – makes Tim 'sad'.

'I loved the patchwork-quilt effect of the different grandstands,' he says, 'the way they come together to form that perfect circle that always looks so spectacular when photographed from above.'

His musing and nostalgic tone changes, becomes sterner.

'I'm also appalled,' he says, 'that the beautiful red-brick facade of the Members is coming down. The architectural travesty that is the Gallery of Sport has obscured it for twenty years, and now it's going altogether. Bloody tragic. I recognise that there are pressures to upgrade facilities, but I don't reckon those sorts of pressures will ever force the SCG Trust, for example, to do away with its antiquated but magnificent Members' and Ladies' stands.'

On that militant note, for the time being we parted.

In the weeks afterwards, plans for my visit to the box became slightly fraught. Time was passing and what with my commitments and absences, the AFL fixtures over the last few rounds of the season and the need to fit in with Tim's ABC schedule, it was Sunday 1 September 2002 – the last day of the whole home-and-away season – before the visit became possible.

The game was Essendon versus Carlton – on which nothing depended, unless it was the impossible hope that Carlton might produce an upset and redeem, however forlornly, their catastrophic year. But I didn't mind who was playing: I was going to watch the best man in the business call a game, and I would see that mighty ground from a vantage point given to few.

I memorised Tim's instructions, pinned the original on the

noticeboard at home, where it hangs as a souvenir, and arrived on the dot of midday at the ABC box.

The severe woman behind the window at Gate 1 glares at me suspiciously. I haven't got the casual, vaguely scruffy mien of a journo but, on the other hand, I don't look classy enough to be the friend of a member. The envelope with my name on it is there all right, however, and the fact that it's *Professor* Brian Matthews – nice little touch of protocol by Tim – gives her a real jolt. I *do* look scruffy enough to be a professor is the message of her mellowing attitude.

In the envelope is my ticket:

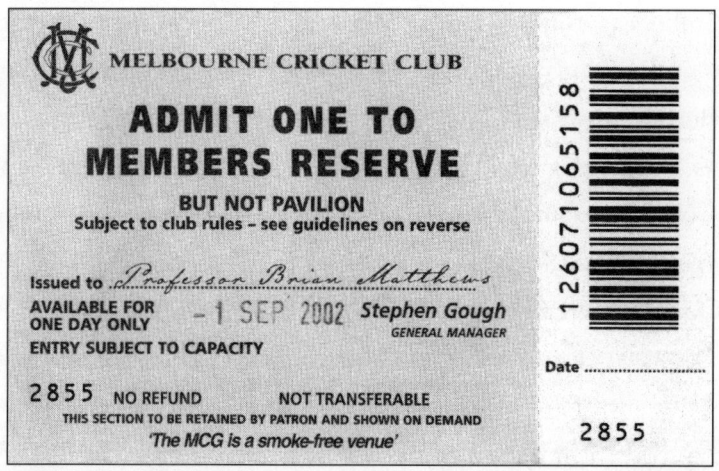

At the end of the day, this card joined Tim's email on the pin-board at home – you don't come by such grand *entrées* to the 'G' all that often. It's hard enough sometimes just to get into General Admission. But there was another reason for my archival initiative. This admission card, with its stern warnings and instructions over the name of Stephen Gough, General Manager, was ironic for reasons only I knew. Stephen Gough and I had corresponded.

I had written him a polite and deferential letter in September 2001, explaining that I had been commissioned by Penguin to do a book on the MCG; that it would not be a history (that had been done and updated by Keith Dunstan) or simply a compendium of great games and signal events. I was pretty convincing on what I was *not* going to write but less precise on what the book would actually be about. This was because I wasn't dead sure myself: I wanted to evoke the place and the presence of the 'G' in Melbourne over all its years, to tap into its mystique, to come at it from all directions – through the pubs you can stop at on the way, through history and yarns, by journeying down the Yarra to Yarra Park, and so on.

I didn't say any of that to Stephen Gough, merely suggesting that it would be a book about the life and times of the MCG, but, one way or another, I seem to have failed to convince him that I might stand a chance of adding something to the vision of the MCG that sat somewhere in the private spaces of most Melburnian imaginations.

When by January 2002 I had received no reply, I sent him a second letter, this one simply a note but, like its predecessor, a model of courtesy and unthreatening cooperation. I wasn't asking for very much, was the subtext of both my letters.

In fact, during the months when I had received no acknowledgement of any kind, it had crossed my mind that perhaps I had been so deferential, courteous and unintrusive that he didn't know what on earth I was writing to him for.

But at last, at the end of January, came the reply. It was lengthy and discouraging. Its burden was that 'a number of factors preclude us [i.e. the MCC] from being in a position to assist you with your publication in the near future'. Essentially, these 'factors' were that my book would be 'in direct commercial competition with some of our intended initiatives' and that 'access to MCG material would be hampered during the forthcoming MCG redevelopment'.

In more detail, he explained that to mark the 150th anniversary of the establishment of the MCG in Yarra Park, the MCC was 'undertaking a number of different historical works. These [included] a detailed history of the MCC and MCG . . .' There would also be 'authorised projects' on particular events at the ground. Until these were published – probably towards the end of 2004 – it would not be possible to allow me 'access to . . . official records or the archives'. In any case, he continued, nailing the whole thing down, because of the redevelopment's demanding relocation of all archives and records, and so on, 'Museums Department staff have been occupied with planning, packing and implementing the move, and therefore resources are not available to assist external research requests'. It might become possible in 2005.

None of this was encouraging for someone whose deadline of 31 July 2001 had already passed! But Mr Gough wasn't finished with me yet. He felt it necessary to point out, as a final *nolle prosequi* upon what I was now realising had been my ludicrously naive hopes of MCC assistance, that 'External projects of a commercial nature may be subject to supervision and access charges, as set by the Secretary of the MCC'. If I backed up in 2005, I would be charged standard fees.

By the time I had read through to the end of this letter, with its intensifying tone of admonition and its rush of rapidly closing options, I felt as if I was trying to get into the Members' Pavilion in shorts, thongs and dreadlocks. It certainly didn't feel like I was dealing with the people's ground.

So, passing through Gate 1 clutching my admission pass authorised by Stephen Gough, and finding the red Food Court sign and then the stairs and the door marked 'Media Centre', and being pleasantly welcomed by the bloke on the door as he ticked my name on his list all rated as a bit of a win, really.

Suddenly there are the doors to all the glass-walled boxes. The ABC den is the last in the row and as I approach, Tim Lane – earphoned and microphoned – happens to turn around and wave. I am introduced to Stan Alves, former Melbourne and North Melbourne champion, and St Kilda's greatest coach since Allan Jeans, Danny Southern, ex-Bulldog defender, the ABC's Dan Lonergan and Jack Cameron, the stats man, and then find myself a spot well out of the way.

The view is immense. Each row of three or four seats is higher than the one in front – the box is like a narrow, miniature dress circle. Tim Lane and Dan Lonergan sit down the front at the picture window commanding the ground, side by side and with Jack over to their left and in easy reach of pencilled notes and scribbles.

Behind them, Stan Alves and Danny Southern, the special comments men, sit at either end of the second row. Then there's me against the glass side wall in the third row, and sports medicine specialist Dr Peter Brukner, who comes and goes as he does interviews on the boundary and in the change rooms. And next to him is a space for any interview guests.

Behind us is Matthew, the producer, with a formidable set of buttons and controls at his ever-active fingertips and connections to the ABC studio at Southbank, to that day's game at Manuka Oval in Canberra and to God knows where else. He and Tim keep up a running series of brief communications and rejoinders and in between Matthew can be heard talking *sotto voce* to the ether.

One of the visiting guests today is Professor Allan Fels, a prominent Carlton supporter. He is being interviewed because of his Carlton affiliations, but Tim Lane takes the opportunity to ask him his professional view on the wrangle between the AFL and the MCC about where Preliminary Finals should be played, because Professor Fels's better-known identity is as chair of the Australian Competition and Consumer Commission.

The dilemma, which has occupied much air time and newspaper space in the last weeks of the season and is being conducted in increasingly acrimonious terms, is that Adelaide look like earning a home final (they did), but the MCC says it will insist on observance of the contractual agreement that provides for one of the two Preliminary Finals to be played on the MCG.

Professor Fels says that if the original contract was valid – and there is no reason to suspect that it wasn't – then there is no case to be brought under the Trade Practices Act, and the MCG is entitled to its Preliminary Final regardless of claims by interstate teams.

Listening to this discussion, it strikes me again what an amazingly complex phenomenon the 'G' is – stadium, symbol, heartbeat, political dynamite, cathedral of sport and sports fans, one of Melbourne's enduring and important physical connections with and reminders of its past.

Professor Fels gives his judgment on the AFL/MCC dispute on air. During a break for the news, when everybody relaxes and chats, he voices a number of other highly incendiary opinions, this time about the Carlton hierarchy and the Blues' disastrous season, a milder version of which Tim Lane elicits from him in the on-air interview that follows the break.

As the ABC's prematch round-ups go, it is all fairly low key. I am a habitual listener, either at home or in a car heading for some ground or other, to the 'Grandstand' program, and I know that for many weeks during the latter half of the season the Saturday prematch discussions led by Tim Lane and featuring Stan Alves; former Carlton strong man Mark Maclure; Lane's colleague and co-commentator Dwayne Russell; *Age* journalist Caroline Wilson; and assorted high-powered guests such as Wayne Jackson, then CEO of the Australian Football League, and various club presidents, have consistently set the agenda for the ensuing week with their revelations, persistent probing and canny questioning. But if the intensity is slightly less than usual, I am not complaining.

The pace is furious: there is a lot happening here on this very last home-and-away round of the 2002 season at the MCG.

But first of all there is the 'G' – the sunlit nave of the great cathedral. With so few people having arrived at this early hour, it is another one of those times when you can see the coloured sweep of the seats – the blocks of red, green, blue, grey, brown gleaming in the sunlight. And the immaculate lines marked on the smooth green of the oval. Like all great works of art, it doesn't matter how many times you see it, there is always some new wonder, some new *frisson*.

For me, on this last day of the season for 2002, I am adding the view from the commentary box to my personal MCG album. No wonder Tim Lane and his colleagues love the job, which, incidentally, they are now doing at a frenetic pace.

When I had arrived, I was aware that some intense discussions were concluding between Tim and Dan Lonergan and Matthew, the producer. They had been canvassing the virtues of taking a direct description of the game between the Kangaroos (North Melbourne) and the West Coast Eagles being played at Manuka Oval in Canberra. This was a vital match for both teams, and the result would materially influence their finals fate.

Because of its importance and because it was starting an hour earlier than the Melbourne game anyway, the broadcast team decides to bring the Kangaroos–Eagles game direct to Melbourne and Victorian listeners.

So, when the Essendon–Carlton game starts at 2.10, Tim Lane explains that they will be giving only periodic scores from that match and asks Matthew for a 'fade' every time there's a score at Manuka so that the MCG score can be updated.

Meanwhile, Dan Lonergan, in a virtuoso performance of the caller's art, follows the local game as it unfolds before us on the 'G', not giving a description in the normal way – because there is no listening audience – but calling the name of each player who gains a possession – *Mercuri short pass, Hird handball, Camporeale mark* – and thus enabling the statistics to be recorded accurately even though the game is not being 'called'. It is, to my eyes at least, a remarkable feat.

All of this amounts to something of a frenzy. On the TV suspended in a corner above our heads, the Kangaroos fight it out with the Eagles in Canberra. With earphones tuned to the Manuka call, one eye on the TV and the other on Matthew, Tim periodically 'climbs into the Manuka broadcast', as he puts it, to update the Melbourne score; and Dan down the front calls the stats, and Stan Alves and Danny Southern watch and take notes in preparation for their summaries of the local game. This latter task doesn't look as if it will be very testing: as expected, Essendon are murdering the Blues.

The moment half-time arrives at Manuka, the windows at the front of the booth are slid open and Tim Lane and Dan Lonergan launch into a full call of the Essendon–Carlton game. Sitting behind them, watching the very same action that they are seeing, you realise what intense concentration and preparation lie behind the apparently effortless, dramatic and vivid call and what amazing fluency they bring to the description, never lost for words yet never dithering or redundant; and never silent, for silence is death on radio.

It is workaday for them but very exciting for me to watch and hear such professionalism, dedication and an enthusiasm that is still fresh – almost boyish – in the cause of sport. This sort of observation is generally written off as 'blokey' in Australia. Though Martin Flanagan, Barry Oakley, Dave Headon, John Harms and maybe some others have, in their different ways, demonstrated that sport is as proper a part of Australian imaginative writing as, say, war and peace, it would be

very difficult in the Australian literary climate to get away with a passage like this one as the opening move in a serious novel:

> . . . In the radio booth they're talking about the crowd. Looks like thirty-
> five thousand and how do you figure it. When you think about the textured
> histories of the teams and the faith and passion of the fans and the way
> these forces are entwined citywide, and when you think about the game
> itself, live-or-die, the third game in a three-game play-off, and you say the
> name Giants and Dodgers, and you calculate the way the players hate each
> other openly, and you recall the kind of year this has turned out to be, the
> pennant race that has brought the city to a strangulated rapture . . . and
> when you think about the blood loyalty, this is what they're saying in the
> booth – the love of team that runs across the boroughs and through the
> snuggled suburbs and out into the apple counties and the raw north, then
> how do you explain twenty-thousand empty seats?
>
> The engineer says, 'All day it looks like rain. It affects the mood.
> People say the hell with it.'
>
> The producer is hanging a blanket across the booth to separate the
> crew from the guys who've just arrived from KMOX in St Louis. Have to
> double up since there's nowhere else to put them . . .
>
> And the engineer says, 'Plus the Giants lost big yesterday and this
> is a serious thing because a crushing defeat puts a gloom on the neigh-
> bourhood. Believe me, I know, this where I live. It's demoralising for
> people. It's like they're dying in the tens of thousands.'

This is part of the opening sequence of Don DeLillo's justly cele-
brated novel *Underworld*, which was rapturously received by Australian
critics and reviewers. Yet it defies belief to imagine that an equivalent
scene – substituting Australian Rules football, a game Australians
invented for themselves, for baseball, a game Americans invented for

themselves – would even be tolerated let alone rhapsodised over. Although there are honourable exceptions, it is by and large *de rigueur* for a significant number of Australian reviewers and critics, male and female, to announce with some pride their total disjunction from, and in individual cases loathing of, sport, especially Aussie Rules.

DeLillo can write with complete confidence, 'In the second innings Thomson hits a slider on a line over third'; those who know baseball – and you can tell he thinks that should be *everybody* – will understand; those who don't should keep up as best they can. But it would be a brave Australian writer in whose serious novel about iden- tity crisis and cross-ethnic relationship there appeared not only a detailed game of footy but also a line like, 'Thomson dummies the handball, switches play to the centre square where Carluccio and Schwartz are one out.'

'Lloyd and McKay one out in the goal square.' Tim's voice runs into my reverie. 'Lloyd knocks the ball in front of him, gathers, goals.' The afternoon races on. Lloyd is kicking goals for Essendon and, when he marks within range for the fourth or fifth time in a few minutes, Tim remarks that he scarcely needs to go through his prekick ritual of adjusting socks, jumper, shorts and throwing a blade or two of grass into the still air, 'but he probably will, anyway'. He does.

By half-time at the 'G', the Bombers are 47 points clear of a hap- less Carlton.

'This could get very ugly,' says Dan Lonergan.

Conversely, a similar convenient blow-out in scores at Manuka, which would enable the broadcast team to leave that match and con- centrate on events at the 'G', does not occur.

At three-quarter time, the West Coast Eagles are two goals in front, but neither side is confidently in control.

'Shit,' says Lonergan – off air of course – as all hope of a foregone conclusion at Manuka vanishes. They are in for the long haul, running two games at once until the final result in Canberra.

But, for the moment, there's a lull – half-time at the 'G', three-quarter time at Manuka.

Dan hands round chunks of delicious 'rocky road' made by his wife and, although he had no idea I'd be there, generously includes me in the handout. Then everyone heads for the coffee and sandwiches in the lobby area on to which all the broadcast boxes open.

I had been fascinated by our neighbours, fully visible through the glass wall separating the ABC box from 3AW. (At least there was a glass wall and not a blanket.) Presided over by the rambunctious Rex Hunt, the 3AW box is full of what looks like about fifty blokes, and it is very noisy. I'd been thinking I might try to talk to Rex Hunt and perhaps ask to join him and Clinton Grybus – formerly of the ABC Sports team – for one of their calls. But being a window's thickness away from them for the entire afternoon makes such a plan redundant. They are highly audible, larrikin, derisive – like a bunch of schoolboys farting and joking down the back of the class. But among their number are two highly experienced, knowledgeable and successful veterans of action on the 'G', Tony Shaw and Robert Walls.

Back in the box with the games cranking up again, the atmosphere waxes and wanes, with the rhythms of the down-to-the-wire Canberra game on TV producing a tension, which the match before us out on the 'G' completely belies.

In the end, the Eagles get home and, with visible and audible relief, Tim and Dan devote their full attention to the last stages of Essendon's reasonably substantial drubbing of the Blues – although it hasn't turned out to be quite the pitiless dismantling everyone was expecting.

'Next year's the year,' says Tim of the shattered Blues, displaying a faith in the future usually reserved for St Kilda supporters who, gratefully conceding the wooden spoon to Carlton in 2002, are expecting miracles in the new year.

Stan Alves and Danny Southern discuss the game and the players as kids of all ages pour on to the ground after the second siren gives them the signal. The centre square is roped off, but everywhere else across the sacred turf a milling multicoloured mob runs and jumps and kicks, and footies fly all over the place, and there are so many boots thudding so constantly on leather that that familiar sound is like some kind of softened military barrage.

As the playing arena fills, some people just stand and look around; whole families congregate, pointing back up into the Great Southern Stand where most likely they've just come from. Fathers who are not actually spearing drop-punts at sons and daughters are picking up bits of turf as if to examine the soil, or are pointing around to illustrate some lecture or other on the great ground that they feel they must deliver to their wide-eyed offspring.

Sunlight slashes down across the city skyscrapers and inches along the Great Southern Stand wing. Shade and light add their play of shapes and colours to the skeining interweaving crowds. Footies float and fly, up into light, down into shadows. Kids run and wrestle and joust and fight – fat kids, tiny kids, blockbuster kids, forty-something kids convinced for the moment that they could have played on this ground if a few lucky breaks had come their way, if the old knee hadn't played up, if they hadn't married so early . . .

Tim Lane meanwhile is broadcasting the day's statistics; Dan Lonergan has headed off to the rooms to interview players, and Peter Brukner is doing interviews somewhere. Stan and Danny are wrapping up their notes and pencils and books.

Quite suddenly, the crowd on the oval visibly thins. Broad stretches of grass show through as the running figures and hovering groups drift away to the boundary and back over the fence. Shadows darken and stretch black fingers from goal to goal; the seats are vacant apart from stragglers lingering in a few sunny pockets. The ground empties.

As I watch through the picture window, looking over Tim Lane's head where he sits at his position, seagulls, hundreds of them, come swooping over the top of us, filling our field of vision, curving and cruising down to the grass. Like pigeons to cathedrals, they assume ownership, bobbing and curtseying and courting, as if to emphasise that even in wondrous, man-made places like the 'G' – only minutes ago seething with humanity – light, shade, nature, earth, air, fire, water are as always the essential elements, the forces which, beyond bricks and mortar and girders and iron, endow such places with their peculiar and inexplicable mystery.

THERE'S A TIME to love and a time to die, as the man said. Everything to its season. At the due time, you can see Parliament rise on a clear day, or watch the ratings period end amid a fireworks display of really bad TV or, as the weather sharpens again, look out for robin redbreasts and footballers with knee reconstructions. At pretty well any time of the year, however, it is not unusual to come face to face with a seagull. You don't necessarily have to be at the beach. Seagulls inhabit not only populous, picnic-studded beaches but also float around city squares, arenas and garbage dumps. They are not known either for finickiness or their retiring, shy dispositions.

In this respect, their only competitors are pigeons. Seagulls and pigeons are the two species of bird that pre-eminently see themselves as sharing space and food, as a matter of right and in the proper order of things, with human beings. In a sense, your average seagull or pigeon does not realise that he or she is a seagull or a pigeon. Moving easily and fearlessly among the rugs and towels and beach shelters, or waddling with imperious assurance among forests of pressing and passing human feet crowding through city squares and plazas, seagulls and pigeons assume an air of proprietorial confidence. The rapid sidestepping of a seagull, if you suddenly wave your arms as it is about to share your sandwich, or the raised eyebrow of a fluffed-up pigeon when you stamp your foot at it, signify not so much fear or alarm as astonishment. They see themselves as the objects not of potential violence or actual threat but of antisocial behaviour among equals who should know better.

Pigeons exude an air of comfortable, almost ecclesiastical serenity. They are the well-fed vicars of the broad parishes they inhabit with such presumption. But seagulls are more temperamental. They conduct continuous territorial bickerings and brawlings among themselves, and they are edgy and querulous in negotiations with their human constituency. If it were physically possible, seagulls would carry mobile phones and be keeping tabs on the NASDAQ, whereas pigeons would carry rolled-up umbrellas and, in fine disregard for fashion and modernity, would wear monocles.

A seagull's eye is like a cartoonist's *idea* of a bird's eye: a perfectly round outer ring encloses a circular black dot, a pinprick almost. It is a cold, unblinking, expressionless orb that seems not to have been constructed for actual *seeing* – a mere gesture towards vision, a parody of looking. Yet this unlikely peeper, voraciously scanning the middle and remote distance, unerringly detects discarded crusts, potato chips, fractured crisps and other detritus and guides every seagull for miles to your dropped, half-eaten sandwich before it hits the ground. Edible and inedible are not valid classifications for the seagull: whatever exists is tucker until exhaustive empirical tests and serial regurgitation prove otherwise.

Yet seagulls are not without finer feelings, even if they seem much less alert to the world of art, music and aesthetics than cathedral-haunting, town-hall-cooing, monument-roosting pigeons. For all their dispassionate and ruthless gaze and their single-minded dedication to the lure of the scavenge, seagulls have to be respected for their love of sport. Forsaking the salt air, the refreshing surge of sea and the rancid delights of overflowing, malodorous and decaying foreshore rubbish, seagulls regularly flock to Test matches and Australian Rules football. And, like their human counterparts, their favourite expanse above all, when it comes to arenas, is the MCG oval.

Bunched down at fine leg or third man, they nod and strut and quarrel with a disruptive and distracting intensity that is the equal of any Bay 13 aficionado's aggro. Like true cricket hoons of modern one-day international infamy, they turn up in large numbers but pay no attention to the game except when the ball is hit for four in their direction, at which point they rise and fall with the mindless ease of a Mexican Wave.

At the footy, where they are more often and more violently disturbed, they circulate around the ground and across the grass of the oval, restless, questing – like John Elliott prowling the MCG or Docklands Stadium looking for a nook to have a smoke.

You might want to say that, when it comes to joining in the hurly-burly with human beings on a more or less equal footing, sparrows also have to get a guernsey. They can be found, it is true, fiercely fossicking beneath the seats of the MCG and flitting through stands and causeways on indeterminate errands. Not to mention their preference for outdoor restaurant tables, hobnobbing with the coffee drinkers and croissant crusaders, bobbing and darting, busy busy busy, as if they were on the waiting staff. Known to some medieval poets as the 'lecherous sparrow', this drab brown little goer does devote a great deal of time to furious, lightning-quick bouts of copulation.

And while this is a preference very familiar to humankind it is an obsession that tends to cancel the sparrow out of much day-to-day, ordinary – as distinct from minute-to-minute sexual – intercourse. Taking it a bonk at a time, sparrows don't apparently lay waste their powers, but they do tend to miss out on the big picture, which may suggest that sex isn't everything, though what the hell, chirps the panting sparrow.

Anyway, it's seagulls and pigeons for mine, if you're looking for the avian punters who play it closest to the human rhythms. And, of the two, I'd back the seagull to rule the world in a manner more recognisable to us lords of the planet.

Pigeons would favour gourmet food, siestas, procrastination, cosiness, sacred places and no ambition.

Seagulls would fight, seek vengeance, undermine, steal and connive – all with a cold eye and a sharp, stabbing beak. If it served the higher purpose, they would eat shit, badmouth their tribe, travel miles to do a colleague down, steal, brawl, scream, shout and generally behave in as frightening a manner as their icy eye suggests. Familiar?

Take a look at them as they swoop down on to the 'G' next time you're at the footy or the cricket or watching a children's display. Talk about 'cast a cold eye on life, on death', as the poet said. I reckon he was frightened by a mob of seagulls at the 'G'.

THE 1902 GRAND FINAL – the first at the MCG and Collingwood's first as a member of the Victorian Football League – had naturally led on, in Wills's magic show, to the Grand Final 100 years later in which Collingwood again featured. But Wills had time only for the first quarter, which was remarkable enough in itself because with only minutes left both teams were still without a goal.

Collingwood finally had the break, and the quarter-time score was an extraordinary Collingwood 1.4 (10) to Brisbane's 0.4 (4). For such scores to be recorded – looking more like one of the earliest games of Australian Rules and not one from the running game of the twenty-first century – was, on the face of it, bad enough, but for it to happen as Channel 10 caller Anthony Hudson remarked 'of all places at the MCG on Grand Final Day' seemed disastrous.

But no one was complaining. It had been a terrific quarter of footy, and the scores were low because Brisbane, the champions, had been shut down. In that first quarter Collingwood laid thirty tackles to Brisbane's thirteen. This was an important Grand Final for many reasons, and the first quarter, regardless of the niggardly scores, had done nothing to diminish that sense of importance.

And so up goes the ball for the start of the second quarter. Collingwood are immediately in attack, but Brisbane captain Michael Voss clears, and Lynch ends up with a mark on the boundary. The violent angle is too much for him, however, and Brisbane's first goal remains elusive. Play sometimes sweeps up the ground but often struggles for space in furious knots of tackling and smothering. There are many mistakes as players rush to dispose of the ball under constant pressure. A scrimmage in front of Brisbane's goal results in the ball bouncing high to McRae. Instead of grabbing it he punches it back across his body to Hart who turns and goals. Brisbane are on the board at last. As if in universal relief, the game settles into more systematic patterns (though it is still as tough) and the sun comes out.

Wakelin and Brisbane's full-forward, Lynch, are having a scorched-earth battle in the goal square. Wakelin marks and whacks Lynch in the guts. Lynch pays him back a few minutes later, and Wakelin gets the free.

Hudson describes Collingwood's build-up from Wakelin's kick as 'a little labour intensive'. Voss misses from about 50 metres and Collingwood's Betheras gets crunched.

Black picks up off the pack and kicks straight, but the ball is touched on the line.

Desperate Collingwood defence through Buckley sets up a rebound down the ground, and Fraser marks, is ironed out by Chris Johnson (who hurts himself more than he hurts Fraser).

With a 50-metre penalty putting him dead in front, Fraser goals. It's a goal 'against the run of play', as comments man Malcolm Blight correctly notes, but Collingwood aren't complaining.

Buckley is everywhere as Collingwood match Brisbane's huge

momentum with individual dashes of brilliance, such as Nick Davis shaking a tackle and landing the ball with Rocca, who taps it to Fraser, and then is scragged.

Rocca takes the free kick and lines up from 35 metres.

You'd back him from 60 metres, muses Hudson, but in this close, 'who knows?'

Rocca goals.

The Pies are in front by eight points, 3.4 (22) to 1.8 (14).

Brisbane's Pike, with a groin injury, joins teammate Beau McDonald, who has a dislocated shoulder, on the bench. The consensus is he won't be back.

On the field, Voss is still deep in the forward line, seemingly resting up for the time being after several shattering first-quarter clashes, and Chris Johnson has obviously strained a hamstring. It's not looking bright for the reigning premiers.

Collingwood attack through the increasingly confident and effective Didak.

When the ball rebounds, Voss is flattened in a big tussle across centre, but he falls and is back on his feet in the one motion, handballs to Black, who goals.

With twenty-five minutes gone in the second quarter, the scores are level, Collingwood 3.4 (22), Brisbane 2.10 (22), and certain players are forging their particular identities for this game of footy. Buckley – tireless; Voss – indestructible; Black – dangerous; Rocca – with luck, the match-winner; Wakelin – impassable; Lynch – explosive.

Much dogged play and counterplay ends with Collingwood breaking out of the back line.

Wakelin to Lonie to Buckley to Burns to Lockyer – goal.

But with only minutes to half-time, Brisbane – always dangerous in time-on when behind on the scoreboard – get a goal after Brown is knocked flat, the ball spills free and the advantage free kick lands with McRae.

In the ensuing centre bounce (or, on this day, throw-up), Fraser is beaten in the ruck, Voss breaks away and his 50-metre kick picks out Lynch who kicks the goal.

At half-time, having fought back valiantly in a quarter in which at one stage they looked like they might be run over, Collingwood are eight points off the pace: 4.4 to 4.12.

Although Wills's magic show would have done it better, that's pretty much how it was up to half-time.

As the teams leave the oval, the crowd is on the move. It's a close one. No one expected it. In pie stalls and bars and corporate boxes and among the members and in the rain-swept seats along the front of the Great Southern Stand, that is the talk. It's close. The Pies might do it, they might just do it.

In the end they don't.

A nerve-jangling second half sees match-stealing efforts from Buckley and Voss and huge exploits from Rocca and Lynch and Wakelin and Burns and Black and Lappin.

Buckley runs riot in the third quarter, mopping up, rebounding, passing with murderous accuracy, occasionally and uncharacteristically 'spraying' a kick, masterminding the midfield.

In two separate ten-minute periods in the third quarter, Buckley has five disposals. One of these occurs when Lockyer marks the kick-off after a Collingwood behind, handpasses to Buckley who, from more than 50 metres and on the boundary, steers through a goal.

Anthony Hudson says it could be one of those 'defining moments' that occur in games and uncannily tip the balance.

But Voss likewise has now come to life, and his nerveless moves and decisions under extreme stress are starting to bring his champion team more into the run of play. Brisbane's bottle-blond motormouth, Akermanis, and Licuria are having a sort of running wrestle, which is becoming increasingly irritable.

Lynch takes an incredible mark to goal, but Rocca answers soon after, then Didak and Tarrant both miss chances to give Collingwood a significant lead in such a low-scoring game.

Brown, on the end of a string of passes, goals from a long way out for Brisbane, and then the amazing Voss launches a 55-metre drop-punt after a centre bounce that goes straight through.

It's four points Brisbane's way at three-quarter time, and the last quarter is for a while a copy of the first – effort and stalemate.

Then Fraser puts a banana kick through from an acute angle close in, and Collingwood hit the front by three points in the Grand Final with about twelve minutes to go. At which point white ponchos and coat collars and makeshift newspaper shelters all snap and flick in the breeze from a new weather front, and the rain begins to fall.

Lynch goals from a free kick almost in the goal square, and Brisbane snatch back a slim lead.

Malcolm Blight says, 'This is serious stuff' and 'They're playing for keeps'.

The rain sheets briefly across the ground, but then slackens. Heavy-legged in the wet and slippery going, both sides look for an ounce more of strength, one more inspired move, one last dogged defence.

'The script is set for a hero,' says Malcolm Blight, and he's right, but probably none of the players is now up to heroics.

A Brisbane runner comes out and is seen talking to Akermanis. We learn later that his message from coach Leigh Matthews is to stay out in front of Lynch the next time he flies for a mark instead of running behind as has been the plan so far.

Within minutes Lynch and Wakelin are part of a pack leaping for the ball only metres from goal. The ball comes off the questing hands and bounces in front of Akermanis, now out in front of Lynch as instructed, and he grabs it and goals.

The lead is nine points. It will stay that way.

Collingwood's last throw comes when Licuria is running on to the ball on the wing. He is for a few crucial instants on his own. Ordinarily, one instant would suffice. But now he is just too exhausted to control the ball, and a couple of fumbles and grabs and he is caught and buried by two Brisbane defenders.

It's all over and the Woods have lost another Grand Final on the MCG.

'Collingwood have made an art form of losing Grand Finals,' writes the well-respected *Age* journalist Caroline Wilson later that evening, 'but surely this was the cruellest loss of all . . . Dusk was descending over the wettest and coldest Grand Final in the history of the AFL and 'The Marseillaise' – Brisbane's theme song – throbbed repeatedly, but only minutes earlier Licuria had held a miracle in his hands on the MCG Members' wing only to learn that he too was only human. The 2001 Norm Smith medallist, Shaun Hart, was running at Licuria from one direction and Luke Power from the other. It was the brave and gallant spirit of Victorian football versus the massive and star-studded threat from the north. In the end the latter was unbeatable, but Brisbane showed it could bleed yesterday and the brave Magpies nearly killed it.'

As with death, so with sporting loss and glory. No matter what the grief, the loss, the shock, the unfairness, the intolerable hurt, the dead man's friends, as Kafka pointed out, get up and go to work next morning. It might seem callous, but they have to. They are still here, and life goes on.

EPILOGUE

When the massive project to rebuild the
northern side is finished in 2006, the MCG
will be unrecognisable as its old self.

Greg Baum, *The Age*, 3 May 2003

And so Jason Edmonds's team of cleaners would move in, as always, and mop up. Michael Birmingham would consult his records and lists and work out how it had all gone. Tony Ware would scrutinise the brutalised turf of the oval and plan his next moves, dreaming no doubt of drop-in pitches.

But there would be one difference after the 2002 Grand Final. It was especially important that the game itself, against all the odds, turned out to be so memorable and that the teams were so brave. Because almost as soon as the crowd had dwindled away in its time-honoured manner, across the parks and footbridges and on to the stations and over to the tram stops and through the park to the cars, shouting or sorrowing according to loyalties, Brunton Avenue was closed off and the big machinery moved in.

Within days, the first chunky lumps had been hammered from the Ponsford Stand and, by the time the cricket season came around, you would be able to see right through the gap to the city's tall buildings. In the football season of 2003, the effect of the wind ripping through this medieval-looking embrasure would preoccupy players kicking for goal and inspire a competition to give it a name commensurate with the great winds of the world – the Mistral, the Sirocco, the Fremantle Doctor. The winning suggestion was the 'Ponsford Spirit', for 'the breeze [that] is there because of what's not there any more'. No one was sure whether, as the Ponsford Stand disappeared, there might not be a great harm done to the giants of the past and to the MCG of the future. But, for a short while at least, the light of the setting sun would shine through the broad, emptied space, as it had on that miraculous day all those years ago when Charlie Dumas and Chilla Porter jumped for gold.

AUTHOR'S NOTE

Many people helped me with this project in a variety of ways, and I wish to record my gratitude to Michael Birmingham, Michael Bisits, the Hon. John Cain, Sebastian Clark, Sir Zelman Cowen, Brent Crameri, Jason Edmonds, Ted Fitzgerald, Martin Flanagan, Richard Hosking, Col Hutchinson, Tim Lane, John McLaren, Marc Marsden, David Matthews, Patrick Matthews, Claire Osborne, Geoff and Hazel Reddall, Jarlath Ronayne, Peter Rose, the late Bob Rose, Tracy Spencer, John Timlin, Ray Tynan and Tony Ware.

To the Penguin team: publisher Bob Sessions, editors Bruce Sims and Katie Purvis, and designer Brad Maxwell. And to Jack Clancy for reading the manuscript, telling me about the Olympic torch saga in Sydney and being generally insightful. To Niky Poposki, my assistant at the Europe–Australia Institute at Victoria University, for tireless researching, tolerance, ingenuity and general all-round loyalty. To Meryl Potter for her stylish and lateral index. To Megan Ponsford, for her photographs.

And, as always, to Jane Arms, for helping me to cajole a sprawling mosaic into a manageable structure.

I also thank the editors of the *Weekend Australian Magazine* and *Eureka Street* for permission to reprint material published in an earlier form.

Select Bibliography

Beardsell, David & Cam, *The Yarra: A Natural Treasure*, Royal Society of Victoria, Melbourne, 2002.

Blainey, Geoffrey, *A Game of Our Own: The Origins of Australian Football*, rev. edn, Black Inc., Melbourne, 2003.

Borgers, Walter, *Olympic Torch Relays 1936–1944*, Agon Sportverlag, Kassel, 1996.

Buckley, Vincent, *Cutting Green Hay: Friendships, Movements and Cultural Conflicts in Australia's Great Decades*, Allen Lane/Penguin, Melbourne, 1983.

Cashman, Richard & McKernan, Michael (eds), *Sport in History: The Making of Modern Sporting History*, University of Queensland Press, St Lucia, 1979.

Christen, Richard, *Some Grounds to Appeal: The Australian Venues for First-class Cricket*, R. Christen, Parramatta, 1995.

Clark, Manning, *Meeting Soviet Man*, Angus & Robertson, Sydney, 1960.

Conrad, Peter, *Modern Times, Modern Places: Life and Art in the 20th Century*, Thames & Hudson, London, 1998.

DeLillo, Don, *Underworld*, Picador, Sydney, 1998.

Dickens, Charles, *Great Expectations*, Penguin, Harmondsworth, 1965.

Donald, Keith & Selth, Don, *Olympic Saga: The Track and Field Story, Melbourne, 1956*, Futurian Press, Sydney, 1957.

Dunstan, Keith, *The People's Ground: The MCG*, 4th edn, Australian Scholarly Publications, Kew, 2000.

Fitzgerald, Ross & Spillman, Ken (eds), *The Greatest Game*, William Heinemann Australia, Richmond, 1988.

Flanagan, Martin, *The Call*, Allen & Unwin, St Leonards, 1998.

Hutchinson, Garrie (comp.), *Great Australian Football Stories*, Viking O'Neil, Ringwood, 1989.

Hutchinson, Garrie & Ross, John (eds), *200 Seasons of Australian Cricket*, Macmillan, Sydney, 1997.

James, Alfred, *Ratu Kadavu's Fijian Cricket X1 in Australia, 1907–08*, limited edition, A. James, Sydney, 1993.

Laughlin, Greg, *The User's Guide to the Australian Coast*, New Holland, Frenchs Forest, 1997.

Macintyre, Stuart, *A Concise History of Australia*, Cambridge University Press, Melbourne, 1999.

Marsden, E. J., 'Cricket in Fiji', in P. F. Warner (ed.), *Imperial Cricket*, London & Counties Press Association Ltd, London, 1912.

—— *The Fijian Cricketers Australian Tour 1907–08*, private archive belonging to Marc Marsden.

Murray-Smith, Stephen (ed.), *The Dictionary of Australian Quotations*, Heinemann, Richmond, 1984.

O'Brien, John, *Around the Boree Log and Other Verses*, Angus & Robertson, North Ryde, 1994.

Office of Regulation Reform, *Yarra River Traffic: Managing Access*, Department of State & Regional Development, Melbourne, 2001.

Olympic Games (16th, 1956: Melbourne, Vic.) Organizing Committee, *Olympic Games, Melbourne, 22 Nov.–8 Dec. 1956*, Australian News and Information Bureau for the Organizing Committee XVIth Olympiad, Melbourne, 1956.

100 Years of Australian Football, Viking, Ringwood, 1996.

Parks, Tim, *A Season with Verona: Travels Around Italy in Search of Illusion, National Character and – Goals!*, Secker & Warburg, London, 2002.

Pierce, Peter (ed.), *The Oxford Literary Guide to Australia*, Oxford University Press, Melbourne, 1987.

Pierce, Peter, & Kirkwood, Rhett, *From Go to Whoa: A Compendium of the Australian Turf*, Crossbow Publishing, Melbourne, 1994.

Presland, Gary, *Aboriginal Melbourne: The Lost Land of the Kulin People*, McPhee Gribble, Ringwood, 1994.

Smyth, Dacre, *The Bridges of the Yarra: A Book of Paintings, Poetry and Prose*, D. Smyth, Toorak, 1979.

Torre, Stephen (ed.), *The Macquarie Dictionary of Australian Quotations*, Macquarie Library, Sydney, 1990.

Vamplew, Wray, et al. (eds), *The Oxford Companion to Australian Sport*, Oxford University Press, Melbourne, 1992.

Williams, R. M., *I Once Met a Man: True Stories from One of Australia's Greatest Folk Heroes*, Angus & Robertson, North Ryde, 1989.

Wodehouse, P. G., *Wodehouse at the Wicket*, ed. Murray Hedgcock, Hutchinson, London, 1997.

NEWSPAPERS AND ARCHIVAL MATERIAL
The Age
The Argus
The Australasian
The Australian
Bell's Life
The Castlemaine Leader
The Central Western Daily
The Daily Record (Rockhampton)
The Gosford Times
The Herald and Weekly Times
The Herald-Sun
The Maitland Daily Mercury
The Maryborough Standard
The Sporting Globe
The Sun
The Sydney Mail
The Sydney Morning Herald

DOCUMENTARY MATERIAL AND CORRESPONDENCE
MCC News, no. 122, December 2002.
Melbourne Cricket Ground Trust, *Annual Report 1996–97*.
—— *Annual Report 1997–98*.
—— *Annual Report 1998–99*.

SELECT MATERIAL ON MEDIA ACCESS:
Assorted correspondence and presentations involving Blake, Dawson, Waldron lawyers; Dr John Lill; the MCC Media Access Committee (viz. the Hon. John Cain, John Harvey, Miranda Milne, Bruce Thompson); Peter French (Assistant General Manager, MCC); et al.

Lill, Dr John (confidential), 'Melbourne Cricket Ground Multimedia Issues
Paper', 7 August 1997.

SELECT MATERIAL ON THE STATUS AND CONTROL OF YARRA PARK:
Harris, Ian (Regional Manager, Department of Conservation, Forests & Lands,
Melbourne), 'The Future Control of Yarra Park North of Brunton Avenue
by the Melbourne Cricket Ground Trustees', briefing note for the
Minister, 21 July 1989.
Wilson, George (Department of Conservation, Forests & Lands), memorandum
to the Minister on Yarra Park as 'permanently reserved Crown Land',
10 November 1986.

SELECT MATERIAL ON THE MCG ACT AND ITS AMENDMENT:
Melbourne Cricket Ground Act 1933 No. 4149/1933: An Act Relating to
a Ground Known as the Melbourne Cricket Ground.
Melbourne Cricket Ground (Amendment) Act 1998: A Bill to Amend the
Melbourne Cricket Ground Act 1933 and for Other Purposes.
Melbourne Cricket Ground (Amendment) Bill: Second Reading Speeches,
8–29 October 1998.
Stevenson, Ross, interview with Premier Jeff Kennett on the subject of the
MCG Trust and management, 3AW Breakfast Show, 21 October 1998.

SELECT MATERIAL ON GENERAL OPERATIONS:
Assorted MCG Trust meeting agendas and minutes.
MCG Trust Business Plan 2000–2004, 15 December 1999.
Melbourne Cricket Ground Operations: Performance Measurement Report,
October 1999.
Melbourne Cricket Ground User Agreement, 26 August 1999.
Thomas, Bryce (Secretary), 'Background to Paul McCartney Concert',
memorandum to Trustees, 8 January 1993.

SELECT MATERIAL ON REDEVELOPMENT:
Proposed Redevelopment of Olympic Stand: presentation by Ernst & Young.
Proposed Redevelopment of the Northern Stand: analysis by John Davies,
Partner Ernst & Young, for John Wylie, Chairman, MCG Trust,
12 October 1999.

Photographic Credits

Pages ii–iii: View from the Members, with seagull (Megan Ponsford)

Pages vi–vii: Winter crowd (Megan Ponsford)

Pages viii–ix: Sunlit boundary fence (Megan Ponsford)

Pages x–1: Looking onto the pitch from the Members (Megan Ponsford)

Page 2: Laying new grass, 1986 (courtesy of *The Age*)

Pages 16–17: The good old days – a muddy centre square (courtesy of *The Age*)

Page 18: Old-style green seat, Members' Stand (Megan Ponsford)

Pages 126–7: At the footy (Megan Ponsford)

Page 128: Queuing in the men's dunny (Chris Beck/courtesy of *The Age*)

Page 203: Aerial shot of St Patrick's Cathedral, 1948, with MCG in the background (Charles Pratt/courtesy of State Library of Victoria)

Page 204: Sleeping and queueing outside the Members, early on Grand Final Day 2002 (Megan Ponsford)

Pages 296–7: MCC Arenas Manager Tony Ware 'worshipping' the earth (Wayne Ludbey/courtesy of *The Age*)

Page 298: After the party's over, 1970 (courtesy of *The Age*)

Page 301: Deserted, wintry top of the Northern Stand (Megan Ponsford)

Cover: Looking onto the ground from the Members (Megan Ponsford)

Front endpaper: Crowd during the 1954–55 Test series (courtesy of *The Age*)

Back endpaper: Aerial shot of the MCG at night (Craig Sillitoe/courtesy of *The Age*)

INDEX

Abbreviations: BM = Brian Matthews; RT = Ray Tynan; Aust = Australian;
Eng = English; NZ = New Zealand; WI = West Indies

ABC broadcasts from MCG 268–9,
273–5, 276–80, 282–5
Aboriginal
cricket teams 40–1, 42
footballers 9
occupation pre-MCG 8–9, 261
Adams, Frank 'Bluey' (Melbourne
footballer) 251
Adelaide, city of 51–3
Adelaide Football Club (Crows) 51,
64, 278
2002 Preliminary Finalists 48, 49,
50, 60–1, 63–5
Adnyamathanha Aboriginal people
41
AFL Park see Waverley Park
AFL/VFL
dispute with MCC over finals
277–8
and Docklands Stadium 122
media access rights to MCG
113–15, 121–2, 123

opposes standing 190
rationalises venues 193, 196
see also Grand Finals
Allen, Brett (AFL umpire) 144
Alves, Stan (ABC commentator) 268,
277, 278, 280, 284
Andrews, Barry (literary historian)
219
Ashes cricket matches 58–9,
179–81, 212, 213, 214, 230, 234,
242
Association for the Study of
Australian Literature (ASAL)
218–24
somewhat larrikin nature of 218
Austral Wheel Race (1886) 94
Australian cricket team 10, 13, 72–3,
130, 133–4, 146–8, 170, 176,
179–81, 212, 230, 232–4, 235,
236, 238, 240, 242, 272
Australian Football League see
AFL/VFL

Australian Rules football 161, 247
  Aborigines and 9, 30
  causes dissension at home 268
  causes distraction in church 271–2
  creation of 27–32, 247
  crowds 91, 122, 123, 176, 183,
    185, 194, 197
  elements of game 29, 177, 253,
    290
  first game at MCG 31, 34
  Gaelic football 141–4
  national competition 49, 60, 63–5,
    268, 277–8
  night games 183
  offside rule 29, 30
  opening bounce 102, 103, 104
  people's game 29
  politics of 110–11
  prekick ritual 282
  prematch entertainment vividly
    described 192
  shirtfront 189, 209, 251
  supporters 102–3, 122, 123
  threat of all-interstate Grand Final
    49, 50, 103
  TV, influence on 123–4, 191, 192,
    268
  see also AFL/VFL; First Semi-Final;
    Grand Finals; Preliminary
    Finals; Qualifying Finals;
    Second Semi-Finals; individual
    team names

baggy shorts 186
balloon ascension 37–8
Bannerman, Charles (Charlie) (Aust
  cricketer) 45–6
banners 49–50, 194

Barassi, Ron (Melbourne/Carlton
  footballer) 142, 177, 251
Barassi (Ron) Lecture 240
baseball 94, 281, 282
Bay 13 15, 154, 50, 154, 225,
  226–9, 223–4, 239–43, 244
  bad behaviour 241–3, 244, 288
  as a classless socialist utopia 241
  Mexican Waves 226–8, 242
  for serious cricket watching 225,
    240–1
Beitzel, Harry (VFL umpire) 142–3
Benaud, Richie (Aust cricketer) 176,
  212, 233, 234, 242
bicycle races 94
Birmingham, Michael (MCG catering
  manager) 65, 67, 68, 96–9, 106,
  299
Bledisloe Cup 115
bodyline cricket series 130, 133–4
bowling green at MCG 112, 247, 248
Bradley, Craig (Carlton footballer)
  144
Bradman, Don (Aust cricketer) 10,
  176, 179
  bodyline Test 130, 133, 134
  centuries 12–13, 134, 145, 148
  Invincibles team 147, 229
  testimonial game at MCG 12–13,
    148, 229, 252
Brisbane Lions Football Club 63, 98,
  291–5
  2002 Grand Finalists 98, 101–6,
    290–5
Brown, Bill (Aust cricketer) 9
Brownlow Medal 104, 183
Brukner, Peter (sports medicine
  specialist) 277, 284

Brundage, Avery (IOC president) 87
Buckley, Nathan (Collingwood
    footballer) 47, 48, 49, 67, 102,
    104, 143
Buckley, Vincent (academic &
    Collingwood supporter) 211–16,
    217, 225, 236, 291, 292, 293
bush ovals 247–8, 254–6
    pose make-up problems for
        umpires 255

Carlton Cricket Ground (Princes
    Park) for Olympics 85, 86–8
Carlton Football Club 84, 122
    1970 Grand Finalists 170, 177
    at MCG 47, 197, 247, 273, 277,
        279–80, 282–3, 284
    players 197, 278
    supporters 64, 122, 269, 271, 277,
        278
Castledine, Rebecca (immigrant)
    41
catering at the MCG 65, 67, 68,
    106
Centenary Test 47–8
Chappell, Greg (Aust cricketer) 264
Chappell, Ian (Aust cricketer) 180,
    181
Chloë (Lefebvre) 266
Clark, Manning (historian)
    cricketer 212, 214, 215
    at MCG 211–16, 217, 225
    theory of Soviet Man 213–16
Clarke, Ron (Aust runner) 92, 139,
    148
cleaning the MCG 66, 67, 69, 299
Collingwood, prototypical behaviour
    38

Collingwood Football Club 47,
    48–50, 90–2, 96, 122, 263
    1902 Grand Final 95, 290
    2002 Grand Final 96, 99, 101–6,
        290–5
    backlash hatred for 50, 64–5, 271
    centenary 183, 197
    coaches 49, 253
    defence against threat of all-
        interstate final 49, 50, 60, 63–5,
        103
    finals 48–9, 50, 60, 63–5, 86,
        253
    games 86, 95, 142, 183, 185,
        188–90, 191–6, 197, 250–1
    Grand Finals 4–5, 48, 90–1, 95,
        101, 142, 170, 177, 183, 251–2,
        253–4, 271
    lose Grand Finals 101, 177, 295
    players 49, 50, 64, 67, 92, 104–5,
        197, 249–54, 291–5
    supporters 4, 50, 65, 102–3, 122,
        185, 189, 191, 192, 193, 194,
        215, 263, 271
Collingwood Rifles football team 47,
    48, 183
Colonial Stadium see Docklands
    Stadium
Commonwealth Games, Melbourne
    (2006) 121
Communist Party, replaced by
    Richmond supporters 240–1
concerts at MCG 173, 182, 197–9
conscription rallies (WWI) 107–9
Coppin, Hon. George Selth
    (entrepreneur) 37–9, 88
Cordner, Don (Melbourne footballer)
    183

cricket at MCG 71
  arcane and devious game 133–4
  Bay 13 225, 228–9, 240–1
  Bradman's testimonial game
    12–13, 148, 229, 252
  Centenary Test 47–8
  crassness of winning too often
    235–6
  Fijian XI 74, 75–80
  first England tour 38–9
  first India tour 9–10
  first Test hat-trick 47
  first Test match 45–6
  hat-tricks 47, 94
  one-day cricket 179–81, 226–9,
    242–3
  Mexican Waves 226–8
  records 129, 133
  somewhat uneven match 39
  as weapon against the English
    134
  wide rule 181
  see also Ashes cricket matches; Test
    cricket; individual team names
Cricketers Arms Hotel 267
crowds 170–1
  behaviour 59, 162, 165, 166, 167,
    185, 194, 226–9, 234, 239–40,
    241–3, 284, 285
  numbers 4, 39, 60, 64, 68, 91, 92,
    95, 99, 101–2, 106, 108, 122,
    124, 143, 144, 145, 156, 160,
    165, 166, 169, 179, 183, 194,
    197
  record numbers 133, 173, 174–5,
    176, 233, 234, 249
Cuthbert, Betty (Aust runner)
  166–7

Dainty, Paul (concert promoter)
  198–9
Dalai Lama, confused by banners
  49–50
Davidson, Alan (Aust cricketer)
  72–3, 212, 233
Davis Cup tennis 100
Delany, Ron (Irish runner) 131,
  139–41
DeLillo, Don (writer) 281–2
Dexter, Ted 'Lord' (Eng cricketer)
  72–3, 230, 239
Dickens, Charles (novelist) 35
  invited to Australia 36–7
Docklands Stadium (Melbourne)
  bit of a joke 196
  construction 122–3
  lockout palace 237
  no threat to MCG 122, 123–4,
    196
Duke of Wellington Hotel 266–7
Dumas, Charles (US high jumper)
  158–62
Dunstan, Keith (writer) 275
Dyer, Jack (Richmond footballer)
  250

East Melbourne Artillery 47, 48, 183
Edmonds, Jason (MCG head of
  cleaning) 66, 67, 69, 299
Elliott, Herb (Aust runner) 170, 171
Elliott, John (businessman) 288
Ellis, J.B. (MCC committee member)
  29–30
England cricket team 34, 39, 42, 45,
  467, 71–3, 130, 133–4, 168–9,
  179–81, 183, 212, 213, 229, 142,
  272

English, very 188, 209, 235
Essendon Football Club 122
    at MCG 48, 95, 146, 253, 273,
        279–80, 282, 283
    supporters 122
Eucharistic Congress, Fourth (1973)
    173

false prophets 4
father–son rituals 90, 134, 190, 284
Fels, Allan (head of ACCC & Carlton
    supporter) 277–8
fiction, sport in 281–2
Fijian cricket team 74, 75–80, 81, 150
Fikotova, Olga (Czech discus
    thrower) 155, 157, 165
finals see First Semi-Final; Grand
    Finals; Preliminary Finals;
    Qualifying Finals; Second Semi-
    Finals
Fingleton, Jack (Aust cricketer) 145
First Semi-Final 1953 86
firsts at MCG
    Aboriginal football team 9
    Australian Rules carnival (1908)
        100
    Australian Rules game 31, 34
    baseball game 94
    cricket match 34, 246
    Davis Cup tennis (1912) 100
    England cricket team 34, 38–9
    football game 247
    game under lights 47, 182–3
    Grand Final, VFL (1902) 94, 95,
        100, 290
    improved scoreboard technology 81
    Indian cricket team 9–10, 146–7
    lacrosse (1910) 100

royal visit 45
rugby game (1914) 100
soccer game (1910) 100
Sunday football match 176
Test hat-trick 47
Test match 45–6
VFL game after WWII 146
Fitzroy Football Club 86, 95, 176,
    191
football see AFL/VFL; Australian
    Rules football; rugby; soccer
footbridge at MCG
    dangerous place to stop 4–5
    new 185
    old 4–5, 131, 136, 184, 185, 210
Forbes, Jack 'Witchetty' 41
Frank Worrell Trophy 176

Gaelic football 140–4
    Compromise Rules 141, 143, 144
Gallery of Sport, MCG 31, 273
Gatting, Mike (Eng cricketer) 168–9
Geelong Football Club 86, 252
gold rush 261–2
Gough, Stephen (MCC GM) 274–5
Grace, W.G. (Eng cricketer) 40
Graham, Billy (evangelist) 173–5
Grand Finals (VFL/AFL) 3–5, 15,
    48, 71, 86, 90–1, 142, 146, 176–7,
    250–1
    2002 68–70, 96–9, 290–5
    catering 65, 96–9
    greatest 176–7
    prematch entertainment 97, 99
    prematch entertainment
        commentary 192
    preparation for 68–70
Grand National, 'Void' wins 188

'Grandstand' (ABC radio program) 268–9, 273–5, 276–80, 282–5

Great Southern Stand 32, 50, 63, 112, 113, 131, 145, 183, 184, 189, 191, 196, 197, 226–8

Grey Smith Stand 100

Grout, Wally (Aust cricketer) 233, 234

grounds, preparing MCG 66–7, 69–70, 116, 168–9, 223, 224, 299
    cricket 66, 69–70, 264–5
    delicate art of 117–18
    drop-in pitches 69, 112, 265, 299
    football 66–7, 69–70
    Merri Creek soil 263–5
    see also Ware, Tony

Hadlee, Richard (NZ cricketer) 253

Hammersley, William (co-creator, Australian Rules) 29

Harvey, Neil (Aust cricketer) 213, 214, 216, 229, 233, 240

Hassett, Lindsay (Aust cricketer) 229

Hawthorn Football Club 108, 146, 268

Healey, Des (Collingwood footballer) 251, 252

Helpmann, Robert (dancer) 255

Hewson, Brian (Aust runner) 139, 140

Hickey, Bernard (academic) 24, 25

Hughes, Merv (Aust cricketer) 236

Hughes, Philip (artist) 221–2

Hughes, William Morris 'Billy' (prime minister) 107–9

Hungarian uprising 164

Hunt, Rex (3AW commentator) 282

India cricket team 9–10, 146

Invincibles (cricket team) 10, 117, 146–7, 229

Ireland see Gaelic football

Irish at MCG 131–44

Irish Australians
    attitudes to cricket 133–4
    attitudes to English 130
    at MCG 131–8
    see also Maguire, Barney; Tynan, Ray

Iverson, Jack (Aust cricketer) 230–3

Jardine, Douglas (Eng cricketer) 130

jellyfish, man-o'-war, traumatised erectile function of 10–11, 12

Jesaulenko, Alex (Carlton footballer) 177

Jock McHale Stadium see Victoria Park

John Paul II, Pope, at MCG 169–73

Johnston, Bill (Aust cricketer) 13, 229, 232–3, 241–2

Johnston, Brian (BBC commentator) 272

Kadavulevu, Ratu (Fijian prince and cricketer) 75–9

Kashkarov, Igor (USSR high jumper) 158–62

Kulin Aboriginal nation 8–9

Kuts, Vladimir (USSR runner) 155, 156, 157, 158, 165

Landy, John (Aust runner) 92, 136, 138, 139–41

Landy Room 220, 222–3

Lane, Tim (ABC commentator & Carlton supporter) 268–74, 276–84

larrikinism 131, 136, 151, 180, 243, 244
and ASAL 218, 219
see also Bay 13

Larwood, Harold (Eng cricketer) 130, 134

La Trobe, Governor Charles, creation of MCG 8, 55, 109–10, 111–12

Lawry, Bill (Aust cricketer) 180, 181
on pigeons 57

leg theory see bodyline

Lillee, Dennis (Aust cricketer) 46, 170, 253

Lincoln, Merv (Aust runner) 139

Lindwall, Ray (Aust cricketer) 230

Lockett, Tony 'Plugger' (St Kilda/ Sydney footballer) 184–5, 186, 194, 195, 196
thighs and groin of 76

Lonergan, Dan (ABC commentator) 277, 279, 280, 282, 284

Longhena, Baldassare (architect) 27, 31, 32

Lord's cricket ground (UK) 234–9
Austrade Chalet at 235–9
lockouts 237
spare tickets sought after 237, 239
suitable dress for 235, 238

McAuley, James (poet), at MCG 213–213, 214, 215

McCabe, Stan (Aust cricketer) 130

McCartney, Paul, MCG concert 197, 198–9

McCool, Colin, drops ball 12–13

McDonald, Colin (Aust cricketer) 117–18, 233

McEniff, Brian (Irish coach) 144

McGuire, Eddie (Collingwood FC president) 49, 102

Mackay, Ken 'Slasher' (Aust cricketer) 233

Maclure, Mark (ABC commentator) 268, 278

Maguire, Barney (friend of BM) 131–8

Maguire, Gerald Xavier (grandfather of Barney) 132–4

Maguire, Patrick (father of Barney) 132, 133

Magwitch (Dickens character) 35–6

Mallett, Ashley (Aust cricketer) 180

Malthouse, Mick (Collingwood coach) 49, 104

Mankad, Vinoo (Indian cricketer) 9–10

Mannix, Archbishop Daniel 53, 108–9

Manuka Oval (Canberra), Kangaroos/ Eagles game at 277, 279, 280, 282, 283

marn grook (Aboriginal ball game) 30

Marsden, Edward J. (businessman/ cricketer) 75–9, 150

Marsden, Marc (organiser 1956 torch relay) 80, 149–52

Marsden, Samuel (flogging parson) 78

Marsh, Rod (Aust cricketer) 46, 47

Martians, comprehend nature of pumps 135

Mathews, Marlene (Aust runner) 166–7

Matthews, Brian
  admitted to ABC broadcast box
    269, 273–4, 276–84
  Bradman's testimonial game 12–13
  considers streaking 239
  exam season 89–90
  father 12, 13, 190, 256, 272
  first visit to MCG 9–10
  as footy coach 110–11
  at MCG 3–5, 9–10, 11–12, 13,
    14–15, 61, 188–96, 190, 269,
    273–4, 276–84
  learns to drive 255–60
  at Lord's 235–9; brandishes
    umbrella 235; abandons
    umbrella 238
  mother 11
  naively seeks assistance of MCC
    274–6
  at Olympics 137–9, 154–62, 163–7
  rarely in Members' area 234
  St Kilda supporter 271
  upgrades accommodation and
    meets a cricketer 230–2; doesn't
    mention the war 231
May, Norman 'Gold! Gold! Gold!'
  (broadcaster) 139
MCC *see* Melbourne Cricket Club
MCG *see* Melbourne Cricket Ground
MCG Trust *see* Melbourne Cricket
  Ground Trust
Meckiff, Ian (Aust cricketer) 212, 234
media access rights for MCG
  113–15, 121–3, 124–5
meeting places 189–91, 265–7
  clocks 210, 266
  effect of mobile phone on 211
  footbridge 131, 210

  at MCG 189, 210, 211
  MCG as 211–16, 217, 223–4
  queue 211
  Young & Jackson's 265–6
Melbourne
  attitude to sport 39, 41, 50
  as a City of Churches 53–6
  MCG as symbol of 5, 6, 7, 117,
    118, 121, 196, 203, 206,
    214–15, 216, 278, 284
  three cathedrals 53–6
  see also Melbourne Cricket Ground
Melbourne Cricket Club (MCC) 8,
  22, 29
  as ground manager 116, 330–1
  hallowed MCG turf 30–1, 116–17
  management of MCG 88, 109–10,
    111–12, 113–25
  Members 56, 61, 112
  and Olympics 84–5, 86–7, 88,
    90–1, 112
Melbourne Cricket Ground (MCG)
  advertising 124
  appearance 6, 32–3, 154, 170,
    220–1, 222, 265, 273, 279
  appearance when empty 217,
    220–1, 222, 223, 224, 245
  archetype for bush ovals 247–8,
    254–6
  atmosphere 9, 92, 118, 124–5,
    157–8, 165–6, 170
  attitudes to 15, 50, 93, 117,
    214–15, 284
  as cathedral 5, 32, 50, 53, 55–6,
    57, 84, 93, 96–9, 109, 153–4,
    158, 196, 203, 206, 214–15,
    216, 217–18, 224, 245, 271,
    273, 285

Melbourne Cricket Ground (cont.)
corporate takeover 32, 62, 65, 66,
    97, 113, 115, 119, 191
establishment of 8, 55, 109–10,
    111–12, 246, 262
gluepot, creation of 69, 193, 265
government and 8, 55, 109–10,
    111–12
Grandstand 82
ground 246
helpful instructions for entering
    188–9, 192
imaginative heart of city 5, 6, 7,
    117, 118, 121, 196, 203, 206,
    214–15, 216, 278, 284
light towers 112, 170, 183, 200
lockouts 192, 193–4, 274
management of 88, 109–10,
    111–12, 113–25, 274–6
as marketplace 33
media access rights 113–15,
    121–3, 124–5
men in grey 193
Mexican Waves, progress through
    stands 226–8
miracles at 170
no peace any more 124–5
people's ground 109–10, 111–12,
    116–17, 118, 216, 234, 241
privatisation 113, 115
pro-conscription rallies (WWI)
    107–9
public ownership 109–10
redevelopment 1980s/90s 112–13
redevelopment 2002 82, 98, 99,
    113, 119, 121, 273, 299, 300
reversible grandstand 81
seats, green jarrah 13, 61–2

staff 62, 65–7, 68–70, 96–9
stands 10, 98, 99, 100
symbol of Australia 117
tour of 244–6
trampling the hallowed turf 30–1,
    85, 168–9, 193, 247, 284, 299
trapdoor, handy 221
women at 175
see also Bay 13; crowds; footbridge;
    Grand Finals; Great Southern
    Stand; Landy Room; Melbourne
    Cricket Club; Melbourne
    Cricket Ground Trust; Members'
    Stand; Northern Stand; Olympic
    Stand; Ponsford Stand
Melbourne Cricket Ground Trust
dispute with AFL on Grand Finals
    277–8
and management of MCG 88,
    109–10, 111–12, 113–25
and Olympics 84–5, 88, 90–1,
    112
Paul McCartney concert 198–9
replaced 114–21
Melbourne Cup 86, 89
Melbourne Football Club 168, 253
coaches 251, 252
games 90–2, 142, 146, 247, 250–1
Grand Finals 15, 90–2, 142, 146
at MCG 31, 34, 47, 245, 247,
    250, 253
players 91–2, 131, 183, 277
Melbourne Military Tattoo 182
members, MCC 88, 96–7, 116, 129,
    154, 234
Mexican Wave refusers 226–8
Members' Stand (Pavilion) 32–3, 63,
    81, 129, 154, 175, 234

Menzies Centre for Australian
    Studies, cricket conference
    269–70
Merri Creek soil 263–5
Mexican Wave 180, 226–8, 242, 288
Miller, Keith (Aust cricketer) 10, 11,
    117, 147, 229
Mimoun, Alain (French marathon
    runner) 165–6
Mithen, Laurie (Melbourne
    footballer) 91–2
Moonlight concerts on the oval 47
Morris, Arthur (Aust cricketer)
    229–30
Mullagh, Johnny (Unaarrimin) (Aust
    cricketer) 40
Murray-Smith, Stephen (academic)
    219–20
    at MCG 223–4

National Gallery (London) 221–2
New Zealand cricket team 253
Next Year, cult of 283–4
Norm Smith medal 295
North Melbourne Football Club
    (Kangaroos) 168, 183, 277
    2002 Manuka Oval game against
        Eagles 277, 279, 280, 282-3
Northern Stand 82, 113, 119, 121
    see also Olympic Stand

O'Hannigan, Pat (prospector) 261–2
Olympic Games, Melbourne (1956)
    84, 153–62, 163–7
    50 km walk 165–6
    10 000 metres 155
    BM and RT at 88–93, 137–9,
        154–62, 163–7

building program 84–8, 112
closing ceremony 85, 92, 173
Day 1 154–62, 165
Day 2 163, 165–6
Day 3 166–7
funding 84, 85
high jump 156–62
illegal entry 137–9
marathon 165–6
at MCG 15, 84–5, 88, 90–1
metric mile (1500 m) 92, 131,
    136, 139–41
opening ceremony 85, 92, 148,
    149, 173
politics 164–5
USA at 163
USSR at 163, 164
venues for 84–8
water polo 164
women's discus 154, 157
see also Olympic torch
Olympic Games, Sydney 122, 196
Olympic Park (Melbourne) and 2006
    Commonwealth Games 121
Olympic Stand (MCG) 63, 82, 112,
    113, 121, 155, 226–8
Olympic torch
    carried by Ron Clarke 1956 92,
        148
    hijacked in Sydney 1956 151–2
    relay 1956 148, 149–52
one-day cricket 180
    Barmy Army 228
    Bay 13 226–9
    behaviour at 226–8, 241–3
    Mexican Waves 226–8
    origins 179–81
    selection for 180

opera, Italian expertise explained 25

Pakistan cricket team 183
piano-playing in the army 28
Pierce, Peter (academic) 219
pigeons 285
  Italian v. Antipodean 58–9
  ownership of MCG 56, 57–60,
    272–3
  participation in cricket 59
  unerring aim of 272
Pirie, Gordon (Eng runner) 155–6
pitch/wicket *see* grounds, preparing
politics and sport 109, 110–11,
  164
Pond, Christopher (hotel owner)
  36–7, 38, 39, 42
Ponomareva, Olga (USSR discus
  thrower) 155, 157
Ponsford, Bill (Aust cricketer) 129,
  264
Ponsford Spirit (wind) 300
Ponsford Stand 98, 99, 121, 155,
  189, 192, 221, 226–8
Port Adelaide Football Club,
  Qualifying Finalists 49
Porter, Charles 'Chilla' (Aust high
  jumper) 158–62, 300
Preliminary Finals 86
  2002 48–9, 60, 62–5, 68
  catering 65, 67
  cleaning 66, 67
  ground preparation 66–7
  people's final 62–3

Qualifying Finals 48
queue jumping, as threat to
  civilisation 208

queues 63, 217
  at MCG 11, 169, 184, 210
  raffish Italian 208–10
  theory and practice of 187,
    207–11
  see also stampedes

radio broadcasts 268–9, 273–5,
  276–80, 282–5
Read, Norman (NZ walker) 165–6,
  167
Reddall, Geoff (B&B owner), and
  MCG door 61–2
religion at MCG 169–75
Richards, Lou (Collingwood
  footballer) 252
Richards, Ron (Collingwood
  footballer) 252
Richmond Football Club 3, 4, 14,
  15, 122, 168, 176, 241, 245, 250,
  268, 272
  supporters 122, 191, 240–1
Ring, Doug (Aust cricketer) 13, 232,
  233, 241
rooned
  BM's attitude 92
  and vagaries of weather 178–9
Rose, Bob (Collingwood footballer)
  249–54
Rose, Robert (Aust cricketer) 253
royalty
  children's displays for 129, 145
  children's display forgotten 176
  Fijian cricketers 74, 75–9
  pine for children's displays 149
  visit MCG 45, 81, 129
rugby, Australia unsuitable for 28,
  29

Rumble, Doug (MCC member) 61
running of the bulls at the MCG 99
  see also queues; stampedes

St Kilda Baths 10–11
St Kilda Football Club 64, 84, 270
  backlash hatred for 271
  games 184–5, 188–90, 191–6, 272
  Grand Finals 3–5, 64, 271
  perennial wooden spoons 271
  players and coaches 147, 184–8,
    195, 277
  premiership, sole 4–5
  supporters 4, 5, 64, 185, 189, 191,
    194, 271, 272, 283; at the
    cricket 238
  see also Next Year, cult of
St Patrick's Cathedral (Melbourne)
  19, 50, 53–6, 57, 109, 153, 171–2,
  217
St Paul's Cathedral (Melbourne) 50,
  53–6, 57, 153, 171–2, 217
Santa Maria della Salute (Venice) 6,
  26–7, 217
seagulls
  assurance and finer feelings of
    286–9
  at MCG 57, 59, 285, 288
  unerring aim of 272
Second Semi-Finals 48, 86, 95
Second World War and MCG 146
security 191
  complete failure of 137–9
  somewhat excessive 187
  somewhat relaxed 242–3
Serle, Geoffrey (historian) 215
Sheedy, Kevin (Essendon coach)
  268–9

Sheffield Shield cricket 145, 241, 265
shirtfront 187, 209, 251
Silvagni, Stephen (Carlton footballer)
  143
Smith, Norm (Melbourne coach)
  251, 252
Smith, Thomas (co-creator Aust
  Rules) 29
Snow, John (Eng cricketer) 181
soccer
  at Docklands Stadium 122–3
  at MCG 100, 143, 182, 183
  at Stamford Bridge 186–8
South Africa cricket team 86
South Melbourne Football Club 84
South Yarra football team at MCG 34
Southern, Danny (ABC
  commentator) 277, 278, 280, 284
Southern Cross windmills, as cow
  fans 135
Southern Stand see Great Southern
  Stand
sparrows at MCG 288–9
Spiers, Felix (hotel owner) 36–7, 38,
  39, 42
Spofforth, Fred 'The Demon' (Aust
  cricketer) 47
sport in Australian imaginative writing
  279–81
sportsmanship
  bodyline 130, 133–4
  Centenary Test 46
  doing a Mankad 10
  fallen bail 233, 234
  Olympics 164–5
  wide rule in cricket 181
Stackpole, Keith 'Stacky' (Aust
  cricketer) 180, 181

Stamford Bridge (oval)
  1993 Chelsea/Middlesbrough game
    186–8
  cop:supporter ratio 187
stampedes v. queues 63, 99, 209–10
  see also queues
standing at MCG 154
  at cricket 229
  at footy 189–90, 191, 192
  at Olympics 154
  see also Bay 13
State of Origin (AFL) 183, 184–5
Stephens, Dave 'The Flying Milko'
  (Aust runner) 156
Stephenson, H.H. (Eng cricketer)
  34, 39, 44
stingray terror 12
Stubnick, Christa (German runner)
  166–7
Stynes, Jim (Melbourne footballer)
  131
Sydney Cricket Ground, preserves old
  stands 273

television, dominance of 123–4, 191,
  192, 268
  see also media access rights
Telstra Dome see Docklands Stadium
tennis courts at MCG 247
Test cricket 71–3, 86, 145, 168–9,
  170, 176, 212, 213, 214, 221, 228,
  229, 230, 232–3, 234, 241, 242–3,
  272
  1955 Tyson's Test 233
  1970 tied Test against West Indies
    176
  1971 Third Ashes Test knockout
    match 179–81

Thompson, James (co-creator
  Australian Rules) 29
Thomson, Jeff (Aust cricketer) 170
3AW broadcast team 283
Tickner, Bill (organiser, 1956 torch
  relay) 149–50
Trumble, Hugh (Aust cricketer) 94
Tynan, Ray (BM's friend)
  billiards and snooker 14, 89
  character 135–6, 151
  at MCG 14, 90
  Olympic tickets 90–3, 134–8
  at Olympics 138–9, 154–62,
    163–7
  Richmond supporter 14, 15
  at school and university 14–15,
    89–90
  takes accelerated beer-drinking
    course 90, 93, 166

umpires 243, 247
  attacked by goanna 257–8, 259,
    260
  make-up problems for 255
  manhandled 144
  perils for bush 257–60
  Tom Wills as 31, 247
University of Melbourne 88–9

Venice
  BM's telephonic adventure 24–5
  BM transported to 24, 26
  epidemics 26–7
  sounds of 26
Verity, Hedley (Eng cricketer) 215
VFL Park see Waverley Park
Victoria cricket team 117, 129,
  168–9, 253

Victoria Park 250, 263

Victoria Racing Club, and media rights 114

Victorian Cricket Association (VCA) and media rights to MCG 113–15

Victorian Football League (VFL) 3–5
see also AFL/VFL; Australian Rules football

Victorian Women's Centennial Sports Carnival 145

Voce, Bill (Eng cricketer) 130

Voss, Michael (Brisbane footballer) 102, 105, 291, 293, 294

Walker, Max (Aust cricketer) 46, 47, 253

Walters, Doug (Aust cricketer) 180, 181, 249

Ware, Tony (MCG Ground Manager) 299
preparing ground for cricket 66, 69–70
preparing ground for football 66–7, 69–70
see also grounds, preparing

Warne, Shane (Aust cricketer & St Kilda supporter) 238

Warner, Pelham 'Plum' (Eng cricket tour manager) 130

water polo 76, 164

Wathaurong Aboriginal people 8

Waugh, Mark (Aust cricketer) 236

Waverley Park (VFL/AFL Park) 143, 190, 196

weather 163
dust storms 163
fog 163
a new wind 300

rain 102, 105, 106, 177, 178–9, 193

seasons at MCG 6, 71

storms 72

summers longer and hotter then 10

windy 71, 146

winters colder then 19

winters foggier then 163

worse at Stamford Bridge 186

West Coast Eagles Football Club v. Kangaroos at Manuka Oval 2002 279, 280, 282–3

West Indies cricket team 13, 61, 176, 232

Western Stand 176
see also Ponsford Stand

Wills, Cedric (brother of Tom) 42–4, 201–2

Wills, Horatio Spencer (father of Tom) 21, 29, 42–4, 201–2

Wills, Tom (Thomas Wentworth) (cricketer, footballer, creator of Australian Rules football)
Aboriginal cricket team 40, 42
and Aborigines 21–2, 30, 40
character and appearance 44, 147, 268
creates Australian Rules 27–32, 141, 269
cricketer 22, 23, 201
death 22, 176, 200, 201–2, 205, 206
family 21, 42–4, 201–2
footy player 201
goes bush 42–4
letters 22, 28
life 21–2, 201–2

Wills, Tom (cont.)
    as phantom 17, 19–20, 23, 34,
        40–1, 45, 74, 81–2, 94, 100,
        129–30, 145–8, 163, 176–7,
        182–3, 197, 200, 205
    on rugby 22
    statue of 31–2
    umpire 31, 247
Wilson, Caroline (journalist) 268,
    278, 295
Woiworung Aboriginal people 8, 9
women's Test cricket 145

Woodfull, Bill (Aust cricketer) 130,
    134
World Cup (cricket) 183
Worrell, Frank (WI cricketer) 232,
    233
Wurundjeri Aboriginal people 9, 263

Young & Jackson's hotel (Melbourne)
    54, 172
    Chloë 266
    lost patrons 190–1
    as meeting point 191, 265–6